DATE DUE

British Television

Mr. Graham Scott in 1972.

British Television

An Insider's History

by

Peter Graham Scott

McFarland & Company, Inc., Publishers
Jefferson, North Carolina, and London

Frontispiece: Mr. Graham Scott, when producing
The Onedin Line, 1972. The author chose early in
his career to use "Graham Scott" rather than "Scott"
as his professional surname.

Partial Library of Congress Cataloguing-in-Publication Data

Graham Scott, Peter, 1923–
    British television : an insider's history / by Peter Graham
Scott.
        p.   cm.
    Includes index.
    ISBN 0-7864-0653-4 (library binding : 50# alkaline paper) ∞
    1. Graham Scott, Peter, 1923– 2. Television producers
and directors—Great Britain—Biography. I. Title.
    PN1992.4.GXX A3   2000
    791.45'0232'092   99-52496

British Library Cataloguing-in-Publication data are available

Manufactured in the United States of America

*McFarland & Company, Inc., Publishers
    Box 611, Jefferson, North Carolina 28640
    www.mcfarlandpub.com*

To Eve Rosemary ("Mimi"),
who had the idea...

Acknowledgments

A life is little without friends.

So, many thanks, for help and encouragement, to: Cyril Abraham, Ken Annakin, Lord (Richard) Attenborough, John and Roy Boulting, Ruth Caleb, Peter Chudleigh, Bernard Cox, Iain Cuthbertson, Dame Judi Dench, Jacques Dercourt, Lesley-Anne Down, Patrick Dromgoole, Elizabeth and John Elliot, June Epstein, John Fabian, Nina and Moris Farhi, Pat Ferns, John Frankav, Seymour Friedman, Sir Michael Gambon, Sir John Gielgud, Peter Gilmore and Anne Stallybrass, Marius Goring, Robert Hardy, Lotte and Hans Hass, Sir Anthony Havelock-Allan, Sir Anthony Hopkins, Glenda Jackson, Joan and Roger Jenkins, Howard Lang, Inge and Clifford Lauriston, Karolyn and John Lord, Kathryn and David McCallum, Patrick McGoohan, Patrick MacNee, Vicki Miller, Andrew Osborn, Joan and Richard Price, David Sullivan Proudfoot, Lord (David) Puttnam, Hope and John Redway, Dame Diana Rigg, Patrick Ryecart, Sidney Sager, Jenny Seagrove, Jane Seymour, Malcolm Slonims, Carol, Paul, Anne, and Susan Stager, Maureen-Anne and John Temple Smith, John Thaw, Barry Thomas, Eileen and Tim Vignoles, Daphne and Ralph Watson, Billie Whitelaw, Lord (Ted) Willis, and Anne and Julian Wintle.

Special thanks are due to Dennis Meikle, who gave me considerable advice and valuable assistance, and to my former secretary, Elizabeth Batty, who transformed the painful scrawl of the first draft into legible English.

Finally, my deepest gratitude for unfailing support must be to my wife, Mimi, my daughters Cherry and Heather, and my sons Robin and Martin.

Contents

Preface

Gentlemen, there is at hand a mighty instrument to banish ignorance and misery and to enrich the sum total of human well-being.

The sole concern of those to whom the stewardship is given—by accident—is to ensure that these basic ideals should be safeguarded so that broadcasting may play its part in the development of the human race.

—John Reith, to the Board of Governors
of the British Broadcasting Company,
April 1926

From the earliest cave painting, human beings have sought to record their perceptions of life around them. Imaginative pictorial expression has found form and continuity in sculpture, painting, photography, and cinema. Now television has become the latest visual communicator, sometimes even fulfilling John Reith's brave aspirations for broadcasting more than 70 years ago.

In Britain after the Second World War television grew rapidly from a few hours of black-and-white broadcasts in London only to five main channels and many digital, cable, and satellite stations all in color playing nationwide from before breakfast until the small hours of morning.

For the first time in history, anyone, without special education or privilege, could enjoy music and drama, gain reliable information, appreciate art, wildlife, and travel, and learn something of our neighbors' spiritual and social problems.

But for these 50 years we have also chosen to pick at the sores

1

of our ailing society and exploit the dramatic possibilities of felony, drugs, murder, violence, and every form of sexual perversion. *What next?* Even more realistic savagery—performed in illiterate monosyllables? Or should television writers be more positively encouraged to explore the effectiveness and beauty of language as Arthur Miller, Edward Albee, Tom Stoppard, and Harold Pinter have in the theater?

Dare we hope for more insight, more values like (if this sort of language may be excused) genuine friendship, pride in family, loyalty, even love—the extraordinary moments of beauty that life (despite all the highly publicized evil and terror) continues to offer? *We must.* Only then can television both profess and preserve its sanity, and move in the twenty-first century from insecure middle age into true sagacity and a responsible level of social influence.

It was my good fortune to have been making television programs from pioneer days. But ideas change with passing time. The concept of society in *The Prisoner* echoed my own in the late 1960s; the views of earlier eras in *The Last Enemy* and *The Onedin Line* reflected a personal truth—when I made those programs. For I was lucky enough to be living through a period of remarkable change, of social and industrial development when ordinary people were at last able to seize great opportunities in education, travel, and accelerating technology.

Alongside the amazing advances in aural and visual communication I hope that I too have matured, in thought and compassion, sustained by a firm belief in the survival of television broadcasting as a public service, always attempting an excellence accessible to all.

I have been part of television's dawn promise, bright noon, and golden afternoon, and now watch its gathering darkness. I can only hope for a new dawn—and *soon.*

1

1923–1952:
Why Me?

*The BBC's choice. Adventures in films
and the dawn of vision.*

"I want to speak with pictures," I answered. "I want to observe
life and interpret it in drama."

Which was judged reason enough. Soon, on a cloudy Monday
morning, September 22, 1952, I cautiously entered a shabby gray
building off London's Marylebone Road, training headquarters for
the British Broadcasting Corporation. Gray was then the BBC's
standard color, possibly in puritanical memory of the first director-
general, John Reith. Walls and doors varied in shade from ash to
slate, and even the pictures transmitted by BBC Television flickered in less than a million homes in ghostly blue-gray. Gray, not
Greed, was the essence of British television.

Certainly we had no false illusions of wealth that day as we
entered corporation service. We were only interested in making programs. Some months before there had been a small gray announcement of a BBC training scheme for producers. Acceptance for the
four-week period was, it was emphasized, no guarantee of future
employment.

In the sad foyer under the none-too-friendly gaze of a bristle-
mustached commissionaire I nervously eyed my chosen fellows,
trying to guess their names from a list I'd been handed. "David
Attenborough" was easy; though as yet unfamiliar from swamp and

3

jungle he had a strong resemblance to his brother, Richard, whom I'd met on the film of Graham Greene's *Brighton Rock.* "Brian Tesler" was the handsome young man in a corner, with perhaps "Michael Peacock" beside him, exuding London-School-of-Economics confidence. Among the others were Ernest Maxin, from Light Entertainment, and Patricia Foy, soon a music producer. Then a familiar face appeared—John Fernald, an experienced stage director I'd met once—waving a script. "Peter Saunders sent me this rubbish this morning! Absolute tosh! Supposed to be by Agatha Christie!"

The play was *The Mousetrap.* John refused the chance to direct it, and thus denied himself a weekly royalty payment for over 40 years when it became London's longest-running play.

Why, I wondered, do all these people want to make television? There were no kudos, very little glamour, and certainly no money in it. Four thousand five hundred cinemas throughout Britain still attracted bumper audiences for colorful stories of romance and adventure. The minority who owned television sets watched mainly for news and sport. Television dramas were usually creaking West End near-successes of yesteryear, clumsily staged in cardboard sets cobbled together from last week's middle-class drawing room. "Repertory in an iron lung." But I sensed an opportunity for creating original images. As a successful feature film editor of 28, I badly wanted to direct, preferably something I'd written myself.

No one in my family was in entertainment. My father Frederick's origins were slightly mysterious; his birth in 1884 had never been registered. His father, George, had come from a good Lowland Scottish family and had married "beneath him," sired five children, then set up house with a younger woman who became Fred's mother. In those days births out of wedlock were common enough. Unrecorded and unconcerned, young Fred learned to read and write, to add up, and to ride a horse. At 16, claiming his age as 20, he enrolled in the Thirty-seventh Squadron, Tenth Imperial Yeomanry, and was shipped to South Africa for the last 18 months of the Boer War. He undoubtedly enjoyed the open-air life trekking across the plains. His campaign medal was duly clasped with the names "Transvaal," "Orange Free State," and "Cape Colony."

Demobilized in 1902 at 18 (officially "22, Conduct Very Good"),

Fred discovered Edwardian Britain's lack of concern for its returning soldiery, and used some of his savings on a steerage passage to Canada, completing the 6,000-mile journey to Port Moody just short of Vancouver free of charge in a series of drafty goods wagons. In nearby Coquitlam wooden houses were being built for eager settlers. After a few months of working as a carpenter, Fred found a partner and set up his own building company. In one of their early developments there is still a "Graham Street" leading to "Scott Place"—Fred's saucy nod to the family that seems to have rejected him.

Pioneering on the West Coast of Canada was undoubtedly the high point of his life, sailing and fishing and drinking with the good old boys. Soon prosperous, he was a popular figure until far-off Britain declared war again in August 1914.

The Great War between Britain, France, and Germany now appears to us as a pointless contest of national arrogance—certainly no reason for returning 6,000 miles to the banal trumpet of "King and Country." But the gallant young Boer War veteran sold up and traveled east (fare-paying this time) to Canadian Army Headquarters at Valcartier, a bleak plain near Quebec, to enlist for "the duration" on September 23, 1914. But the "Fifth Western Cavalry" he joined was a cruel fiction. The approaching European battle had already been foreseen as a relentless struggle of infantry against murderous artillery and machine guns. None of the would-be horsemen ever saw a horse. Instead they were herded into merchantmen and bucketed across the unfriendly Atlantic to shiver through bitter winter in soaking tents on Salisbury Plain.

In January 1915 the Canadians were shipped to France, into the line before Ypres, the Belgian market town captured by the Germans early in the war to create an untidy bulge in the straight front line that affronted military minds. Over the next four years thousands of increasingly younger men were maimed and slaughtered in a vain attempt to repossess a few hundred yards of this evil "Salient," their monument at nearby Mons Gate inscribed with names from pavement to skyline (among them my wife's uncle, Sergeant Bryce Martell, killed at 21), a sobering reminder of the meaninglessness of that war.

At dawn on April 22, 1915, a troop of Canadians scrambled out of the stinking slime of their trenches to slither through the mire in one of the hopeless sorties dignified as "The Second Battle of Ypres," to be struck down by accurate machine gun fire. Fred was among the last to fall, his left leg shattered, to lie with blood pouring into the mud for the next 12 daylight hours, until he could be recovered and dumped among the piles of wounded in a makeshift field hospital. The exhausted surgeon who finally examined him, suspecting gangrene, performed a rapid and clumsy amputation. During the long months of recovery Fred came to believe, bitterly, that with more care his leg might have been saved. Fitted with a primitive artificial limb he was promoted to corporal and because of his facility with figures given a job in Canadian Army Records in Whitehall. It was then that he met Connie Cornish.

Connie's story was the stuff of Dickensian melodrama. In 1895 at age 15, her mother, Hannah Cornish, had traveled from the West Country to become housemaid to the Lethbridge family in Putney. Catching the susceptible eye of Horace, the youngest son, she became pregnant at 17. When the truth was revealed, father Lethbridge behaved in true Victorian fashion. Horace was dispatched to South Africa to make his way, Hannah was dismissed without pay or reference.

The bewildered girl, fearful of returning home, sought the grudging aid of public assistance, and on July 3, 1897, my mother, Constance, was born in Wandsworth Workhouse, her birth certificate inscribed ILLEGITIMATE with chill Puritan disdain. It must have been some relief to discover that handsome Fred's origins were similarly murky!

Raised by a stern grandmother while Hannah found work elsewhere, Connie turned out to be a bright child, and she started to collect a small library of school prizes. About 1909 the now prosperous Horace Lethbridge returned unexpectedly from South Africa hoping to marry Hannah.

But she had found a new admirer, and with appalling timing was pregnant again with Connie's half sister. After spending a day taking Connie around the London Zoo (the only time they ever met) he took the next boat back to Port Elizabeth.

By 1917 Connie was a secretary at the Ministry of Munitions, once encountering the formidable but unpopular minister, Winston

Churchill. On November 18, 1918, against the fierce opposition of Grandma Cornish ("Why marry a cripple?"), she married Fred Scott and set up home in a pleasant apartment in East Sheen near Richmond. Fred stayed on in the army for a couple more years, and after more operations his ruined left leg was fitted with a Desoutter artificial one, strapped to the remains of his thigh and suspended by heavy braces over his shoulders, hampering his mobility. They lived quite well, with frequent parties for comrades returning to Canada, spending the proceeds of the Coquitlam business. But apart from odd bookkeeping jobs Fred wasn't fully employed for some 15 years. My brother Raymond was born in 1921, and I appeared on October 27, 1923.

Times became harder as savings ran out. My mother salvaged £75 ($100) as a deposit on a small, three-bedroom house being built near Hounslow Heath in Middlesex, price £675 ($1,000). We moved in 1925. It was spartan and jerry-built with no heating except a crude copper geyser in the tiny bathroom, but it provided basic shelter. Our new neighbors were nearly all ex-servicemen, five or more with missing limbs, wives struggling to feed young families on meager pensions. With the heath nearby we had the illusion of living in the country; milk, coal, and greengrocery goods were sold from the back of horse-drawn carts at our doorstep. Fred acquired a rusty bicycle, but otherwise we had no transport and walked everywhere. We had few books, no pictures, a wind-up gramophone, but no radio or camera. My mother fed us on plain, nourishing food: tripe and onions, Irish stew, and suet puddings. As Grandma Hannah was now a housekeeper to a family with two small sons, we were well supplied with hand-me-down clothing.

But my mother's life must have been very cramped, for with no hobbies and little to occupy his mind Fred had taken to drink. Every night, even on weekends, after rising late and drifting through the newspaper's racing pages in search of certainties that his few shillings seemed only to discourage, he would leave the house regularly at six for the local pub, The Plough. Connie would be left alone with her two young sons, her knitting, and perhaps a library book. With intelligence enough to earn her own living she was caught in the old matrimonial trap.

Having performed well in school plays, she had had a secret

ambition to become an actress. But Grandma Cornish had blocked that certain road to ruin. During her lonely nights Connie must have dreamed of future triumphs for her sons, to make up for Fred's lack of material success. In the right mood Fred could be wonderful company—full of stories of his early adventures. But beneath the laughter was an increasing anger at the way his life had been curtailed by his terrible wound when he was only 31.

The marriage became increasingly bleak. I don't think Connie had every truly enjoyed the pleasures of love, and with contraception primitive and crude, my parents, like many others at that time, found abstention the easiest course. (Indeed, my mother once confided to my wife that after I was born she had "shut the shop.")

The Wall Street Crash of 1929 affected us worse than other families. The Canadian dollar plunged against the pound, and the Dominion government drastically cut war veterans' pensions. We now began to experience near-poverty. Connie's pride wouldn't allow her to default on the mortgage payments, so she managed to let the front room to a couple for 17 shillings and sixpence (about a dollar) a week to cover the cost. Unfortunately for me their name was Hoare. For one of my first essays at school I was caned on both hands for "impudence," for I had innocently written, "My mum lets off her front room to a couple of hores."

My brother and I had been enrolled at the Grove Road Primary School, a rundown Victorian institution where the three Rs and fear of God were instilled with the rod. Learning was ladled out without a hint of enriching the mind: history as written by victorious empire-builders, geography as a catalog of exploitable raw materials, the great English language reduced to a means of correspondence. Originality of thought ("rebellion") was not encouraged. It was assumed that if you could learn to write adequately and grasp basic arithmetic you would (if lucky) end up in some pen-pushing role in business or the civil service, or as an underpaid teacher, unquestioningly obedient to authority and the Crown. The only escape lay in "The Scholarship," an examination taken at age 12 which decided whether you gained one of the few places at the County School Isleworth, or went to the more attainable Spring Grove Secondary, or languished with the rest at Hounslow Central School. My brother, of course, won a top place with ease, and with a certain difficulty I followed him to the County School, a pleasant three-mile cycle ride from our house.

By this time, 1935, the year of King George V's Silver Jubilee, my father had sobered up enough to get a job. As an assistant relieving officer in one of the saddest parts of Paddington, West London, he had daily to listen to pleas for financial help, stories of appalling poverty and misery that made our minor hardships seem trivial. I remember his taking us one Sunday to watch a column of South Wales miners on a hunger march to Whitehall. Soaked through, their tattered raincoats belted with rough string, some with feet bound in rags, they were an impressive sight as they came marching by with remembered military pride.

We lived a mere ten miles from the very seat of government, and yet the thought of people like us wielding political power was still remote. Politicians were stone-faced masters in black bowler hats and long coats glimpsed only rarely in newspaper photos, their voices as yet unheard on radio, making furtive decisions to withdraw from the gold standard or to cut benefits for the unemployed, without concern for the suffering of millions.

Meanwhile in Europe Mussolini ranted, Daladier dithered, Franco plotted the rape of Spanish democracy, and Hitler consolidated secret military muscle, while in Britain Stanley Baldwin, presiding over an unhappy coalition of opportunists and fools, was portrayed on huge billboards as a bland, pipe-smoking image of "sound common sense." With reason, our aging, bearded monarch, George V, glared angrily at photographers, his ancient queen's chalky death mask veiled beneath her perennial toque-turban, and occasional cinema newsreels gave us glimpses of the heir to the throne, Prince Edward (soon to be discredited as the Duke of Windsor), a skinny dwarf in riding breeches and an oversized army peaked cap, smirking and giggling among real men—while others broke land speed records, flew anew across desert and oceans, ballooned to new stratospheres, all in the name of "progress."

Life for us eased in the early thirties. My father's wages, such as they were, enabled Connie to buy her first radio and to involve herself in local politics and amateur dramatics, which meant my brother and I had to sit through hours of appalling dramatic tosh in draughty church halls, waiting for the enlivening moments when

Mother finally appeared as a comic maid, or once, splendid in shiny red rayon, as a Tart with a Heart of Gold.

In 1937 she had somehow saved enough to buy a secondhand Morris Minor that took us to the sea in Devon for our first proper family holiday. Fred attempted to drive at first, but after a few hair-raising miles, difficulties double-clutching with his artificial leg made him yield the wheel to Mother.

When we arrived home from the holiday a large brown envelope awaited. It had been opened and resealed several times, but had somehow found its way at last to "Miss Constance Cornish" in Hounslow, and was from a firm of solicitors in Port Elizabeth, South Africa. Her father, Horace Lethbridge, had apparently died in 1922, but his partner, Walter White, a bachelor, had survived him by 13 years, and on his instructions their combined estate was now left to daughter Connie.

Lethbridge and White had owned a well-patronized music shop in Port Elizabeth, with a flourishing import trade in violins, trumpets, and particularly pianos for the emerging South African white middle class. (Presumably fastidious Afrikaners insisted their children should play only white notes!) The proceeds were substantial.

For the next few months (as the old king died and the new one decided to abdicate for the sake of marrying a curiously domineering, twice-divorced American, Wallis Simpson) we slowly came to terms with newfound affluence. Mother bought us a grander house in the Grove, Isleworth, a broad boulevard sheltered with ancient trees, a new, larger Morris replaced the Minor, and the rest of the money was safely invested. Fred was not allowed to touch a penny. Brewery profits were high enough already.

Then one of Fred's army friends, Ted Bartholomew, turned up from Canada and amazed his old comrade by revealing that he was the father of Freddie Bartholomew, a child film star currently appearing in Hollywood epics like *Kidnapped* and *David Copperfield*. For days my mother went around with a peculiar gleam in her eye, then announced her startling plan. I was to become the vehicle for her frustrated acting ambitions. My brother was more studious, I was the clown able to get cheap classroom laughs with instant mimicry of masters. Connie Cornish had no doubt that *her* son, bursting with talent as he surely must be, needed only proper training to become a much bigger star than the offspring of the wretched Bartholomew.

I wasn't so sure—but early in 1937, before I could argue, I was enrolled for acting classes every Wednesday night and Saturday morning at Miss Italia Conti's Stage School, over a dingy engineering works in Theobald's Road, Holborn, in Central London.

I welcomed the change from ordinary schoolwork, reading Shakespeare's plays for the first time and discovering how scenes could be brought to life and transformed by inflection, pace, reaction, and actors' inner energy. My fellow pupils included Richard Todd, Leslie Phillips, and George Cole. Soon I was considered proficient enough to be sent to professional auditions, and appeared in the summer holidays at the Open Air Theatre in Regent's Park as Mamillius in Shakespeare's *The Winter's Tale*, with Jack Hawkins and Fay Compton, directed by the outrageous old ham Robert Atkins ("You may have heard my Belch, but wait till you see my Bottom!"), and in the autumn at the Old Vic as Prince Edward in *Richard III*, with Emlyn Williams and Angela Baddeley, directed by Tyrone Guthrie, where I immediately noticed the considerable difference between actors' reactions to the flatulent direction of an old windbag like Atkins and the close attention paid to Guthrie's every word.

Tall and rather fey, with a soft Anglo-Irish accent, Guthrie unwittingly taught me how to speak to actors, how to encourage with properly judged criticism, and most importantly, why in rehearsal a director *must* create a positive and creative atmosphere.

I also appeared in *Peter Pan* at the Palladium for four weeks of the Christmas holidays with Anna Neagle, and in *The Zeal of Thy House*, by crime writer Dorothy L. Sayers, at the Westminster in the summer of 1938. Sayers, a fiercely amiable Cheshire cat in fur-trimmed drag, successful author of the Lord Peter Wimsey thrillers, had written this "serious" play about the conflict between the Church and an architect's ego over the rebuilding of Canterbury Cathedral in 1174 after it had burned down four years previously (having been the scene of the murder of Thomas à Becket). The chosen architect, William of Sens, was arrogant and lustful, but effective and imaginative. An unexplained accident ("Either the vengeance of God or the Envy of the Devil") prevented him from completing his ambitious design.

The play was a trial run for the committed Christianity that Dorothy Sayers was to display three years later in her radio (and later television) series about the life of Jesus Christ, *The Man Born to Be King*. Her use of language was admirable, achieving rhythms worthy of Auden or Eliot. Harcourt Williams played William of Sens, with Marie Ney as his lover, Lady Ursula. He also directed, quite differently from the inspirational Tyrone Guthrie. An old-fashioned ranter, Williams played everything straight out to the gallery—a style of acting I saw only once more, from the outrageous Donald Wolfit.

All this experience persuaded me *not* to pursue a career as an actor. The professionals I had met seemed shallow and superficial, always worried about where their next engagement was coming from. But I had discovered a real ambition. That same summer I had been chosen for a tiny two-line part as a hotel page boy in a film being shot in the newly opened Pinewood Studios called *Young and Innocent*.

Dressed in a tight uniform, I was not immediately needed, but was allowed to watch the crew setting up. The whole studio was dominated by a short, chubby man with a protruding stomach and a Cockney accent, the director. I asked his name.

"That … is Mr. Hitchcock." And although *Young and Innocent* is not one of Alfred Hitchcock's finest cinematic achievements, it contains a complicated crane shot. From a high view of a hotel ballroom crowded with fox-trotting dancers the camera moves relentlessly forward through the revelers, nearer and nearer to the dance band and crooner on the stage, right into a huge close-up of the eye of the drummer, at the moment when the man's nerve breaks (as he sees a detective enter, out of shot) and his eye begins to twitch nervously—revealing him as the murderer and thus proving fugitive Derrick de Marney's innocence.

It was this key shot that I was privileged to observe at age 14 in my first day in a film studio. There were no zoom lenses in those days: the camera had to travel all the way, slowly gliding down on its huge, cumbersome crane arm, complete with camera operator and focus-puller to the final dramatic moment of truth.

I watched, from first rough rehearsal, the laying of boards for the crane to run on, the careful orchestration of dancers, waiters, and main actors, to the final cue for the drummer's reaction. At last came the great moment when camera and sound rolled for a take—the slap of the clapper-board, Hitchcock's muttered "Action," the start of playback of previously recorded band music, dancers springing to life, and the slow movement of the camera crane to its objective, dancers skillfully parting just out of picture to let it through, all the way to the guilty drummer's eye—again and again, 16 times, until the director was satisfied and said, "Print."

From then on I had no doubt. Though actors receive most of the public's acclaim, it is the director who essentially chooses the subject, casts it, shapes and delivers the final work. While often expressing powerful emotion and truth, an actor is only an interpreter of someone else's words and thoughts. I wanted to control and communicate my own message.

My mother was disappointed, but the acting classes ended. Chamberlain met Hitler for the useless Munich "agreement," making another war with Germany inevitable. But unlike the long conflict that had ended my father's vigorous life, this war was to be fought for a credible moral purpose—the destruction of a foul tyranny based on the crudest form of racism, intolerance, and national greed. I realized I had about four years to complete my education before having to join the army. I forgot the theater and film and concentrated on real history, true geography, mathematics, and the invaluable English language.

War was declared, food was rationed, France overrun. Bombs fell near our house in Isleworth throughout the winter of 1940-41, shattering the windows many times as we all slept on mattresses on the ground floor. My brother postponed his training as a chartered accountant, volunteered for the tank corps, and was commissioned second lieutenant from Sandhurst in 1942. My father's duties in local government now included organizing air raid precautions and overnight fire watching in his Paddington office—pressure that brought on the first of his heart attacks, which forced him to give up work in 1942. Unfortunately this also gave him greater leisure for serious drinking. Often my mother and I would be awakened on his return after eleven at night by a loud thump as he tripped over the doorstep and collapsed on the mat, before being hauled upstairs.

The government started producing weekly five-minute propa-

ganda films to be shown in all cinemas, on every subject, from how
to tackle a German paratrooper to saving waste paper. As a relief
from tutorials I wrote several trial scripts and sent them hopefully
to "The Minister of Information." Surprisingly this led to an appointment with the poet John Betjeman, who had some sort of ministry
job (and expected a mature writer, not a beardless student), and to
a further meeting with Basil Wright, noted documentary filmmaker,
whose *Song of Ceylon* had successfully experimented with sound
and visuals before the war. With his help I was assigned in the summer vacation to Strand Films, a company producing sturdy patriotic documentaries, as a literary "keeper" to an as-yet-unknown
Dylan Thomas, who was supposed to be writing a script about the
newly formed Arts Council, then called the "Council for the Encouragement of Music & Arts." Dylan arranged to rendezvous at Hene-
key's Bar in Holborn at 10:30 A.M. Not used to pubs I diffidently
sipped tomato juice until he arrived about lunchtime, belching and
farting like an evil cherub. For a couple of hours we played with
his rough draft, Dylan displaying dazzling verbal skill but not writing very much down. So it was for the next two weeks at haphaz-
ard intervals, until a virtually unchanged script was delivered, and
shot by a variety of directors. (In John Brinnin's book on Dylan
Thomas I am noted "P. Scott" as a contributor to the film. I have
chosen to use "Graham Scott" as my surname to avoid confusion
with another "Peter Scott," the wildlife preservationist and son of
Antarctic explorer Robert Falcon Scott.)

I also picked up from Strand Films a production that none
of their elegant directors would touch: a cheap and cheerful instruc-
tional for the Ministry of Agriculture to teach farmers to culti-
vate their own vegetable seeds. At 18, with equally young cameraman John Burgoyne-Johnson and an ancient clockwork camera, I
wrote, directed, edited, and delivered a 20-minute film on a budget
of less than £350 ($500) and returned a small profit to the company.
I was thus able legitimately to write "Film Director" instead of "Student" under "Civilian Occupation" when I was called up for the
army in autumn 1942. I reported to Warley Barracks in Essex, unprepared for the shock of induction. Hair shaved to the bone, our shivering bodies solemnly inspected for God-knew-what scrofulous
infection, we were issued ill-fitting battledress and viselike boots,

and set to polish, scrub, and march our way to victory. There was never any hot water at Warley. After a cold shave you could be screamed at by some maniac sergeant for a single visible bristle— or a speck of mud on a just-polished boot.

After six weeks I was transferred to Lochmaben in the Scottish Borders to train with a new unit, the Reconnaissance Corps, a fast-moving commando unit designed to probe ahead of the main army with small groups of assault troops to gain intelligence of enemy positions. Our instructors, mostly ex–Royal Marines, were at least proper soldiers, not parade-ground sadists, and the training, though hard—using weaponry, running up and down mountains, and embarking across the loch in flimsy canvas boats, conducted in continuous icy rain—at least made sense. For moments I was even able to appreciate the beauty of purple heather and moorland in the country of my ancestors.

After three months I was selected as a "potential officer." Vacancies that week were in the Royal Artillery. I traveled south to an officer cadet training unit near Wrotham in Kent, and after six more weeks I graduated to the final unit in Catterick, a stark army enclave on a bare Yorkshire hillside. Here I made my first real friends in the army: Rob Richardson, who sadly was killed in Normandy the following year; and Peter Chudleigh, a charming gnome from Cornwall with a wicked sense of humor, who survived to become a successful merchant banker. We met again recently, and although he was over 75, his boisterous laugh had not faded. But my most important friend, as it turned out, was Royston Morley, urbane, mysterious, and older than most of us, who astonishingly revealed that before the war he had worked as a producer in fledgling BBC television. His faith in the new medium seemed perverse and extraordinary at that time. I was committed to film, as shown in thousands of cinemas all over the world, but Royston could already foresee a future society with television sets in every household.

As we pushed the heavy and ancient 25-pounder cannon across the wind-scoured moors, I began to be convinced that in the end television must inevitably become the medium of the future. But it would take time to establish. My immediate prospects after the war would be in film. At the end of November 1943 we were all passed out with military music and dispersed to our various units. I was posted to the 145th Field Artillery Regiment, near the port of Dover. Originally a "territorial" unit formed of weekend volunteers who had all been called into service at the beginning of hostilities, 145 was known as the "Berkshire Yeomanry," its officers' mess a last bastion of British snobbery. From captain upward most of the officers had been at Eton College together, with nicknames like "Squiffy" and "Pongo," their country-house servants pressed into uniform as batmen. New officers like me were deemed to be "WOGs" (War Office Gentlemen) and given all the rough tasks, like all-night orderly officer duties and inspecting the camp latrines.

Not surprisingly the unit had not been selected to be part of the spearhead of the forthcoming summer's invasion of Occupied France. Instead we were given the task of deception as a "ghost army." Strategy dictated that the Germans, who had built their strongest defenses near Calais, 20 miles across the Channel from Dover, should be led to believe that the main invasion would come from there. In fact the Sixth American and Second British Armies were well concealed in the southwest of England from Portsmouth to Plymouth, ready for a much longer sea voyage to invade east and west of Cherbourg.

Our division, plus a mass of dummy tanks and cardboard airplanes parked at random under trees, was the decoy. We created an impression of massive movement by driving our trucks and guns up and down the leafy lanes of Kent from morning to night, clogging the main highways, occasionally boarding old landing ships at night careless of noise and flaring light, to venture into the Channel in the hope of luring enemy E-boats with their deadly torpedoes. (Luckily none appeared!) Obvious as this may sound, it worked. The German High Command became convinced the main Allied thrust would come from the Kent ports, keeping at least two crack divisions in Calais until it was too late, when the Americans and British had already secured firm footholds in Normandy.

Before D-Day, however, in mid–May, I was sent for further battle-training to Westgate near Margate. Pre-invasion tension was making instructors careless with live ammunition. Two days after I arrived, a corporal, blithely explaining how long one could hold a grenade after pulling out the safety pin, managed to blow his hand off, showering his startled class with shrapnel.

We were divided into platoons irrespective of rank, captains rubbing shoulders with sergeants, and daily trucked to the wooded countryside to run and crawl through the undergrowth while live bullets flew over our heads and earth exploded all around us. Late one morning, crossing a river weighed down with a heavy Bren gun, I slipped and fell in three inches of mud. As I lay exhausted, the rest of the platoon ran past. Perhaps the explosives instructor couldn't see me—or maybe he felt I needed a shake-up. He pressed his plunger: the bank before me erupted. I was thrown several feet—and woke up, badly bruised, with a broken collarbone and a splitting headache. Arm in plaster, downgraded to Medical Category C, I was posted to Woolwich Depot, another shabby Victorian pile overcrowded with middle-aged officers and other ranks temporarily out of action with every complaint from hernias to hemorrhoids.

We paraded daily at 8:00 A.M., spending a whole hour on roll call, then whiled away the rest of the day on pointless route-marches or map-reading exercises. Nights were empty; once dinner had been served there were only bores at the bar as entertainment.

Meanwhile the Allies had fought on in northern France and begun their painful advance to the Rhine. The Berkshire Yeomanry embarked for the Far East, complete with regimental silver but without me. My one salvation was the local librarian, who began to visit every week with a useful supply of books on filmmaking: Arnheim's *Cinema*, Pudovkin's *Film Technique*, Roger Manvell's *Film*, Field's *Art of Walt Disney*, and Gilbert Seldes' *Movies for the Millions*. But I felt trapped, almost like a prisoner-of-war, without the impetus of some daring plan for escape.

Meanwhile my brother, having fought in North Africa, had now gone on to win the Military Cross in Italy for rescuing his driver from their blazing tank and rounding up 25 prisoners. But my headaches continued. There was no escape from Category C.

As battle lines froze in winter, the War Office uttered a muted offer: If any downgraded officer could find a war-related job he might be granted temporary release. Not sure whether they meant it, I approached Basil Wright and his friends in the Ministry of Information.

A Colonial Film Unit had just been set up and was now proposing a weekly African Newsreel to impress the inhabitants of Kenya,

Nigeria, and other empire territories with vivid proof that we were winning the war. An interview with Bill Sellars, a cheerful ex–district commissioner, slightly puzzled at being asked to run a film unit, led (on the strength of my having made one film—on vegetable seeds!) to my being appointed film editor on the newsreel, under white-haired silent-film veteran George Pearson. My release meant that I could live at home, wear civilian clothes, and travel to Soho Square every day by underground subway. The newsreel was simple enough to construct: we would take appropriate stories from the biweekly *Movietone News* and edit in new sequences of the battles in Europe and Southeast Asia from the army's own specially shot footage.

Two mornings a week I would attend the War Office screenings of the latest material from army cameramen, much, alas, not very usable. It was there that I saw the first terrible pictures of Nazi concentration camps as they were liberated, images of starvation and suffering beyond the most violent and depraved imagination, and not then allowed to be shown to the British public, as the cruelty and despair were felt too harrowing.

In these days of rapid information and freedom from censorship it is difficult to realize how ill informed people used to be, even as recently as 1945. Newspapers, radio, and choppy cinema newsreels gave only a glimpse of the realities of international tension or social injustice nearer home. Spiritually there was true poverty. Only the educated few listened to music, read poetry, visited art galleries or the serious theater. Life for most of the British was painfully inhibited. There might be tenderness, love, and compassion within the family, but otherwise people seemed embarrassed by any public display of emotion.

Because the war had uprooted millions into cheerless army camps and hospitals, cinemas were packed, showing polished Hollywood unreality and more plodding fare from our own studios. British films were not bad, but they had little resemblance or relevance to the real life that people knew. (David Lean's well-meaning *In Which We Serve*, Noel Coward's story of life aboard a Royal Navy destroyer in wartime, showed a lower deck manned entirely by West End actors trying to hide their cultured accents with impeccable stage–Cockney!)

Studio-bound British films lacked imagination, passion, and daring. Denham and Pinewood had become moribund, sources of easy money for uninspired hacks. If the producers of wartime stinkers had ever been in a provincial audience and heard the catcalls of the licentious soldiery they might have reconsidered their creative standing!

At this time I was lucky enough to be able to attend private showings of captured German films like *Baron Munchausen* and Vittorio de Sica's Mussolini-vintage *Our Children Are Watching Us*, as well as old films like Marcel Carné's *Le Jour se Lève* and *Les Enfants du Paradis*—all confirming my belief that there was a better way of telling stories visually than the good old British photographed stage play.

Royston Morley had now transferred to an army radio unit and was able to provide me with authentic battle sounds for the newsreel. (We had only to provide music and sound effects; local commentaries were added live on the spot in each territory.) But I was getting priceless experience making the best of often inferior film, and I would be at least a year ahead of my contemporaries seeking a job in the postwar film industry, while they waited for transport home from Germany or the Far East.

What else had I to offer? Youth, of course, energy, and some idea of the needs of our future audience. But I had little of what John Grierson called "hard root experience." My childhood had been happy (though I had secretly observed my father's bitter cripple's frustration turn to boozy acceptance). I'd seen British class prejudice at its worst, and when visiting a convicted absentee gunner had been shocked by the degradation of our prisons, but I'd escaped the suffering the war had brought to so many. And as an unintentional survivor, I might at least bring a few fresh dramatic ideas to the egalitarian postwar world we were blithely hoping to create.

How little I really knew....

At last, on May 8, 1945, hostilities in Europe ended. The African Newsreel was terminated, but I was immediately offered another job by producer Ralph Keene as film editor for Greenpark Productions, and the War Office agreed to my release. Based at the rundown Merton Park Studios near Wimbledon, we made several documentaries on postwar reconstruction, the replanning of London (which in the event never happened), and a film on English criminal justice directed by ambitious Ken Annakin, later director of *The Battle of the Bulge* and *Those Magnificent Men in Their Flying Machines*, with whom I formed an instant and lifelong friendship.

Ken and I discovered that there were a number of important classic films, both sound and silent, we had never seen. Lacking the means to hire and screen them we teamed up with a local lawyer, John Terry (later Sir John, head of Britain's National Film Finance Corporation), and formed the Kingston Film Society for like-minded film buffs, holding weekly meetings in a cramped room over the gas company showrooms in the town (they happened to have a 16mm projector for hire), where we viewed everything available from the British Film Institute: *The Birth of a Nation, Intolerance* (both by D. W. Griffith), Flaherty's *Nanook of the North*, Wiene's *Cabinet of Doctor Caligari, The Blue Angel, Kameradschaft, The Plow That Broke the Plains*, and Eisenstein's *Battleship Potemkin*.

Unfortunately a young reporter from the *Kingston Times* attended the last two performances and decided to make a name for himself by denouncing our use of government gaswork premises for "Communist propaganda." We lost our projector, and the society died.

I continued to edit documentaries for Greenpark through 1945 and much of 1946. My headaches had eased, and I was restored to fitness. I was enjoying the work, but I was already 22—aging fast— and desperate to direct. Good technicians with far more experience were returning in large numbers to the expanding British feature film industry. My one-year lead was running out.

I wrote careful letters to the most distinguished producers of the day, among them Anthony Havelock-Allan (David Lean's producer on *Brief Encounter* and *Oliver Twist*), and to Roy and John Boulting, the lively twins who had graduated from low budgets to make a brilliant version of Robert Ardrey's *Thunder Rock* in 1942, and more recently *Desert Victory*, a strong account of the British feat of arms against General Rommel in the Egyptian and Libyan deserts. Havelock-Allan saw me and said, "Keep in touch." (I did, and edited a couple of films for him in 1951–52). Roy Boulting took me to lunch and explained that although he and John were keen to help young technicians, they already had a first-class editor, alas. Then the Rank Organization, which owned over half of the larger cinemas in Britain, decided to imitate the successful American series of short topical films *The March of Time* with their own *This Modern Age*. Ken Annakin casually told me he had been offered one, about the forthcoming independence of the Sudan, and had turned it down! This was my chance. With Ken's blessing I hurried to the local library and read everything I could find about the Sudan—particularly its history, and the present political situation. It was, I discovered, a vast area of eastern Africa below Egypt, desert in the north, swamp and jungle in the south, traversed by the Blue and White Niles, nearly as big as Western Europe. Conquered by General Horatio Kitchener in retaliation for the murder of General Gordon by the religious leader el-Mahdi in 1885, the huge country had been an Anglo-Egyptian "joint-dominion" for over 50 years, effectively run by British district officers with Egyptian and Sudanese assistants, keeping an uneasy peace between the Muslim north and the pagan and Christian south. With independence imminent, a power struggle was developing between the Ashigga (right wing) and the Umma (workers) parties.

I wrote a treatment and went to see George Ivan Smith and Sergei Nolbandov, producers of *This Modern Age*. Surprised at my youth, they didn't think much of my script of barely digested facts either, and after a polite hearing I was shown the door.

Walking home, I resolved I would not take "no" for an answer. I knew I could deliver the film they needed. The next morning I rang Ivan Smith. Under pressure to produce a film every week he too had had second thoughts and talked to Ken Annakin. I was invited back, and to my delight Ivan (who had worked for the United Nations organization in its earliest days) began to explain the sort of visual energy he was hoping for—exactly what I wanted to give them.

Five hours later, my mind an overstuffed memory bank, I left with my first directing assignment—after less than two years in the film business.

I told Roy Boulting. He was intrigued and had a suggestion.

He had recently finished directing Howard Spring's *Fame Is the Spur* and was still editing, but his brother John was due to start shooting Graham Greene's *Brighton Rock* quite soon and they had not yet assigned a new editor. Could I be back from Africa in time to take over?

Could I? I rapidly assented and prepared to fly to Cairo, our first stop, with a three-man team: Ted Moore, who later shot several James Bond movies; Ian Grant, his assistant, soon a respected contributor to Independent Television News; and, as researcher and production manager, the Honorable Peter Rodd (son of Lord Rennel of Rodd and estranged husband of society novelist Nancy Mitford), recently retired colonel of some superior regiment, who was reputed to "know the country." The scruffy individual I first met in London in October 1946 completely belied this impressive pedigree. In a somewhat alcoholic mumble he informed me that he had been at Oxford University with Evelyn Waugh and was the original of "the bounder Basil Seale" in Waugh's novel *Put Out More Flags*. But there was no time to doubt Rodd's suitability. Next day we began a grueling flight by ex–RAF Dakota (refueling at Nice, Malta, and Sidi Barani) to arrive in Cairo 24 hours later.

I had never been farther than a one-week trip to Denmark. Cairo—with its heat, mad traffic, dust, flashing neon signs, crowded markets aromatic with spice and sweat, perfumed ladies, and hideously deformed beggars—was a loud and raw experience. For the first time I was in the midst of real starvation and suffering, and not sharing it—as Brendan Behan later described it, "floating round a sewer in a glass-bottomed boat"—which is always the fate of film and television crews in foreign locations. No matter how caring and compassionate we try to be, we simply record pain and cruelty and injustice—and then pass on, *having done nothing to rectify it.*

But there was also the magical vista of the Pyramids, epic monuments of the past, the Sphinx, in those days still unfenced and open for tourists to clamber over for snapshots, and the stifling dusty museum, dominated by monumental effigies of Rameses II and the golden mask of the boy-king Tutankhamun.

In Egypt the British flag had been lowered forever earlier that year (as it was soon to be lowered in many old empire-pink parts of the globe), beckoning a future independence, an incredible mixture of shameless corruption, and flickering hopes of freedom. The new Egyptian government wanted to hold on to the Sudan as a dependent colony and opposed the British determination to grant full independence. The Egyptians supported the rightist Ashigga Party, which was now barred from Khartoum, Sudan's capital, and had made Cairo its base. My brief was to get an interview with the party first.

With a suspicious flourish Rodd produced a group of shifty-looking "politicians" in blue suits whose extreme views we duly recorded on the veranda of Shepheard's Hotel. Later I discovered he'd rounded up a few Sudanese clerks and waiters and told them what to say. I was furious. The assignment was difficult enough without practical jokes from a retarded schoolboy. With all the lofty arrogance of my 23 years I threatened the seedy aristocrat with a swift passage home. "No one would have noticed," he muttered. "All politicians are crooks anyway." But from then on he behaved responsibly and well.

His contacts were indeed excellent. Officially the Egyptians had strict controls on foreign film units. But it was important to show the poverty in their own country as an argument against Egypt's taking over the Sudan. I discussed the problem with Rodd, who simply bribed an Arab tout lurking on the pavement outside Shepheard's to conduct us to his village on the Nile delta where Ted Moore captured uncensored coverage of scrawny cattle and fly-infested half-starved children. Another call by Rodd to Lord Kinross at the British embassy secured an RAF plane to fly over the Suez Canal for further unauthorized filming.

At the end of the week we caught one of the last Empire flying boats, following the glittering ribbon of the great Nile below us southward towards Khartoum, via Luxor, Wadi Halfa, and Atbara. In those days the "world's favorite airline" actually cared about its passengers and laid on lunch at the Winter Palace Hotel after we had skimmed down onto the Nile at Luxor, followed by a leisurely tour around the ancient temple, before flying on to land at last in tropical night's black velvet warmth on the old river in the Sudanese capital where General Gordon had met his unfortunate end.

Khartoum's Grand Hotel sprawled like an exhausted courtesan on the broad shoulders of the Nile, lofty marble halls busy with ghostly servants in long, white galabieh nightshirts gliding courteously to answer the last few imperious hand-claps of perspiring British expatriates. Though the city was now rapidly emptying of army and RAF officers on the eve of independence, vestiges of Khartoum's British society still remained, a miniature version of Kenyan Nairobi's "Happy Valley," with occasional brawls in the whites-only Sudan Club over repossession of one or another of the tanned and scrawny ex-beauties wafting about in chiffon and Chanel.

We were welcomed with a certain suspicion (the taking of cinematograph films was *not* a career for gentlemen), while Rodd addressed his mind to the problem of transporting us through the length and breadth of this vast dry country. Always believing in starting at the top, he contacted the governor-general, Sir Hubert Huddleston, for help.

Before long we were sitting down to dinner in the governor's palace with the full panoply of the Last Days of the Raj. Huddleston turned out to be the finest type of colonial administrator, who understood that in a democracy the best propaganda is to reveal the truth. Thanks to him we met all the people who mattered, including members of the real opposition party and the murderous Mahdi's grandson, Sir Sayed Abdel Rahman el-Mahdi, in his peacock garden. In addition Huddleston lent us his personal railway coach, complete with luxury stateroom, a cook, and a valet, to enable us to tour the enormous country in some style.

We set off from Khartoum station at a leisurely ten miles per hour (saving fuel!), traveling through infinite scrubland punctuated by umbrella thorn, pausing to film the well-irrigated cotton fields between the Blue and White Niles. We rumbled on east to the parched towns of Gedaref and Kassala, dominated by tall hills with curiously rounded and polished domes. We drove on by truck with Camel Corps escort into lawless Eritrea and Ethiopia, rattling north for Christmas on the Red Sea at Port Sudan with beery British emigrants en route to Australia. A further trip down the coast took us to the deserted old Arab slave port at Suakin, its eerily crumbling houses reflected in a glazed lagoon, and we returned at last to Omdurman and Khartoum by way of the clanging railway sheds at Atbara. A second rail excursion took us far west deep into the desert of Dongola and the hills beyond El Obeid, where the naked Nuba performed a spectacular dance for us. Finally we boarded a patched-up Wellington bomber to fly south to the steamy swamps of the Sudd and the relentless heat of Malakal and Juba. The trip showed Rodd at his best. He seemed to know everyone with any influence, even in the remotest Saharan outpost, and had a buccaneer's contempt for obstacles. Had he wanted to, he might have made a career as a location organizer in difficult countries. But even toward the end of our shoot he became bored and tried to set up another safari into Ethiopia, buying a clapped-out station wagon to penetrate the Highlands, until a firm cable from London told him to stop wasting Lord Rank's money.

Africa was the beginning of my real education, both politically and intellectually. Poverty in Egypt and the Sudan was even worse than I had imagined. Yet despite the heat, insects, and endemic disease, there was a popular will to survive utterly different from the stoic acceptance of privation I'd known in wartime Britain.

On our last day, Rodd persuaded me to fly back via Paris to deliver a large carton of soap powder ("Can't get it in France, old boy") to his wife, Nancy Mitford, with whom he hadn't lived for some years. I found her, elegant, witty, and charming, in her apartment in the Rue Monsieur. Her novel *The Pursuit of Love* had recently been a runaway success. She seemed puzzled by the gift of soap powder but gave me an excellent lunch, and was quietly pleased to hear that Rodd was actually gainfully employed.

A few weeks later I received a typical postcard postmarked Marrakesh: "Many thanks for delivering the hashish. Nancy delighted. Love Prodd." Another of his jokes?

The finished film, which I couldn't have made without Peter Rodd's help and Ted Moore's superb camerawork, was judged one of the most effective of the *Modern Age* series. I didn't see Rodd again until many years later, when he was being wheelchaired down Piccadilly by a rather horsey lady. Practically *non compos mentis*, he just barely remembered our expedition together.

Back in England, and still only 23, I began to edit my first feature film, *Brighton Rock*. Graham Greene had written a powerful melodrama about prewar Brighton racetrack gangs who offered crude "protection" to on-course betting bookmakers—and violent

Filming in Sudan with Ted Moore (*right*), 1947.

razor-slashing to defaulters—a story overlaid with Greene's special
brand of Catholic skepticism. His protagonist, Pinkie Brown, 17-
year-old leader of a sleazy razor-gang, was haunted by his own private demons. Once an unlikely hope for the priesthood, now a sadist
and pervert, secretly afraid of physical contact, the boy was obsessed
with his own sense of evil and a certainty of the fiery hell awaiting
him. When forced to marry a little waitress to prevent her from tes-
tifying to his involvement in the particularly brutal murder of a
reporter, he attempts to coerce her into a suicide pact, still conscious of his own unforgivable mortal sin. Yet despite its violence
Greene had somehow managed to invest the tale with a certain quality by fine writing and his undoubted spiritual conviction. It did,
however, seem a strange choice for the (then) socially aware Boulting twins.

At the time the book was considered no more than a routine
thriller from the author of *A Gun for Hire* and *Stamboul Train*. A
play version adapted by Terence Rattigan had had a successful run
in the West End of London, but Greene himself wrote the screenplay for the film.

The backers, Associated British Picture Corporation (ABPC),

owners of a major cinema chain, were rebuilding their main studios at Elstree after wartime occupation by the army, and Roy and John were forced to use a converted tobacco factory in Welwyn Garden City, some miles farther north. Because the cramped space would cause delay in building and striking sets, John, directing rather than producing for the first time, was able to demand a 14-week shooting schedule, plus five more weeks on location in Brighton.

On the first day I cautiously watched him from the shadows as he rehearsed the opening scenes in the gang's seedy house. The atmosphere was tense and expectant, but no one had any idea we were participating in the creation of what would become a cinematic classic.

The next day we saw the scene realized on film, enhanced by Harry Waxman's atmospheric lighting. It began after gang leader Kite's death, with boastful Dallow, shifty Cubitt, and aging hanger-on Spicer gradually accepting the dead man's order that his favorite, 17-year-old psychopath Pinkie (Richard Attenborough), should become their new leader, and ended as the boy convinced them they must murder the newsman responsible for Kite's death.

John had given me precise editing notes, and in the cutting room it seemed to assemble quite well. But then I ran it for Roy, the producer. The viewing room lights went up to total silence. At last Roy said quietly, "Let's put it all together and start again, shall we?" I muttered some sort of protest, but he was adamant. I broke the scene down, painstakingly reinstated each shot to full length, and together we looked at the material afresh. I began to see Roy's point. There were moments, small reactions in individual close-ups, that would add strength to the whole scene, heightening the tension between members of the vicious quartet. We began to assemble once more, adding extra nuances to John's basic concept, orchestrating a series of shots to build up Pinkie's gradual acceptance and final domination of the other three as the scene moved on to its powerful climax.

I never forgot that lesson—*always study every foot of material before editing any sequence*—and I was even more grateful for Roy's intervention when Karel Reisz approvingly quoted my work on *Brighton Rock* in his well-researched book *Film Editing*, demonstrating the elaboration from director's notes to editor's final version.

Roy also allowed me to shoot pick-up shots with a second unit, particularly for a swiftly cut sequence in a seaside pier "ghost train" where the unfortunate reporter meets his death—fast zoom-ins of phantom faces, glimpses of glittering sea below as the train gathers speed, subliminal images of falling as he is suddenly pushed out of his seat to crash to his death in the raging ocean—which are all visible in the final film.

At last the shooting finished; the film was cut to everyone's satisfaction, Hans May composed a powerful score, and the film opened early in 1948 at London's Rialto. John's precise direction and Richard Attenborough's brilliant performance ensured an enthusiastic reception. (And in the Sunday *Times* Miss Dilys Powell gave me an approving nod.) For me it was the climax of a year of rich opportunity, the colorful trek through Africa and the priceless experience of working with two master filmmakers. I looked forward eagerly to the future.

That Easter I went to stay with old friends Bill and Helen MacAlpine in South Leigh, near Oxford, where some of my schoolmates were still studying. They had rented a cottage to be near Dylan Thomas, now famous through the radio broadcast of *Under Milk Wood*, who was living with spouse Caitlin in a small house lent them by Oxford don A. J. P. Taylor's ex-wife. Unfortunately Bill and Helen had invited too many guests. I was assigned an ancient army Bell tent at the bottom of the garden, next to the privy.

On Saturday night the local intelligentsia turned up to meet the great poet, who was as usual in a belligerent mood. As I now possessed a prewar Morris Eight sedan Helen asked me to stand by to run Dylan home by midnight—before he became impossible. I waited, yawning, until about 1:00 A.M., but Dylan refused to leave. I retired to my tent and fell asleep. After about half an hour I was rudely awakened. Dylan was confidently reported to be ready to go home. Donning a raincoat over my pajamas, I returned to the house. But the poet had changed his mind once more and was now engrossed, listening to some ancient hermaphrodite droning Hebridean songs in original Gaelic. After waiting another hour I retreated once more to my canvas shelter and settled into deep slumber.

Suddenly the tent began to rattle violently. "Peter!" Dylan roared in those deep organ-pipe tones that had thrilled so many listeners. It was past three, and he wished to depart at once. But I was too warmly tucked in for a second foray. "Bugger off, Dylan!" He protested for some time, then stopped. I heard a sound like heavy rainfall, felt a splash, and realized he was relieving himself all over me through a flap in the tent. Someone else was awakened to take him off. In the pub the next day he airily dismissed the whole incident. "It is obviously your fate, my boy, to be pissed upon by genius!"

A prophecy not entirely wrong.

I was next approached by a young producer, Roger Proudlock, to direct *Panic at Madame Tussaud's*, a second-feature comedy about a pickpocket pursued into London's wax museum who hides a stolen necklace round the neck of one of the waxworks, returns later but finds the figure has been removed, and then endures all sorts of nocturnal adventures with rival crooks, a mad night watchman, and the full experience of the Chamber of Horrors in an effort to find the jewels. It wasn't a bad script, but, as I discovered, there wasn't enough money to pay for good actors.

Roger's deal with Madame Tussaud's allowed us to shoot for three weeks every night after closing time, from 6:30 P.M. until 11:30. In just five hours I had to get four minutes of screen time. I planned as much as I could, but with inferior actors and a scratch crew it was very hard. However, somehow it was all finished on time and went the rounds of provincial cinemas. I had had my first taste of direction—of a sort—but with a certain relief I returned to editing, this time at Denham Studios, a sprawling gray complex (now demolished, alas) in a pleasant woodland on the banks of the river Colne, built by Alexander Korda before the war.

The film, for Rank, *The Perfect Woman*, had been rather obviously adapted from a stage farce and starred Stanley Holloway, Nigel Patrick, and Patricia Roc, directed by ex-cameraman Bernard Knowles. I was amazed at the amount of time Bernard seemed to waste on set gossiping and joking with crew and cast, then producing results that were predictable and dull. The story, of two buffoons who accept a commission to pass off a robot woman, the creation of a wild-eyed professor, as a real live female in a public restaurant for a whole evening (not realizing the professor's lively niece has taken the place of the automaton), offered plenty of antic scope, but for some reason Knowles didn't shoot enough cover close-ups on the niece's reactions throughout, with the result that I had to use one particular shot of her about 17 times. After the champagne excitement of the Boultings this was small beer indeed!

Just as I finished, Ken Annakin offered me *Landfall*, with Michael Denison and David Tomlinson, an early Second World War story by Nevil Shute about an RAF pilot suspected of having attacked a British submarine, mistaking it for an enemy U-boat—good old stiff-upper-lip stuff—but as usual Ken made it into an entertaining film.

The newly built Elstree studios of Associated British, a gaunt, utilitarian, redbrick barracks, was an unlikely setting for high romance, but in 1949 during *Landfall* I met a delightful, golden-haired bank manager's daughter, Eve Rosemary Martell, assistant to the distinguished production designer Terence Verity. Though still very young she had already contributed to *The Hasty Heart*, with Ronald Reagan, Patricia Neal, and Richard Todd, and was later to work with the redoubtable Alfred Hitchcock on *Stage Fright*, with Marlene Dietrich and Jane Wyman, and on Raoul Walsh's *Captain Hornblower*, with Gregory Peck. Totally dissimilar to Puccini's frozen-fingered "Bohème," her family nickname was Mimi. And Mimi she remains.

I had kept in touch with Royston Morley when he returned to BBC television, and one night I went to see him transmitting a live television play by John Pudney, featuring Kenneth More from Alexandra Palace. It seemed extraordinary and exciting to be able to shoot 90 minutes of live action, delivered straight to home viewers, with actors moving from set to set, changing costumes en route, and Royston calmly directing his cameras from the control room.

I was amazed at how much apparent production value could be created with a number of simple sets in two small studios. Each prewar camera had only one wide-angle lens. Close-ups were obtained by moving in very close on a clumsy, heavy trolley to the actor involved, the cameraman having to rely on a primitive optical parallax viewfinder whose picture was upside down and reversed! So whenever Royston directed the cameramen to pan left, they would duly obey and see their top-to-bottom image moving right. It must have been very unnerving.

Mimi and I spent most of that summer together, at the theater, on the river, or finding one or two good restaurants starting up on the outskirts of London. Just as we became engaged, Anthony Have-lock-Allan, who had left the comfort of the Rank Organization for the hazardous waters of independent production, asked me to accompany him to Rome and Venice to edit *The Shadow of the Eagle*, with Richard Greene and Valentine Cortese, a swashbuck-ling eighteenth-century melodrama loosely based on a treacherous plot by Catherine the Great to induce a certain Count Orloff to kid-nap Elizabeth, pretender to her throne of All the Russias.

I traveled out with Dennis Vance, a young actor with only one scripted line as Orloff's servant, who had resolved somehow to stay on location in Italy for the whole shooting period—and finally managed it! Because the film was a coproduction with an Italian company (loaded with black market lira), the settings were sump-tuous—Venetian palaces, perfect Italian gardens, and a riotous car-nival. But after the first director was fired for wasting time, his knockabout successor tried to turn the whole adventure into a B-picture Western, leaving the unfortunate actors to flounder unaided through great gobbets of lumpy "eighteenth-century" dialogue. But when we again fell badly behind schedule, I was allowed to direct many of the action sequences with a second unit (with survivor Dennis Vance assisting).

I loved Italy. Every day I sent Mimi a new photograph of some interesting view or statue, and we resolved to return together.

We were married the following June. No sooner had we found a pleasant little house in Radlett, Hertfordshire (about 15 miles north of central London), than Tony Havelock-Allan reappeared with another film to edit in Italy. *Never Take No for an Answer* was a story by American Paul Gallico set in Assisi about a small boy and his efforts to take his sick donkey into the cathedral crypt. Filmed as *The Small Miracle*, directed by Maurice Cloche and Ralph Smart, it became an unexpected success.

Winter in Umbria was a delightful additional honeymoon, with the bonus of visual feasts—the frescoes of Cimabue and Giotto in Assisi and Perugino's fine oils in Perugia. Then in Rome we set up house in a room above the Pensione Pinciana in the Via Veneto, close to the huge park of the Villa Borghese, and we scoured the city from end to end, in and out of the frantic traffic, on a belching little Vespa moped (with Mimi a brave but terrified pillion-passenger), in search of treasure: the first brilliant sight of the interior of Saint Peter's; the Vatican Museum, with its Greco-Roman sculptures; Raffaello's huge wall paintings; Michelangelo's Sistine Chapel; the Castel Sant' Angelo; the Colosseum; Canova's lifelike reclining nude figure of Napoleon's sister, Paolina, in the Villa Borghese; and all the riches of small churches around the capital.

The year 1950 ended for us with a powerful emotional and spiritual experience as we stood among packed thousands being blessed by the pope in the forecourt of Saint Peter's, before he sealed up the holy door to mark the end of the holy year.

We returned to Radlett in the spring of 1951 to find that my father was seriously ill, not with the angina he had suffered from for many years, but with rapidly developing lung cancer—he was a heavy smoker. Removed to Saint Mary's Hospital in Paddington, he seemed to have shrunk to a very sad old man in the four months we had been away. I held the shriveled bones of his hand one night as, dulled with drugs, he muttered his last rambling thoughts. I gave him the news that Mimi was expecting our first child. It seemed to cheer him, but I was soon asked to leave. He died early the next morning at the age of 67.

His life had been full of promise until he was 31, when he had offered his very life (for the second time) for an obsolete ideal of "King and Country." Then one grim morning he had been struck down and condemned to limp through his remaining years, hampered by heavy braces and a false leg, unable to play games with his sons, or to dance or to run or be free. Original and uncommitted, all too often fuddled with alcohol, he became at last too resentful of the joys he had missed. But we still remember his laugh and his terrible jokes. Beside his tragedy my next job seemed trivial.

Dennis Vance and I had been collaborating on a script about two families living next door in Cable Street in London's Docklands, reflecting the change in citizens' attitudes from the solidarity and friendship of wartime bombing to the seething racial conflict already beginning to emerge. We had talks with British Lion, a well-established distributor, and left encouraged by the prospect of my directing, and Dennis's producing and playing a leading part.

Then they asked us, quite suddenly, to go and see a popular radio singer, Donald Peers, performing at Kingston Empire. Paunchy and gray haired, he had no less an engaging style and pleased his family audience. But what had he to do with *Cable Street*? Ah—some Wardour Street genius had decided that if Donald Peers could be "fitted in" to our story it might give it a bit of "name value."

After a great deal of argument we agreed to make the film they wanted (we both needed to work!), but with a totally different story about a young songsmith from a Welsh village based on Donald's early success. They agreed to my becoming director, and to Dennis's playing a comic press agent, but *not* to him as producer. Instead, a humorless accountant was foisted on us who made every day a Gradgrind misery.

As was the case with my first film, the budget was far too little. Sets built in Merton Park's low-ceilinged studio were cramped and sparsely furnished, but the real shortage was in acting talent. Donald himself did his best, but apart from good old Dennis the rest were nearly useless.

Having edited five major films with excellent casts I found it frustrating to have to rehearse scenes with actors who brought nothing brilliant or original to their characters, no matter what I suggested, and then to roll the camera on a dud first take and be told to "print it" by our tight-fisted producer. Thus *Sing Along with Me*, made for about £33,000 ($50,000), deservedly disappeared after its first ABC circuit showing. We never heard any more about *Cable Street* from British Lion either.

Then at the Bolton's Theatre in Chelsea I met Royston Morley again. He told me he had been hoping to become the BBC's head of television drama but that they were appointing Michael Barry instead, so he had accepted "head of training." (Thus at a stroke the BBC had robbed itself of its two most able creators of television drama, turning them into not-too-skilled administrators. Royston returned to production a few years later, but Michael Barry terminated a bright career as writer and director.)

Royston was about to set up several television production courses. Would I be interested in three months at the BBC as a trainee director? The salary, he added hastily, would be minimal, about £15 ($23) a week—barely enough to live on and a fraction of what I was making as an editor. It didn't seem possible. Our first child, Cherry, had just been born. I had a wife, a child, and a mortgage to support. However, I agreed to look out for the advertisement and apply.

At the beginning of 1952 I was offered the codirection of *Escape Route*, with over-the-hill George Raft and Sally Gray, but with a considerably bigger budget than either of my first two directing efforts. My fellow director (put in for the American half of the money) was Seymour Friedman, a cheerful young Californian I didn't meet again until 30 years later. By then he was head of production for Columbia Pictures Television in Hollywood. The script contained the usual stunt clichés, car chases, and fights on warehouse rooftops. With a short schedule, Seymour concentrated on the studio scenes and gave me the priceless experience of shooting all the action with a second unit.

At last I was invited to my first searching interview at Broadcasting House. What was I looking for from BBC television? My answer was quite simple—a chance to direct better actors and have a hand in scripts, free from anxious film-business constraints of "Is it Box-Office?" The atmosphere warmed a little. The board seemed impressed that I had actually *seen* television in production. A woman asked if I had any script ideas.

A Young Girl's Diary, by Anne Frank, a moving and true account of the thoughts and emotions of the youngest daughter of a Dutch Jewish family hiding from the Gestapo in a factory loft in occupied Amsterdam, had recently been published. I had found out that the television rights were still available, and proposed it as my first program. It must, I pointed out, be relatively cheap to stage as all the action took place in an attic. There were nods of approval. I left feeling encouraged.

But euphoria vanished with an embarrassed call from Royston a few days later. Although I had been accepted as a suitable trainee, the one and only place in drama for the September course had already been assigned to John Fernald. Would I be interested in reapplying for spring 1953? I thought fast. Could I be accepted for some other department? Royston paused. "Talks?" Sorry. I didn't know enough about BBC features. But I had edited several documentaries and directed another. Could I be called a "documentary" producer? Royston promised to find out.

A week or so later I was called for another interview and was accepted. The trouble was that there was no Documentary Department to join when I was trained. But Royston was vaguely confident that I would be taken care of. I asked if anything had happened with the Anne Frank idea. Now he sounded embarrassed. The Drama Department felt it should be a "play" not a "documentary," so Michael Barry had sent the book to his script editor, Sir Basil Bartlett, to be "read."

Slightly discouraged, I began to wonder what I was doing. Television was clearly expanding, slowly, but it might be some time before I could write and direct my own productions. Had I the right to inflict the strains of financial hardship on my young wife and baby when I could earn a much more comfortable living in the still-thriving film industry, with five major studios producing at near capacity? Mimi encouraged me to try. She knew the frustration I had suffered on the Donald Peers rubbish and understood why I had to work with a better class of actor. (For some reason well-established actors were prepared to work cheaply for BBC television.)

Two events made up my mind. I met Douglas Fairbanks, Jr., who had plans to make a number of half-hour films for American television, but he was dubious about letting me direct one of them. But a friend from Rome, Noel Charles, appeared with a script idea: During the fall of France in 1940, two British officers, both in love with the same girl, have a chance of one seat on a departing aircraft. They toss a coin; the loser won't accept defeat, knocks out his companion, and takes the flight home. He marries the girl, and later they hear that the friend he left behind has died in a prisoner-of-war camp. The wife finds out how her husband cheated to escape—and reveals that she truly loved the dead man. It seemed good enough for a television half hour. In three evenings Noel and I wrote a script and sold it to the dazed Fairbanks when he was still short of material.

Then I was contacted by a friend of the Boultings, Max Gumpel, who had acquired some rough footage of early underwater diving by Hans Hass and Jimmy Hodges, plus some shots of Lord Louis Mountbatten spearfishing off Malta. Max was sure the cinema public was tiring of trivial British second features and would accept an interesting and well-edited supporting documentary instead. He agreed to my editing his film *Beneath the Seven Seas* every evening and on weekends when I started at the BBC. (And he subsequently made a fortune from the film on the major circuits.)

But for the moment my economic problem was solved. I began to look forward to a future in television.

2

1952–1954: Opportunity and a Royal Success

Live TV drama, warts and all.
The Queen's coronation brings kudos.

Strangers still, our little group of potential producers was greeted by a smiling Royston Morley, seated at classroom desks and introduced to chief instructor Roland Price, veteran cameraman of the 1937 King George VI's coronation and a valuable link with television's earliest days.

We were given a short history of the BBC to date. In 1952 the management still considered radio the most important medium, with television a minor craft that might one day develop into something better. While radio's Broadcasting House in Portland Place, London, was an imposing Germanic building surmounted by a pair of controversial Eric Gill nude male figures, television's shabby old Alexandra Palace in the gloomy suburbs remained a financially starved outpost.

British sound broadcasting had begun in 1919 when the Marconi Company was licensed by the government for experimental transmissions of "speech and music" from its headquarters in Chelmsford, Essex. In June 1920, the enterprising Lord Northcliffe, owner of the *Daily Mail*, who had already realized radio's potentially vast audience, persuaded Marconi to mount an hour-long concert that was picked up all over Europe and even (it was claimed) in Newfoundland. Amazingly, the success of this broadcast delayed radio development for several vital months. A discordant chorus of puritans, theater owners, and record-player makers denounced the attempt to seduce their audience. Wireless, they claimed, should remain a purely private communication service. The Post Office promptly canceled Marconi's license, giving Americans a lead that the British never really recovered. In the United States radio stations opened up all over the huge continent, but not until 1921 were eager British amateurs and a fledgling radio industry able to persuade the government to license elementary wireless once more.

In November 1922 the "British Broadcasting Company" took over London transmissions from the old 2L0 station in the Strand. Birmingham and Manchester followed, and within a few months the nucleus of a national network was on the air four or five hours every day.

The first general manager of the BBC was the legendary John Reith, then 33. A wartime bullet wound had given him a permanently ugly grimace. Beetle brows and an uncompromising Scots accent complemented his Scrooge-like countenance. From the beginning he insisted that his unseen news readers should wear dinner jackets at the microphone, but the purity of his vision went much further. He demanded that the BBC should remain free from any form of state control, and should offer not just popular entertainment but classical music, argument, literature, and religion.

At the beginning, primitive wireless sets were mainly built by enthusiasts in garden sheds and back rooms, but as the system developed, several enterprising companies produced cheap home radios. On January 1, 1927, the British Broadcasting Company was reborn as the British Broadcasting Corporation, with John Reith as director-general, and a government charter giving him what he had always wanted, an organization free from political control, financed by annual licenses bought by listeners.

Therefore during the 1926 nationwide general strike, Reith argued that the BBC must report all news impartially, firmly resisting Chancellor of the Exchequer Winston Churchill's demand for the transmitters to be commandeered as a one-sided channel of official information. But later, under further pressure, Reith had to agree to a broadcast statement by Prime Minister Stanley Baldwin, which decisively influenced public opinion and broke the strike. Reith believed he had saved the independence of the BBC. But neither Churchill nor his supporters forgave him for his original stand against them, and 12 years later, on June 30, 1938, John Reith was forced to resign and was shifted sideways to run Imperial Airways. (During the Second World War he was reduced to a lowly rank in the Admiralty and never held major office again.)

Despite his shortage of charm, his obstinacy, and lack of humor, we have John Reith to thank for establishing the high quality of British public-service broadcasting.

The service continued to expand. During the war the Home and Forces networks were the main instruments of information and entertainment until the armistice in May 1945.

Radio's early popularity caused imaginative minds to consider the possibility of sending moving pictures with sound by wireless — "television." The theory was simple. Any image could be divided into lateral strips, each read (or "scanned") from left to right as a series of dots, black or white, sent as electrical impulses and reformed as an identical black-and-white picture in a receiving set. At first there were two different methods of scanning, mechanical and electronic. In 1926, with a mechanical system, John Logie Baird had demonstrated a primitive process for sending pictures by electricity. Using a simple disk punched with concentric holes to produce an image with 22 lines running across it horizontally, he managed to transmit a picture by wire from one room to another in his offices in Frith Street, Soho, and then devised a method of transmitting these pictures by radio waves. The BBC helped him begin a series of experimental broadcasts from studios in Long Acre, and several hundred Baird "televisors," with unwieldy decoding disks spinning noisily at the back, appeared in the homes of perceptive and wealthy patrons. But it became increasingly obvious that a mechanical system could never deliver the greater number of lines necessary for high-definition broadcasting.

Electronic scanning offered a better alternative. As early as 1908 the Scottish engineer Campbell Swinton had proposed a magnetically deflected cathode ray scanning an image focused on a mosaic screen of photoelectric elements within a glass tube.

Essentially this was the system devised by the American Philo Farnsworth and Russian-born U.S. émigré Vladimir Zworykin in the United States in 1923—the "iconoscope" camera tube, further refined by RCA and Westinghouse and successfully demonstrated in 1932. Improved versions of their basic inventions deliver the crisp, color-correct television pictures viewers enjoy today.

By 1936 EMI (Electrical Music Industries) had successfully demonstrated its own electronic process. Baird too had hastily acquired the rights to a German high-definition system. The BBC decided that the only fair way to choose was to operate each one alternately. But the lack of flexibility and high cost of the Baird system, which actually photographed the images onto film developed at high speed for transmission one minute later, made it uneconomical. In the end, the world's first high-definition television service, initiated by the BBC, concentrated on EMI equipment.

Twenty companies exhibited new home television receivers at London's "Radiolympia" in 1938, with prices from £20 ($30) for the smallest model. By 1939 there were over 20,000 in use. The service had already featured several important public events, like the coronation of King George VI in 1937, a glimpse of the Davis Cup tennis finals at Wimbledon, the Derby at Epsom, test cricket at the Oval, and the (soccer) Football Association Cup final.

The BBC had also transmitted a number of plays, some simply imported with cast, sets, and props from London theaters, including a production of *Twelfth Night*, with Michael Redgrave and Peggy Ashcroft, and *Macbeth*, with Laurence Olivier. Program Organizer Cecil Madden was an ingenious innovator of new programs, including a weekly magazine, *Picture Page*, a rich mélange of popular art, cooking, gardening, zoo animals, and, once only, George Bernard Shaw.

Alas, all this bright endeavor was suddenly switched off on September 1, 1939, on the eve of the declaration of war against Germany. British television screens stayed dark for the next seven years.

But on Victory Day in June 1946 the service reopened in a burst of enthusiasm with a full broadcast of London's Victory Parade by the impressive legions of Allied troops who (with American help) had destroyed Hitler's Third Reich. Later that night Michael Barry produced his own adaptation of the French wartime novel *The Silence of the Sea* for an estimated 100,000 viewers in the Greater London area, watching mainly on prewar sets.

Despite the determined opposition of cinema owners, who saw their audiences being whittled away, television began to find its own actors, vaudeville acts, and personalities. Unknown MacDonald Hobley and Sylvia Peters became popular announcers, as well as Mary Malcolm, in private life Lady Bartlett (wife of script editor Sir Basil), and Leslie Mitchell, a survivor from prewar television.

Worthy programs were devised for children. Conductor Eric Robinson began his series *Music for You*; ballet became an immediate favorite, with economy-size versions of *Swan Lake* and *Giselle*. But while talk and factual programs succeeded, most television drama seemed dull compared with the excitement and glamour of film. The audience naturally expected (and failed to see) Hollywood-quality lighting, camerawork, and acting on the small screen. But poverty-stricken television producers were usually obliged to take some three-act stage play, cut it to 90 minutes, and photograph it with static one-lens cameras within the confines of a single set.

Of course not every producer was content to work at this low level. In particular, Royston Morley and Michael Barry often made vivid adaptations of novels and original stories which made the rest look stale. But they were the exceptions, well ahead of their contemporaries. Before their promotions (to head of training and head of drama, respectively), they had made imaginative attempts to break free from the imprisonment of unreal sets, poor lighting, and stodgy pictorial composition. Some of us hoped to follow their lead. (It was appalling to have an old retainer look out of a stage window at a painted backcloth and say, "The young master's just driving up now," when a film shot would *show* it in half the time.)

But because there was so little money for television drama, film inserts were rare; the cameras were still prewar Emitrons resolving their pictures on a huge glass globe like an upturned lightbulb, and cameramen still struggled with inverted viewfinders, panning left and watching their upside-down image go right.

However, the BBC had at last bought bigger premises, the old Gaumont-British studios in Lime Grove, Shepherd's Bush, West London, with five sound stages built on top of each other in two hefty towers.

Unlike the Alexandra Palace fixed wide-angles, the Lime Grove cameras, with turrets of four different lenses, promised a varied choice, from long shot to close-up. Cameramen began to take pride in being able to swing their turrets swiftly and silently, adjust composition, and refocus in less time than it took an actor to speak half a line. With more mobile tracking dollies, instead of the old rubber-tired farm carts, it was becoming possible for directors to achieve a smoother filmic style.

A drama director now had four cameras and three sound booms. During rehearsal he would decide which camera would cover each line and part of the action, orchestrate a visual rhythm between long shots and close-ups, and write a camera-script describing every shot in sequence. Camera and boom positions would then be marked and lettered, from *A* onward, on the designer's studio set-plan. Since each camera trailed a heavy cable plugged into the studio control gallery, it was vital to plan each position with care, in order to avoid tangling cables as the cameras crossed and recrossed between sets. The director's camera-script would detail each chosen camera and its position for the particular shot—2 G would mean camera 2 in position G, and so on—with a clear description—C.U. for close-up, L.S. for long shot, M.C.S. for medium close shot—and the concurrent movements of camera and actions—"Crab left as John crosses right. Zoom into C.U. John." All this was on the left of the page. The name of the set and dialogue were on the right.

These are typical pages from one of my *Onedin Line* scripts as recorded:

Shot No.
    1. **Cam. 3 Position A SCENE 1. INT. OSIRIS SALOON DAY.**
        Boom B pos. 1.

Close two shot JAMES/BAINES.	(JAMES IS GOING THROUGH THE ACCOUNTS WITH BAINES)
	JAMES: A hundred and twenty days?
	BAINES: Might be. Have to be on the safe side.
Widen shot as JAMES stands.	*JAMES:* But the whole point of this voyage is speed.

CRAB LEFT to POS. B holding 2-shot as JAMES crosses left of table. TRACK IN to C.U. JAMES as he comes forward.	Cargo of first crop tea has to be with the merchants in three months. first clipper in gets top price—and I mean to have that price.

Cut to:

2. Cam. 2 Pos. A

2-shot BAINES/JAMES becoming 3-shot as ANNE enters between them.	*BAINES:* (GLUMLY) Aye, sir. *JAMES:* Load all this extra provender and the crew'll lie down and enjoy life. But men that know it'll be hard tack after ninety days will dance to your tune lively enough.
TRACK IN to MCS BAINES.	*BAINES:* No man alive can predict the whims of wind and weather.

3. 3 B

M.C.S. JAMES.	*JAMES:* Get the price down by five percent.
(Stand by Telecine Machine No. 34 for telecine insert 2.)	*BAINES:* (PROTESTING) Can't do that, sir— *JAMES:* Or go and tell the chandler we'll buy our stores elsewhere.

4. 2 A

Close 2-shot ANNE/ BAINES. BAINES stands and exits L. Hold on Anne and CRAB LEFT as JAMES enters RIGHT of frame and moves to chart-table. HOLDING 2-shot ANNE/JAMES.	*BAINES:* (GRIMLY) Aye—sir. (TIGHTLIPPED, HE LEAVES). *ANNE:* Tight-girthed as ever, James. *JAMES:* The men won't starve. If rations run short after ninety days, there's salt pork and biscuit enough to keep life in 'em at reasonable cost.
CRAB R. to POS A. HOLDING close 2-shot ANNE/JAMES as JAMES moves over RIGHT.	*ANNE:* So we're back to thoughts of "profit"? *JAMES:* On this voyage, what else? *ANNE:* There's self-respect.

5. **3 B**
    Close-up JAMES.   *JAMES:* Mine?
    (RUN TELECINE 34)
                                ANNE: No. Captain Baines.'

6. **2 A**
    Close-up ANNE.   Destroy his authority and you'll
                                destroy the man.

Cut to:
    INSERT TELECINE 2.

In practice I found it best to block all the actors' moves right through the play as quickly as possible, preferably on the first day of rehearsal, and write the camera script at night. (With 400 or more camera cuts a red-eyed chore, this ruined any social life.) But it gave my production assistant time to type it all out, print 50 copies on the heavy Gestetner duplicating machine—this was before photocopying—and prepare small cards for each cameraman, giving him a full list of his own shots. I could then spend the rest of rehearsals on the actors' performances without worrying about technicalities.

Some directors preferred to leave their camera scripts almost blank, keeping their options open until they faced the bank of monitors in the control room (one for each camera, one for telecine film inserts, one for preview, and one for the final transmitted program). This didn't work for me. If a better idea emerged in the studio I could always change a shot, but there was no substitute for proper planning. There was little enough studio time to line up every shot, check lighting and costume, and make a stumbling run-through for the now-or-never live performance.

But even with the best-considered technical script, disaster still lurked. A camera could suddenly lose its picture without warning on transmission, leaving the unfortunate director no option but to cut to the next available shot and rapidly rewrite his camera script for the rest of the show. (A useful test of mental agility, but not, on the whole, recommended.)

I quickly discovered, however, that television had one great advantage for a director—I could *see* precisely the shot achieved by each camera and correct it where necessary. In films, no matter how carefully I described a particular composition, even sometimes lining it up through the camera, it was always possible for the operator to misjudge the exact framing I had imagined on the final take. In television I was always sure of what I was getting. (Nowadays, of course, feature film directors have "video-assist"—a small television camera monitoring the shot as seen by the film camera.)

The studio was controlled by a floor manager, gently relaying the director's instructions—but *not* as heard on his headphones ("Tell that silly bitch to wipe the grin off her stupid mug" becoming "Darling, could we be a little more serious, please")—removing unforeseen obstacles as cameras and booms raced into place, cueing actors to enter or to speak, and generally keeping the show running throughout 90 hectic minutes. Everyone on the floor wore rubber-soled shoes, and sets were constantly erected or dismantled, props set and struck by stage managers moving like ghosts just off-camera, as the whole performance ran to its conclusion.

All this knowledge was absorbed like folklore from the experienced producers who solemnly lectured the Course of '52. Some of the more pompous were given a pretty rough ride. A certain head of music was howled down when he tried to explain the difference in emotional effect between a close-up and a long shot, and retired hurt. A powerful lady with an Eton crop, "Johnny" Bradnock, head of make-up and wardrobe, was asked whether she agreed that a director should have the final word on costumes. "No one poaches on my territory," she answered fiercely. Luckily she left the corporation before the poachers were let loose.

As soon as tutorials ended each evening I would grab a hasty sandwich in the BBC canteen and drive to Wardour Street to commence about six hours' more work editing Max Gumpel's *Beneath the Seven Seas*, which mercifully was soon completed.

During the last two weeks of the course, each student had to prepare a 15-minute production. I envied David Attenborough the ease with which he mounted his own show, reading the words to Prokofiev's *Peter and the Wolf*, with a sketch-artist and a couple of friendly musicians in support. Michael Peacock devised three fictitious party political broadcasts from the Tories, the Socialists, and the Liberals—all using the same words and the same clichés, but delivered in totally different accents: upper class, working class, and something in between. The politicians were all played by the same actor, a young economics student called Ron Moody (later to find fame as Fagin in the Dickens musical *Oliver!*), whom I was not to meet again until 25 years later when we made *Into the Labyrinth* together.

John Fernald had chosen the last part of Bernard Shaw's *Candida*, and although I wanted to adapt an O. Henry story, Royston thought it would be more interesting if I produced the same piece as John. Fernald, a friend of Sir Kenneth Barnes, then director of the Royal Academy of Dramatic Art, had the pick of RADA students, including a delightful young Sian Phillips as Candida. I had to go slightly downmarket to the London Academy (in Hammersmith), and my production, though faster cut with much more camera movement, was not considered as "polished" as John's.

However, during the last few days of the course, I was approached by Ronald Waldman, head of light entertainment, to join his department as a director with producer Michael Mills on a series of theatrical biographies, part drama and part staged musical numbers, *The Passing Show*. Since I had heard nothing from Michael Barry about *Anne Frank* or anything else, it seemed an excellent chance.

Michael Mills, a short, bearded bachelor with a talent for ignoring any opinion but his own, made it clear he didn't *need* a director. He would rather have had a groveling assistant or even a loyal batman. ("But Waldman insists," he growled). He considered that he was quite capable of directing actors and cameras himself, but his workload for the next few weeks was daunting. However, during our nine months association we managed to work together cheerfully enough, even though Michael persisted in introducing me to actors as "our trainee."

The first *Passing Show*, "The Great George Edwardes," was due to rehearse with Tony Britton as the Edwardian manager of Daly's Theatre, London. I duly reported to the Sulgrave Boys' Club, Shepherd's Bush, an echoing and far from fragrant gymnasium reeking of active youth and strong disinfectant, and did little but watch as Michael plotted the action with his cast on imaginary sets marked out on the floor with adhesive tape. The script had been written weeks before, and I had no chance to comment on the performance that emerged, a series of short scenes with songs and dances and precious little dramatic conflict. George Edwardes had, it seemed, sailed through life from success to bankruptcy and back to success with few problems.

Transmission was scheduled for a Sunday night. On the previous morning we moved into Studio D, one of the smaller upper stages at Lime Grove, where designer Stephen Bundy had crammed in a proscenium stage for the musical numbers, a few tiny sets, and a huge screen on which black-and-white transparencies of various interiors were to be projected as backgrounds for other short scenes. The back-projection system was cheap, but it restricted camera movement and choice of angles, as each shot had to be taken at an angle of exactly 90 degrees to the screen or the effect was spoiled.

I sat in the shadows at the back of the control room watching Michael with a certain envy as he worked his way slowly through the show, cueing in actors, singers, and Eric Robinson's orchestra, arrayed in an adjoining studio, accompanying the vocalists from a television monitor, as well as bits of film from telecine and extra sound effects. During a pause on Saturday night the sound effects operator, Elsie Grey, suddenly let out a shriek of delight. Surreptitiously checking her football pools coupon she discovered she had won a small fortune. Elsie decided I was her lucky mascot. We made a pact to work together. Promoted, she became vision mixer on all my next BBC programs and for another eight years at Rediffusion until 1962.

Michael's production assistant, a striking, raven-haired girl called Yvonne Littlewood (who became a successful producer herself), had typed the scripts, organized rehearsals—and most of Michael's life. In the control room she called each shot and previewed the next, suddenly screaming, "Close-up on 3!" when a cameraman misread his crib card.

Michael Mills's camerawork and grouping seemed to me stodgily conventional, showing his theatrical background. However, I marveled at his cool demeanor as we sat in the control box on Sunday night, waiting for the last seconds to tick up to eight o'clock, then the countdown from Master Control—"Five, four, three, two, one. On you, Studio D"—and into a nonstop 90 minutes that would be seen live, warts and all, in thousands of homes all over the country. In fact, it went smoothly and was well received. Four days later it had to be rehearsed and performed all over again on Thursday night. I'd hoped Michael would let me take over for the second transmission, but in his wisdom he decided I was too green.

The second *Passing Show* planned for Christmas 1952 was to be on the life of John Logie Baird, a man who had had the dream of television, made a mechanical process work, but was beaten by superior technology. With Willoughby Gray as the eccentric inventor, we started filming with an early "Televisor" copied from a Baird original in Kensington's Science Museum. As the grumbling pulleys and chains gathered speed, the great perforated metal scanning disk suddenly flew off into the air like a lethal flying saucer, whirling dangerously around the small studio before clattering to the floor, fortunately without injuring anyone.

It seemed to be an omen. I was already worried about the script, such as it was. The *Passing Show* format was essentially a mix of feel-good drama and musical numbers. Baird's tragedy hardly fitted in with the comic music hall turns Michael insisted on inserting between brief incidents in Baird's close-fisted Scottish upbringing and continuing struggle all his life, ending in disappointment and utter failure.

Several senior BBC engineers, hearing of our project, pottered into the office to tell us politely that Baird's cranky invention had never stood a chance against the reality of electronic scanning. We attempted a last-minute rewrite, evolving a hopeless "race-against-time," with Baird making every effort to improve his mechanical system against all the odds, but it refused to work. In the end, with actors booked, the start of rehearsals a few days away, Michael confessed our problem to Ronnie Waldman, who agreed it would be better to remount the show by simply expanding all the musical sequences and dropping Baird's biography completely. (Nothing is ever wasted, however. While Michael transmitted his songs and dances on his own, I kept all the research and directed a straight drama based on Baird's life some years later for Rediffusion.)

The third *Passing Show* was to be based on the life of Marie Lloyd, an early–1900s music hall queen, and her colorful story of disgraceful husbands, rags-to-riches, and back again. Colin McInnes, a contemporary writer of sleazy teenage novels like *Absolute Beginners*, filmed in the eighties, had been commissioned to create the script. On the appointed delivery date, Colin drifted in, hungover—and empty-handed. The rich, full drama of "Our Marie's" life had completely eluded him, and he had been unable to put pen to paper!

Transmission was set for Sunday, February 8. It was already mid–January and rehearsals were imminent. With a cast including Pat Kirkwood as Marie, Guy Middleton, and Peter Bull already booked, we could hardly go back to Waldman with another tale of woe. But who did we know who could deliver a script in a few days?

I suggested Alfred Shaughnessy (who later was a key writer on the television series *Upstairs, Downstairs*), and Michael added Christopher Barry (son of Gerald Barry, who had recently planned and executed the "Festival of Britain," London's proud postwar exhibition of art and technology). With a bemused Alfred we piled into Michael's monstrous prewar Daimler (once owned by Anna Neagle), with an engine three times as long as the tiny passenger cabin behind, and drove to Christopher's cottage in the Cotswolds. Although just recovering from influenza, young Christopher rapidly became enthusiastic and seized the research materials, and within a very few days he and Alfred had delivered a working script.

Marie Lloyd, born Matilda Wood, first appeared on stage at age 15 in 1885. She soon became a solo star, able to achieve immediate audience contact with a wink and a double meaning. Once even prosecuted for "vulgarity" (unsuccessfully), she topped music hall bills for nearly 30 years, married three times (each time disastrously), was invariably overspent, and died on stage in 1922.

Alfred and Christopher managed to pack all this, with 30 costume changes, 15 numbers, and about 50 different settings, into their two-hour teleplay. Apart from necessary short film sequences it all had to be performed live on the appointed night.

The production was allocated Studio G at Lime Grove, longer and wider than D, with Eric Robinson's long-suffering orchestra in the draughty scene-dock next door. Because our script was so late, Stephen Bundy again had to rely on back-projected photographs for most of the sets, using neutrally painted doors and flats set at right angles to the BP (back projection) screen for exits and entrances, forcing me into an unwilling close-up technique. I was at last allowed to plot the actors' moves myself, although Michael tried to correct and change here and there. We moved into Studio G on Saturday, and I was able to complete blocking scenes with cameras right through the two-hour show by late evening.

On Sunday afternoon we started to stumble through a catastrophic dress rehearsal that hadn't even finished before the supper break. Less than an hour later we returned to the control room to watch the clock. At eight o'clock precisely, for the first time in my career, I cued Eric to start the first bars of "My Old Man Said Follow the Van"—one of Marie's rumbustious songs—faded up the opening captions (on cards in front of two cameras in the studio), mixing from one to the next on every fourth beat, and signaled Irene Handl to light a gas jet as I faded up the first shot. The flame of the taper in Irene's hand flickered, and the gas jet suddenly flared wildly—burning out the whole picture in a brilliant white eruption before disappearing into ignoble blackness. Stunned, I gazed at the dead monitor as the orchestra sputtered into silence. Behind me an engineer muttered, "'Peel-off.' Always happens with these CPS cameras."

"Peel-off," it appeared, was a new and special hazard. Someone had dipped the taper in paraffin to make sure it lit property. The abrupt brilliance had been too much for the electronic camera to cope with, and we had lost the picture.

I stared at the transmission screen for several more seconds, unable to believe my bad luck, first time on the air live. From the darkness behind me Michael's voice said calmly. "Put up the Normal Service caption, quickly." Somewhere among the captions the oft-used card was found, and the vision-mixer faded up, NORMAL SERVICE WILL BE RESUMED SHORTLY.

The technical problem was quickly solved. "Ready to go again?" Michael asked. I nodded. "Right. Tell Master Control." I was counted down through ten seconds and cued the opening music once more, ran through the opening titles, and watched Irene Handl successfully light the gas with a very subdued flame. The camera panned left to reveal young Marie's first performance as a child in an East End London pub, and the show rolled forward.

From that first disastrous moment fate relented completely. No one missed a cue, set changes were made rapidly and correctly, film sequences cut in on the split second. Pat Kirkwood ran from set to set, sometimes changing her costume as she went, to enter calmly and play a difficult scene or effortlessly burst into her next song. Edward Barnes, our stage manager (later the BBC's head of children's programs, begetter of *Blue Peter* and *Grange Hill*), held the whole studio together. My confidence soon returned, and two hours seemed to pass in a matter of minutes.

The next day the press notices were all anyone could have wished. Pat Kirkwood, effervescent and delightful all the way through the lively songs and lusty melodrama, rightly drew all the headlines for her remarkable marathon. In the *Daily Telegraph*, Marsland Gander, doyen of all critics, complimented us on "a masterpiece and an important milestone on Television History." Leslie Ayre in the *Mail* considered the whole show "splendid entertainment," and Cyril Butcher in the *Sketch* called it "a stupendous triumph."

Which was all very well, but on Thursday we had to go through it all again, live, and like many second performances this time "Our Marie" turned into a shambles. The actors had lost their excitement, and the studio crew delivered the equivalent of a bad dress rehearsal. Which was no one's fault; it simply proved the difficulty of repeating a live success.

While Michael Mills went on holiday, I was able to talk to Michael Barry, head of drama. He told me his script unit had had "insuperable problems" over the rights of *Anne Frank*. (I don't think they tried very hard. I was a new boy and unknown. The book was of course later adapted as a very successful Broadway and London play by two American writers, and made into a Hollywood film eventually shown on BBC television. About 40 years later both BBC and Yorkshire television made new versions of this powerful and moving story.)

But Michael Barry *did* have a 50-minute play for me to direct almost immediately. I left his office clutching the yellowing script of *William's Other Anne*, by Ivor Brown, Shakespearean expert and theatrical critic of the (Sunday) *Observer*. As I read it, however, my heart sank. I knew at once that this was a "dog," refused by all the other producers in drama. Although it was a fair example of Brown's erudition, very little actually happened. The whole plot revolved round the return of a successful William Shakespeare to his Warwickshire village to meet his first love, Anne Whateley (not Anne

Hathaway, but the "other Anne"). Restricted to a small room in a cottage there was little chance for movement. But it was a start—and I would be free to find a good cast and run my own control room without the father figure of Michael Mills at my elbow.

At that time Michael Benthall was producing the complete canon of Shakespeare's works at London's Old Vic. The young Irene Worth had been well reviewed for her Portia in *The Merchant of Venice*, opposite the Shylock of Paul Rogers. I hurried to see her, bearing the *Other Anne* script, and she accepted. I also negotiated with John Gregson, then a fashionable film star after his big success in *Genevieve* (with Kenneth More), to play William.

The cast was completed with reliable actors Richard Wattis, Joan Young, and David Horne. With very little money, designer Freddie Knapman created a richly textured cottage interior, and James Hartley wrote a simple musical theme to be played live during the performance from the back of Studio D. Rehearsals were a joy. At last I was able to direct actors and try out camera movement without interference. Michael Barry came to see a run-through and went away smiling, though he seemed preoccupied with other problems.

The whole play had to be set and performed in one studio day, March 4, starting blocking at 10:00 A.M., with a late-afternoon dress rehearsal, and going on the air at five minutes past nine. The last run went smoothly enough, but for some reason I found the transmitted final performance slightly disappointing, even though Irene Worth was warm and touching as Anne Whateley and John Gregson suitably amusing as William Shakespeare.

Again the press was encouraging. Leonard Mosley in the *Daily Express* described Irene Worth as "one of the most potent young players we have in Britain. A lovely young face that could turn your heart at the tremor of a lip or the change of expression in her eyes." He went on to note the play's "moments of tenderness and poetry, a dewy and ingenious *Midsummer Night's Dream*." In the *New Chronicle* Ian Low concluded, "All praise to Peter Graham Scott for his sensitive production. This young film director is a handsome asset to Lime Grove." (I am sure this final flourish had been generously prompted by the BBC's new press officer, who was to rise high in the corporation and prove an inspiration for all those who wished to make quality programs—Huw Wheldon.)

Michael Mills had telephoned me as soon as I came off the air. "Not a bad first effort"—which from him was praise indeed. Following the notices I waited all day for some word from Michael Barry. At 4:00 P.M. I phoned his office to be told he was "in a meeting." (In the BBC at any time 90 percent of the staff are "in a meeting.") By 5:30 it seemed that no word, good or bad, would be forthcoming. I wandered along the corridor to the washroom. As I was drying my hands, Michael entered quietly and stared at me almost sightlessly. "Everything all right, Michael?" I asked anxiously.

He looked at me again, sighed, and went into one of the cubicles, firmly locking the door behind him. I never heard his opinion of *William's Other Anne* or even whether he had seen it. I was quite unnecessarily hurt by this. I valued his judgment. But I should have realized that running the drama department, with its constant economic worries, was consuming all his energy.

But there was no time for concern, for within four weeks Michael Mills and I had to mount another *Passing Show*. This time we were to unveil the life of Charles B. Cochran, the larger-than-life impresario who had encouraged so much theatrical talent between the wars, including Noel Coward, writer A. P. Herbert, director Wendy Toye, composer Vivian Ellis, and designer Oliver Messel. Once again, in the beginning was the Word, and once again that was the problem. The script of "Charles B. Cochran Presents..." by revue-writer Diana Morgan was no more than a series of quick sketches, starting with a two-minute sequence of Cochran as a very old man telling his story to the camera.

This was the first mistake, as it would have to be prefilmed with the actor in his "old man" makeup (he had to start "young" in the early live scenes), and telecine quality was still not very good. This mini-lecture was followed by a number of quick-fire scenes of Cochran's early life as an immigrant to the United States, where he lived as a hobo before getting a break as a comedian's feed in burlesque. We then settled down (at last!) to a straightforward account of Cochran's return to London to set up with no experience and little money as a theatrical manager (cue for musical excerpts), emerging at last from failure after failure to success with *Cavalcade* and *Bless the Bride*.

Once again we'd not had enough preproduction time, but even with much of the studio taken up by the theater stage for musical numbers, Stephen Bundy was able to build more sets and rely less on back-projection than on "Our Marie."

Casting Cochran himself proved an unexpected problem. There was so little conflict in the script (except for predictable backstage screaming matches) that no reputable leading man felt inspired. Finally, Frank Lawton, a likable actor but by no means our first choice, was signed, with Dennis Price as Noel Coward, Melissa Stribling, the delicate and charming wife of director Basil Dearden, as Cochran's wife, and Vanessa Lee as herself.

Rehearsals commenced at the Sulgrave Boys' Club. Dennis Price had a small problem. He would arrive every morning bearing an important-looking gladstone bag, which he deposited in the evil-smelling showers. One day I was politely asked by the caretaker, a First World War veteran, if I would ask Mr. Price not to leave his "empties" behind. He showed me a huge pile of beer bottles. Dennis was secretly consuming over a dozen pints a day—yet he still managed to retain his composure, and delivered a fine and witty performance as Noel Coward on the night of the production.

Because Michael Mills was more interested in staging the musical numbers with choreographer Freddie Carpenter, I was left alone to direct the actors, until one day Michael burst in, watched for a short while, and bossily suggested numerous changes (none were made!).

Two days before we went into the studio we had our first combined run-through. I had tried my best with the bitty scenes (and with non–Americans playing Americans), but the opening seemed very patchy. Then, with the first musical number, the whole rehearsal room came alive, to sink into boredom with the next piece of "straight" acting. So it continued all the way through. Flat and superficial sketches followed well-staged singing and dancing, right to the deathly hush at the end.

I took my cast away and furiously told them that we somehow had to make it more lively despite the weakness of the script. Years later, Clement Freud, whose wife, Jill Raymond, had a small part as Wendy Toye, told me I'd "reduced the cast to tears." Perhaps I had. I've never been so savage with a bunch of actors since. But with two days to go I began to see more energy, and by transmission day our ramshackle show was just about together.

Once again the notices were undeservedly good. In the *Daily Mail* Emery Pearce described it as "the TV show-business event of the year, a night to remember, with Cochran quietly and sympathetically played by Frank Lawton, and the plum role of his friend and colleague Noel Coward ably and deliciously played by Dennis Price. Memories came tumbling back, Little Nellie Kelly, This Year of Grace, Bless the Bride, and of course, the Cochran Young Ladies. The dancers were vigorous and the singers decorative in a production that by all standards was as extravagant as its subject."

"TV did its audience proud with its biggest and best-ever musical show," chorused Leonard Mosley in the *Express*. "Charles B. Cochran was a showman with entertainment in his blood. Everything he touched made theatrical history. TV caught the dancing spirit of a man who could succeed with a boxing match, a religious play and a risqué revue—all in the same year."

"A spectacular coup," gushed Peter Black enthusiastically in the *Daily Mail*. "As popular entertainment the story couldn't miss. The Cochran shows span so many years there was no song that failed to bring back a happy memory."

However, I was not so happy, because I knew we'd just got away with a show that was substandard. The marriage of our separate talents was simply not working. Visually, "Cochran" had lacked an overall style, and there were one or two unfortunate miscuts that could have been avoided if we'd had more studio time.

Michael was like a whirling dervish, throwing off bright ideas that he often failed to realize on the screen. My concern was to discover the quality and truth of actors' performances and to present them in the best way pictorially. Michael ignored my aims. He wanted to make Big Shows, with his name attached in large letters. He had all the arrogance of genius, without, alas, the final magic touch. I was grateful for all he had taught me—how to count bars and time captions to music, how to speak to actors and cameramen with a mixture of friendliness and authority, and above all how to maximize the use of precious studio hours to make sure the show was ready to go on the air. But it was now time for me to move on, alone.

My doubts were put aside as we began urgent preparations for the last *Passing Show*, "All Our Yesterdays," for transmission the night before Queen Elizabeth II was to be crowned in Westminster Abbey.

The coronation was a major event demanding national coverage by the BBC. It had only recently completed building its five main transmitters, and to ensure reception in the north of Scotland, Northern Ireland, and parts of northeast English, government help was needed for temporary booster stations to serve these smaller population centers. But by mid–1953 the BBC had raised its television coverage to 84 percent of the population—more than any other country so far.

Originally there was some doubt about how much of the enthronement ceremony should be seen. But the Duke of Norfolk and the Archbishop of Canterbury were finally persuaded, and the newspapers went into raptures about the chance of a worldwide broadcast. The organization of the massive broadcasting effort (the placing of scanner trucks and a master control room, and the choice of camera positions along the route from Buckingham Palace and in the Abbey) was the responsibility of S. J. Lotbiniere, head of outside broadcasts. Former RAF fighter pilot Peter Dimmock was to direct the whole daylong performance, its success or failure in his hands.

But all this was yet to come. Michael and I concentrated on our offering for the preceding night. "All Our Yesterdays," by former Ealing Studios scriptwriter Angus McPhail, was probably our most polished script, a sub-*Cavalcade* of incidents in a typical (upper-class, naturally) English family on the eve of five coronations: those of Victoria, Edward VII, George V, George VI, and the present one of Elizabeth II. It was interesting enough, but a more socially aware writer might have produced an honest and popular saga. In the event, despite some last-minute rewrites by—who else?—Michael Mills, it was a cap-doffing patriotic yawn, livened up by topical songs from each period, and climaxing with energetic excerpts from *Guys and Dolls* (which had opened in a London theater that week with Sam Levene and Vivian Blaine), finishing with show-stopping Stubby Kaye in "Sit Down, You're Rocking the Boat!"

Such critiques as we had on the day itself were mercifully

indulgent. Viewers' eyes were already on the main event. All the world loved the coronation of 1953, a spectacle of impressive grandeur presented with prodigal disregard of the cost. Not since victory in Europe in May 1945 had London seen such crowds or so much popular enthusiasm. (In these days of tabloid mockery it is salutary to remember how much genuine respect and admiration the British public once felt for the royal family.)

From the beginning Peter Dimmock's team surpassed itself, with superb close-ups on a massive 25-inch lens of the young queen riding in her carriage from Buckingham Palace to Westminster Abbey, and powerful high shots within as noble figures progressed slowly up the aisle. Richard Dimbleby's hushed commentary echoed awe and majesty to perfectly timed cuts of the boy Prince Charles and his royal relatives watching the moving ceremony, an unforgettable television triumph, as many viewers still recall. As never before, cameras caught the splendor and solemnity of a historic religious ritual with all its traditional pageantry and emotion.

Queen Elizabeth was crowned amid the affection of her people. In Britain more than 20 million people watched, as, without a single hitch of camera or sound, the queen, in a purple velvet robe, wearing the imperial state crown and carrying the orb and scepter, drove in a two-mile procession back to her palace. All the way, crowds of cheering people who had waited all night in rain and cold went wild, surging around the royal coach. With the bells of London pealing joyously above the cries of the multitude, the radiant queen was caught once more in close-up by a brilliant cameraman as her coach entered the palace gates.

Later that day Her Majesty Queen Elizabeth II and her family came out onto the balcony before the ever-present cameras, to acknowledge the tumultuous loyalty of the crowd once more. With a theatrical flourish, as the rain clouds opened to let the sun struggle through, a flight of RAF jet fighters roared through the sky to salute the newly crowned sovereign.

Finally, in a moving and intimate broadcast from within the palace, the queen pledged herself to the service of her people "as you are pledged to mine. Throughout all my life and with all my heart I shall strive to be worthy of your trust."

The whole day had been a great demonstration of the power

of television to the world, a personal triumph for Dimmock, Lotbiniere, and their crews. From this success there was no looking back. The demand for television sets rose by 50 percent, and radio's audiences began to shrink. Large numbers of the opinion-leading class who had not bothered with television had been amazed to see how good it could be. The nation's most popular mass medium became recognized as a powerful propaganda tool. Politicians began to encourage contacts within the newly built Television Centre at White City. A new strain of telly-bore began to breed.

But whatever the promise of the future, the immediate present at the BBC was grim. All the resources that had rightly been expended on coverage of the royal event now had to be recouped with ritual belt-tightening. Freelance producer-directors like me with contracts expiring in the summer were dispensed with.

I was not surprised. I had been to see Michael Barry again and given him what I hoped was a clear-sighted assessment of my work so far. My tension in the control room had eased. I could now watch four cameras on monitors, time cuts precisely, and judge the final dramatic effect in performance on transmission. Above all, I could see a way of writing scripts not for films but for original television, without theatrical verbiage, using imagery instead of words.

"More sets, more film inserts," Michael Barry yawned. He must have been very tired. "Money we simply don't have. Not this year." His future plans seemed slim, harnessed to the very sort of stage-bound old warhorses I didn't want to ride. So that was that, as far as BBC drama went.

It seemed extraordinary that the BBC, having spent money and time turning me from an uncertain newcomer into an experienced director should not now want to retain my services. But this was happening to many of the corporation's first trainees.

On my last day in Lime Grove I knocked on Program Controller Cecil McGivern's door. His deputy, pioneer Cecil Madden, was with him, and both surprised me by revealing how much of my work they had seen. But, busy and overworked, they couldn't be expected to bother with the problems of a new (ex-)recruit.

However, a few days later I had an offer of an original children's television play, *Desert Adventure* by Peter Ling, from Freda Lingstrom, the affable head of children's programs, and a promise of further work. A film producer friend, Julian Wintle, had already asked me to edit three consecutive low-budget features at Nettlefold Studios. So for the rest of 1953 I commuted between Shepherd's Bush and Walton-on-Thames, building up the bank balance once more.

Desert Adventure, performed live on a Sunday afternoon with a boisterous pair of children and even a real camel (and repeated on a Thursday just like an adult drama), was judged a success. Then Michael Mills asked me to take over a Saturday night comedy special, with comedians Jewell and Warris, when he ruptured himself in a fit of rehearsal enthusiasm. And at the beginning of 1954 I returned full-time to the BBC on a new three-month contract as "general children's director," which Freda Lingstrom cheerfully explained meant "dogsbody."

In fact it was the most useful 13 weeks I'd had to date, yielding exactly the experience I needed. Away from the heavily publicized *Passing Show*s I secretly learned my trade. (There was no press interest. The only time my name appeared in print, spelled wrongly, was when a lump of scenery fell on my head at Lime Grove.) I was in the studio practically every day, including Sundays. The rest of the time I was rehearsing for something or other.

I directed one more full-length play, winner of a children's writing competition, *Johnnie's Night Out* by 13-year-old Sean Barrett (later an adult director), designed by the very young Eileen Diss. I staged innumerable comic sketches and game shows, and, best of all, three episodes of *All Your Own*, Huw Wheldon's junior talent show. At that time Huw was simply the BBC's press officer, doubling as presenter of youthful talent found by the inextinguishable Cliff Michelmore. Sunday's studio schedule would start at about eleven with Cliff handing me a list of the week's turns. "Puppets again? Oh, not another girl ventriloquist! Just see what Huw does to *her*!"

I would quickly block a rough camera script. Huw would erupt into the studio by lunchtime, and we would spend the next hour in the pub, with Huw rapidly telling me what he planned to say, before entertaining the assembled regulars with outrageous stories of his wartime paratroop exploits. During the afternoon we'd stagger a run-through with cameras and young artists, have tea, and then go on the air live for 50 minutes of free-fall television. Pigeons escaped from cages, eager young poets "dried" as words fled their brains, and a trained dog once leaped up onto the gantry to rain liquid criticism on Uncle Huw.

But Huw was unflappable. I kept a camera permanently on his face for vital cutaways that would make it all seem skillfully planned. Fifty minutes passed as seconds, and at last we rolled the end-captions on an ancient machine that often jammed in vision and had to be wound up painfully by a prop-man's calloused hand, finally releasing a camera to focus on either Sylvia Peters or Mary Malcolm, sitting in a corner waiting to announce the rest of the evening's entertainment.

It had been 18 months since I'd set foot in the corporation's gloomy Marylebone training room. My experience, live, on-air, was invaluable and probably unobtainable anywhere today. I'd had microphones dangling in shot, even half a camera once, too much sound or none at all. But I'd also had moments of brilliance, of emotional depth where I'd seen none in rehearsal, and of sudden dazzling power and occasional truth.

The people of Britain in 1954, reeling from endless bad news, economic depression, memories of the war against Hitler, bombing, rationing which had lasted into the fifties, shortages of everything—transport, shoes, even drink—deserved something better than the pap they were still getting from Pinewood and Elstree—and television was now delivering it. As you passed another house bearing the huge H of a television aerial, you could imagine a few more of the 4,000 fleapit cinemas closing. Television, crude and clumsy as it might still be, was here to stay.

And the people at the BBC, loyal, hard working, incredibly conscientious, leather patches on sleeves, darns in their socks, had supported me as I had never been supported elsewhere. It was a wonderful place to work. *Then.*

I'd learned a great deal. How to give a word of encouragement over the talkback to a flagging studio crew, and above all, when to praise and thank the right people after the show, good or bad. But I'd already turned 30, and although I'd polished my technical skills, I'd only delivered three cheap films and a few musical comedy memories—nothing of contemporary significance.

When was television going to provide that real opportunity?

3

1955–1956:
Dreams and Disaster

*Commercial television arrives in
Britain—and nearly dies—*

"Stand back!"

I crouched against the side of the dusty staircase as a deep
rumble heralded the sudden collapse of the wall above in a tumbling mass of old bricks and soot.

"All right. You can go on now." I clambered past the wreckage, up another flight into a huge, brown room littered with brand-new desks, chairs, and telephones. From above and below came
sounds of further demolition as the old Air Ministry building in
London's Kingsway was gutted to prepare for its future as Television House.

The destruction was symbolic. By order of Parliament, single-channel BBC was soon to be challenged by "commercial television," showing six minutes of advertising every hour between
programs, a concept initiated by Norman Collins, controller of
BBC-TV from December 1947 until October 1950, when he had
resigned on learning that George Barnes, director of the spoken
word, was to be appointed over his head to become director of television. Collins, committed as he was to the new medium's rapid
development, was insulted by the appointment of a man he considered expert only in the ponderous ways of corporation administration. More than most he disliked the unfairness of the BBC's

monopoly and wanted to devise a scheme paid for by nonlicense revenue.

Early in 1951 Collins energetically lobbied the Conservative government's broadcasting group, and at last a 1952 White Paper cautiously advanced the possibility of ITV, "independent television." To many members of Parliament who had just discovered the magic of appearing before the cameras, advertising meant "sponsorship," which rapidly became a bogey-word. Others thought television with commercial interruptions was being planned to "kill the BBC," and suggested that universities and other worthy organizations might be invited to run a competitive channel. But after furious debate and many amendments the Television Bill was finally passed on July 30, 1954, and an ITV service was announced for the London area to commence on September 22, 1955.

The first night was awaited nervously by enthusiasts and skeptically by nonbelievers. Program content had to be supervised by the Independent Television Authority (ITA), under Chairman Kenneth Clarke, a distinguished art historian but not yet a household name, and Director-General Robert Fraser, a senior civil servant who had had a hand in drafting the new charter.

The ITA would build and control the transmitters planned for London, the Midlands, and the North of England, with central Scotland, Wales, and other parts of the United Kingdom scheduled for eventual coverage within four years. Programs would be provided by "contractors who would recoup their costs by selling advertising airtime." Before ITV began, no one had any idea whether this could work commercially; consequently applications for providing the service were not exactly numerous. Rediffusion (allied to its parent company, British Electrical Traction [BET], a conglomeration of bus companies, laundries, and cable radio for new town housing) was one of the few companies to bid. Although hostile originally, the BET board had been persuaded by Chairman John Spencer Wills.

Wills had had a remarkable career. Trained as an accountant, he had transformed BET's sprawling empire of provincial bus companies into a highly efficient transport network that had defied the postwar Labour government's attempts at "nationalization." Looking around for new investment, supported by Paul Adorian, an amiable radio engineer of Armenian extraction, he had established cable television networks in Bermuda and Montreal, and considered that this gave them sufficient experience to launch a program company.

Contenders for program contracts were interviewed between September 28 and mid–October 1954, and one week later the ITA announced the award of the London station (weekdays) to a consortium of Associated-Newspapers (owners of the London *Daily Mail* and *Evening News*) and Rediffusion, to be called "Associated–Rediffusion."

Saturdays and Sundays in London had been claimed by the father of independent television, Norman Collins, allied to C. O. Stanley of Pye Radio in the Associated Broadcasting Company (ABC). They failed, however, to attract sufficient finance for equipment and trained personnel, and in the end were incorporated with theater-owners Howard & Wyndham and Moss Empires, the Grade Agency (run by brothers Lew and Leslie), and bankers S. G. Warburg, to become "Associated Television" (ATV).

Norman Collins's vision of quality weekend entertainment for Londoners became somewhat eroded by the appointment of this obviously "show-business" group, who showed their intentions on the second night with the popular *Sunday Night at the London Palladium*. The founder members, Chairman Prince Littler, Managing Director Val Parnell (superseded later by Lew Grade), and Norman Collins, deputy chairman, all made huge personal fortunes. But still not satisfied, and sensing a need for balance with more current affairs programs, Collins tried to involve a national newspaper but failed, although he succeeded in procuring a certain amount of capital (but little else) from the *Daily Mirror* a year later.

Programs for the North (Lancashire and Yorkshire) for Monday to Friday were to come from Granada TV, an offshoot of Granada Cinemas, ably run by Sydney Bernstein and his brother, Cecil. They were expected simply to demonstrate the same show-business expertise as Parnell and the Grades at ATV, and it was a refreshing surprise when Granada developed its own individual character, with many programs on contemporary social and political problems.

Weekends in Midlands and the North was first of all allocated to Kemsley-Winnick, a curious mixture of Lord Kemsley, owner of the salacious *News of the World*, and band leader/impresario Maurice Winnick. The odd partnership soon withdrew, however, leaving Clarke and Fraser at ITA with the problem of finding a credible replacement in a hurry. After urgent persuasion, the gap was filled by another major cinema group, Associated British (ABPC). Although this meant competing for their own cinema-going customers, it proved a beneficial decision. Within a few years, many of ABPC's cinemas had been closed and the remnants sold off to Thorn-EMI.

Meanwhile, in April 1954, when my contract with the BBC was up, I was taking stock. I had done better than expected with *William's Other Anne*, but the nearest I had come to lively television was with Huw Wheldon's children's talent show. I could see little chance of developing popular contemporary drama at the BBC, though Dennis Vance had tried to do some interesting work, and Alvin Rakoff had produced a fine adaptation of Irwin Shaw's *The Troubled Air*. Tony Richardson breezed in from a subsequent training course but soon departed to better things at the Royal Court with George Devine. The weary old guard in the Plays Department maliciously grumbled into their half pints of beer that all these "young Turks" didn't stay very long, and at last Michael Barry announced an ambitiously titled *Twentieth Century Theatre*—which eventually turned out to be no more than the same old grave-digging from dead playwrights better left undisturbed, rather than an effort to find present-day writers with something positive to say. The BBC-TV drama settled back into its comfortable torpor as a rest home for superannuated theatricals.

I had in any case an offer to edit a very interesting film, *Under the Caribbean*. Hans Hass, the distinguished underwater explorer and marine biologist, had recently returned with thousands of feet of new Eastmancolor, shot with a pressure-resistant camera and newly developed underwater lighting equipment, and he needed to compile it all into an adventure feature film for German cinema. We soon completed the production with original German dialogue. Hans next decided to make an Anglo-American version, dubbing the dialogue into English. Freddie Shaughnessy, who had helped me to success with "Our Marie," delivered an accurate and witty script, which we duly transferred to the screen. *Under the Caribbean* opened at the Empire Leicester Square at Christmas 1954 and scored a considerable success for Hans Hass.

By early spring new ITV companies were rumored to be opening offices in London. But before I could seek them out, BBC Controller Cecil McGivern, having seen *Under the Caribbean*, asked me back to the BBC to take a trip to Liechtenstein to persuade Hans Hass to make television films. At first Hans was extremely dubious, but over an enjoyable weekend I managed to convince him that the thousands of feet of film he had locked in his vaults (some dating back to before the war) could be turned into a successful series. Hans and his glamorous wife, Lotte, duly became household names all over Europe with the BBC's *Diving to Adventure*.

But for me the opportunities of ITV drama seemed more exciting than BBC underwater. Dennis Vance and Desmond Davies had already joined Norman Collins's company to record West End revivals with star-casts on a system called "high definition," a crude way of filming television cameras' pictures from a superfine monitor. The results, alas, were as gray and drear as a wet day in Glasgow's Sauchiehall Street, and high definition, completely belying its proud title, disappeared shortly after ITV went on the air.

A great vacuum of broadcasting hours had suddenly been created. Though the space was bound to be partly filled with American soap operas, cheap homemade game shows, and other time-wasting junk, surely in the first year, at least, there would be room for experiment, originality, and the sort of subjects the BBC was too craven to attempt? The problem was, *which* of the new companies, variety-led ATV, or cinema-based Granada or ABC, might be most receptive to my ideas?

Strangely enough, the company that intrigued me most was Associated-Rediffusion, nominated to be first to transmit, in London. I soon discovered that Lloyd Williams, who had been my BBC floor manager on *All Your Own*, had been appointed assistant controller. But after several attempts on my part to contact him, he was not encouraging. Only when Peter Cotes, elder brother of the Boultings, became Associated-Rediffusion's senior drama producer was I able to penetrate the frantic muddle for an interview with Roland Gillette, newly named program controller.

He kept me waiting for over two hours. Eventually I was

ushered into the presence of a sleek executive in a shiny Dacron suit and a carefully assumed American accent. "Didn't mean to stand you up. But I've just been seeing Orson Welles."

I wasn't as impressed as he'd obviously hoped. Though Welles had astonished the world in 1942 with *Citizen Kane*, his subsequent directorial performances had been somewhat patchy. I'd met him briefly in Venice in 1949 when he was hustling around Europe trying to raise money for various enterprises—and selling his powerful talent in other people's movies.

"What's Orson Welles going to do for you?" I asked.

"Plenty." (The American accent now seemed slightly Cockney.) "We're planning a series, *Around the World with Orson Welles*."

I didn't respond enthusiastically, doubting whether Orson would ever have the commitment to deliver a weekly series on time. (He eventually begat three programs, the first devoted to a long and turgid conversation about bull fighting with Kenneth Tynan as they sat in an empty bull ring. Scarcely riveting television!) Roland Gillette admitted he had not seen any of my films or television programs. I confessed I'd not heard of him either. He was reputed to have done very well in American television. But this prompted the question, why on earth should he have left an industry that paid huge salaries for the uncertainty of a new British venture? (We were soon to learn the answer!)

He promised me a further interview with Captain Thomas Brownrigg, A-R's general manager. But for the next few weeks I heard nothing more. Luckily I had another interest. Over the previous year I'd had time to write a stage play, *The Breath of Fools*—from a quotation by George Granville, "What is this 'fame,' thus crowded round with slaves? The Breath of Fools, the bait of flattering knaves."

Set in a studio production office, it was roughly based on the real-life conflict I'd observed between director John Boulting and Carol Marsh, the girl he'd chosen as Rose in *Brighton Rock*. In his novel Graham Greene had insisted on a depressing ending with Rose, the little waitress whom gang leader Pinkie had cynically married to prevent her from giving vital evidence against him, learning at last how much the dead villain had despised her. With a barely credible trick using a hiccuping gramophone record, John Boulting had caused Rose to believe Pinkie really loved her—a surprising revelation of "the appalling strangeness of the mercy of God"— which I still feel spoiled the whole film's strength in its closing minutes. The changed ending was a cause of serious dispute between inexperienced actress and director. The theme of innocent belief versus cynical unbelief became the theme of my play.

Many of us who had survived the war had considered the possibility of a merciful God. But no matter how powerful our ingrained religious impulse, another more rational voice within continued to demand, "Why should my particular survival have been so arbitrary? Why *me* and not others more deserving?"

At times, pondering the new world we hoped (and failed) to build, I longed for some great religious revival. But it never occurred. Yet Graham Greene seemed able to make philosophical sense—to himself at least—of the world's deceptions, corruption, and pointless pain a part of some lifelong divinely inspired assault course ordained to toughen and indeed enrich our spirits.

In my play I made my fictional novelist a cross between the austere Greene and a more affable Irishman, the sort of pragmatist who would answer, "I believe in Belief." His antagonist was John Hagerman, whom I made much crueller and more cynical than the quiet and well-mannered Boulting, a misanthropic director who selects the innocent Catholic girl Ann for his free adaptation of the story of a miracle in a nineteenth-century Irish village, deliberately rewriting it as an exposé of what he perceives as the Church's exploitation of the gullible. But in real life the girl believes in the simple truth of the original story and continues to challenge Hagerman's interpretation all through the production of the film.

I enjoyed exploring and inventing the struggle between the young actress and her Svengali, her (fictional) Hagerman-inspired seduction by the leading man, and the final near-destruction of her moral certainty, building the clash of belief and nonbelief to what I hoped was a strong theatrical climax.

Never having written a play before, I found it a useful and demanding discipline to force all the action into one set—exactly what I wanted to avoid in television! Casually I entered the play in the Q Theatre national play competition and had a pleasant shock when it won a top prize. The Q Theatre was a former cinema near

Kew Bridge in West London converted for weekly repertory by Jack de Leon and his wife, Beatrice. They had struggled to keep going since before the war, desperately presenting a different play every week. The contest had been a cheap way of finding new material, but part of the prize was a full showcase production.

Dennis Arundel, known mainly for his superb opera productions at Sadler's Wells and elsewhere, agreed to direct. In rehearsal it was fascinating to see my characters come to life through the confident performances of Reginald Tate, Nigel Davenport, and, as the young girl, Ann Stephens. But of course, as the play grew, I began to wish I had insisted on directing it myself. Reginald Tate had far too pleasant a "leading man" personality to attempt the real, utter villainy of my Hagerman, and Dennis, though sympathetic and patient with my criticism, failed to create the true spiritual violence of the older man's confrontation with the young girl. For the first time I knew the anguish of a writer whose work has not been properly understood in production.

My wife, Mimi, and I were expecting another child, and two days before the play's opening, on Sunday, April 17, 1955, our second daughter, Heather, was born. The following day the national newspapers went on strike, so on Tuesday's first performance no leading critic saw the play. I doubt whether the critics would have affected its fortune, although several managers came, and one or two were even complimentary afterward. But I had to admit that the production didn't merit a transfer to London's West End, and my hopes of becoming a successful playwright died on that Saturday.

I was back in the doldrums, needing work. I couldn't see any point in chasing A-R again, but I composed new letters to Granada and ABC. Ford Motors advertised for a chief films officer, a highly paid hack job organizing all their publicity films. I applied and was offered the post.

Having attended my medical at Dagenham, I was suddenly called by Captain Brownrigg's secretary from Associated-Rediffusion. The publicity for the Q play had jolted his memory and the forgotten appointment was set. Thus for the first time I encountered the remote and patrician figure of Captain Thomas Marcus Brownrigg, R.N. (retired), C.B.E., D.S.O., talent-spotted by Rediffusion boss John Spencer Wills when general manager of Bracknell New Town. (He had been "helpful" in setting up Rediffusion's cable radio there.) Compared with the executive talent chosen by other new program companies, Brownrigg was indeed a strange choice. The ATV had for instance selected Bill Ward, an ex–BBC veteran of Alexandra Palace, with a clear understanding of lively television entertainment. Granada, in addition to the Bernstein brothers with their lifetime of cinema expertise, had film producer Victor Peers and former director of the British Film Institute Denis Forman, a man of taste and refinement with a deep love of music and the arts whose contribution to intelligent programming over the next few years was simply incalculable. The ABC had probably the best chief executive of all in Howard Thomas, a wartime radio producer who had invented *The Brains Trust* and had recently been making films. If ever a man understood the needs of popular television it was Howard Thomas. Against such stalwarts it is difficult to discern Brownrigg's appeal.

Born in 1902, he had had a classic naval career. Educated at the Royal Naval College at Dartmouth, Devon, he had become a midshipman in 1919 and had risen to master of the fleet in the first three years of the Second World War, when Britain reeled from defeat to defeat. It was rumored that he had made many enemies. He was passed over for admiral, and his subsequent early retirement surprised few of his colleagues. His idiosyncrasies were many, but he had joined Associated-Rediffusion determined to run "his" company on well-disciplined lines (or as a wag put it, "on true Nelsonian principles of rum, buggery and the lash"). If his newly chosen career had been in making a simple consumer product, like beef sausages, Brownrigg might have been an acceptable manager. But his knowledge of television was, as Company Secretary Arthur Groocock admitted, "fractionally greater than zero."

Television programs demand many diverse skills. Made with apparently identical ingredients, they can be anything from appalling to brilliant. The difference lies in some strange fusion of passion, style, energy, and wit, from people of uncertain temperament and talent. Lacking understanding of any of these qualities, Captain Tom was almost certainly the world's worst candidate to run the show.

Thus, while ATV, ABC, and Granada presented images of slick professional showmanship, A-R was usually dismissed as "doggedly decent." Poor Brownrigg even had a problem deciding whether producers, writers, and directors should be considered to be of "commissioned" rank or strictly lower deck. This became clear as he kept me standing throughout our interview and delivered a weighty lecture about the formation of A-R. As my attention wandered, I suddenly caught something about my becoming a permanent drama director. He even mentioned an annual salary. I argued that it was far less than what the Ford Motor Company was willing to pay me. He dismissed this with contempt. At A-R I would be a pioneer in an exciting new venture. (Who had told him, I wondered.) If I showed up well, my salary would be raised. (A promise he kept after a year.) I accepted, and Karel Reisz took the Ford job.

So, on May 1, 1955, I entered the newly christened "Television House," selected one of the new desks, and sat down to wait. I was joined by a young girl called Vicki Miller, whom I had met briefly weeks before while waiting to see Roland Gillette. We decided on the spot we would like to work together, and for the next eight years we formed an effective partnership in the control room.

A fledgling Drama Department was being loosely assembled under Norman Marshall. Born in Rawalpindi (then in India), educated at Edinburgh and Oxford, after starting as an actor and stage manager Norman had run the small Gate Theatre in London for five years before the war, and had directed several plays in New York and London, including the acclaimed *Victoria Regina*, by Laurence Housman. Looking like a stern old colonel, he could suddenly burst into peals of fruity laughter. But he encouraged us from the beginning.

Peter Cotes, senior drama producer, tried at first to supervise the younger talent, but later he became so involved in his own shows that his effective producing ceased. The original directors included John Llewellyn Moxey, now a Hollywood director, Philip Saville, an ex-actor of real talent, and Cliff Owen, writer and former assistant director on *Brighton Rock*. Cyril Coke, latterly chief assistant to Frank Launder and Sidney Gilliat, was also there, as well as Tania Lieven, purveyor of the old-fashioned BBC style of "well-made plays." Lurking within the company, her great talent as yet unrealized on pop programs like *Cool for Cats*, was the dignified figure of Joan

Kemp-Welch, who later brilliantly illuminated everything from ancient Greek tragedy to modern Harold Pinter, and became a considerable force in A-R drama.

During the first few days, directors were expected to be seen but not heard, uninvolved in the frantic editorial meetings where schedules were heatedly argued by Roland Gillette and his assistants, Stephen McCormack and Lloyd Williams. Peter Cotes sometimes attended, to emerge white-faced some hours later. Gillette's ideas for commercial television appeared to be scrappy, quickfire programs of half an hour or less, with "pace" and "attack"—but no real substance.

Meanwhile a Script Department under Donald Bull, with playwright Giles Cooper, Jessica Morton, John Letts, and Robert Irvine (whose daughter Lucy later wrote the best-seller *Castaway*), was trying to find good television dramas. Gillette proudly announced the blind purchase of 50 old American radio scripts, but we rapidly discovered that material that might have sold beer in Milwaukee in the thirties was hardly hot stuff for modern British viewers.

By now A-R had bought the near-derelict Fox-British studios at Wembley and was busy converting them for live television, but for the moment A-R was stockpiling drama programs on film in three small stages (E, F, and G) at Shepperton Studios in Middlesex.

Rather than hunt vainly through the old radio scripts, I persuaded Donald Bull to buy a play I'd seen at the Bolton's Theatre, *A Call on the Widow* by James Doran, soon adapted as my first television film. The story was simple. During a heavy rainstorm two detectives arrive at a lonely cottage to interview the widow of a rich man after his sudden death. As they question her, the floodwaters rise around the cottage, and they are marooned. Their enforced stay lasts three days, the younger detective falls in love with the widow, and then finds incontestable evidence that she has poisoned her sadistic husband.

In his adaptation Robert Irvine had cleverly spread the four-handed action (two detectives, the widow, and an old retainer) through the various rooms of the cottage, tautened the conflict and dialogue, and heightened the sexual jealousy between the older policeman and his assistant to create a gripping final confrontation.

Jean Kent, playing the widow, was still a star of British films, and Clifford Evans a fine character actor. With the then unknown Michael Craig as the younger detective, we began rehearsing for two weeks before filming. I was expected to shoot the whole 50-minute piece in four days at the unheard-of rate of 12½ minutes per day, when the average those days in British studios was only two minutes. However, I knew that with a skillful cameraman and a swift operator I could make as many as 35 set-ups a day. Planning ambitious camera movement and dramatic angles with care, I completed just on time, with Jean, Clifford, and Michael delivering powerful performances (usually in the first take), aided by Brendan Stafford's crisp black-and-white photography.

Before I could start editing, I was handed the script of *The Guv'nor* by Tudor Gates, an original black-comedy about an academic burglar operating his nefarious enterprises under cover of the sales force of an ultra-respectable encyclopedia. Michael Hordern created one of his charming, dithering eccentrics as the learned crook, tempered by Coral Browne's bitter lemon as his not-too-adoring secretary. The cast included Nigel Davenport, Jimmy Hanley, Sam Kydd, and a young Robin Ray. Again we rehearsed for two weeks and shot the whole hour in five (not four) days at Shepperton.

It was a particularly lovely summer that year. Stages E, F, and G hummed with the new activity, and there was a great spirit of optimism as we gathered for drinks in the garden of the old house at the end of each filming day. Only Cliff Owen was more realistic. He foresaw, correctly, that when the first injection of capital had been spent, pruning knives would come out, rapidly. He had reason for gloom; he had been saddled with one of Gillette's American radio retreads, and his next assignment was to be *Can I Help You?*, with Godfrey Winn, a toupeed women's magazine journalist of uncertain gender pouring syrup on bogus women's problems of the heart. Cliff soon left us for the more serious world of Granada, where he directed some outstanding plays by Clifford Odets and others.

My last Shepperton film was *All Correct Sir*, from a story by a friend, Bill Naughton (who was later to find fame as author of Michael Caine's film success, *Alfie*). In his youth Bill had spent a short sojourn in Strangeways Jail, Manchester, where the governor told him how a wild and intractable girl prisoner had finally been rehabilitated. Commissioning new writer Barbara S. Harper to adapt the story, for the first time I was able to influence a script from inception to rehearsal. Adrienne Corri was an attractive young redhead who had just been released from a career-stifling Rank contract (having made *Lease of Life*, Robert Donat's last film, and Wolf Mankowitz's *Make Me an Offer*, with Peter Finch). Wasted by inhibited Pinewood producers whose feeble idea of screen sex was like a furtive peep into a schoolgirls' changing room, she had just the fire and energy to portray my impetuous girl prisoner, driven by weeks of thoughtless punishment to smash up her cell in a final act of defiance.

The governor of Holloway Women's Prison allowed us a visit. Adrienne was locked in a cell for half an hour and emerged looking very thoughtful. With Bernard Lee as prison governor and Megs Jenkins as chief female officer, I was allowed six days' filming, for the best result so far.

I returned to Television House in early September as Captain Brownrigg and Associated-Rediffusion were anxiously preparing to be the first ITV company on the air on the night of September 22, 1955. For some extraordinary reason the opening program was to be an outside broadcast of a Guildhall banquet in the City of London attended by honored guests from Parliament, mayors of London boroughs, so-called celebrities, even the chairman and director-general of the BBC, and a few friendly pressmen. (Naturally no one vulgar enough to be involved with real program-making was invited.)

At 7:15 precisely, after an opening fanfare and a few dull shots of London, A-R's live cameras focused on the completely unknown faces of Guildhall guests as they arrived. At 7:30 Sir John Barbirolli and the Hallé Orchestra launched into Elgar's "Cockaigne" and "God Save the Queen." At 7:45 the lord mayor, the postmaster-general, and the chairman of ITA, Kenneth Clarke, made hopeful but overlong speeches. After all that, those viewers who hadn't been so bored that they'd switched back to the BBC were actually treated to a taste of the future: a 40-minute live variety show produced by Bill Ward of ATV from the Wood Green Empire.

At 8:12 the program faded out, replaced by sharp cinema-type advertisements for toothpaste, drinking chocolate, and margarine— to be greeted with riotous applause from the Guildhall revelers. The great television adventure had, rather hesitantly, begun.

The next day, programs settled down to a regular pattern, and viewers and critics began to see what all the fuss had been about. There had never been any question that ITV was going to be "popular" television, but in the early days some attempt was made to provide a sprinkling of "culture" too. The A-R even scheduled a full concert by Barbirolli and the Hallé Orchestra every alternate Thursday. Newspapers' response depended on whether or not they had invested in a program company. Associated-Newspapers' *Daily Mail* and *Evening News* were fulsome, naturally. ITV, they claimed, offered an alternative most people wanted and new aerials and new sets were selling well, even in the Midlands and North before transmission up there had started. For years the BBC had tried to "improve the minds of the public." But here was exciting new *entertainment*, challenging all the high-minded ideals of established broadcasting.

The *Daily Express*, however, with no money in ITV, fearing the novelty as a growing rival for its advertising revenue, was loud in its condemnation of some of the rubbish being shown. The *Daily Telegraph*, Sunday *Times*, and *Observer*, whose middle-class readers were not yet the prime target for commercials, were more balanced, occasionally singling out a quality ITV program for respectable mention.

The ITV set up its own organization to assess the audience, not in the BBC's "audience appreciation" terms, but simply to measure the gross numbers watching. Television Audience Measurement (TAM) and Nielson delivered massive reassurance. In the first month three out of every four homes with sets converted to ITV chose the commercial channel in preference to the BBC. Some months later the BBC's own figures still showed a more than 60 to 40 lead for the newcomer.

The ITV's top ten programs became hot news. For program makers it would have been more helpful to know how much any show had been *enjoyed*, but the ratings never told us that. When Midlands and Northern transmitters revealed ITV to 75 percent of the entire population, the airwaves had been won for working-class voices and regional accents talking straight to viewers with a mateyness they had never had from the stuffy corporation.

The message was optimistic—from friendly comics Hughie Green and Tommy Trinder, from playwrights like Ted Willis and the crop of new young directors—reflecting life either as we perceived it or as we hoped it would become. Though our message could be funny or sometimes painful, it would at least be true to our own experience. The small flickering rectangle of the television screen began to predict the possibility of a world without fear, without hunger, without oppression. Alas, it was impossible that someone of the limited imagination of Captain Thomas Brownrigg, R.N. (retired), could in any way grasp the extent of this shared vision. In his eyes we were no more than hired hands, paid to do a job.

Within Television House the hammering and drilling had now more or less stopped, and directors were moved from the large general office, abuzz with noise and ringing phones, into tiny "bullpens," makeshift compartments with flimsy partitions that gave little quiet or privacy. Other departments, documentaries, current affairs, and light entertainment, had been set up in a great hurry. Peter Hunt from the BBC, journalist Daniel Farson, pioneer Leslie Mitchell, and filmmaker Peter Morley were busy finding new faces and new ways to present hard facts, rejecting blandness and evasion. Robert Tronson and Roger Jenkins were new boys in Children's Hour. The Light Entertainment Department was officially run by Kenneth Carter, formerly of Lime Grove, but aging band leader and impresario Jack Hylton had been contracted at a vast fee to supply old-fashioned vaudeville—which didn't attract big audiences no matter how hard he tried, for A-R could never match the resources and talent of the Grades at ATV.

Early in A-R's formation Brownrigg had admiringly studied the BBC's overmanned administration before copying it, filling his upper deck with military and naval rejects. "Captain" this and "Major" that appeared all too frequently on A-R's first telephone list (though Vicki Miller dissuaded me from readopting my war-emergency rank of second lieutenant). Rapidly, however, these bellicose figures disappeared from active service—one for over-indulgence at the pink gin fountain on Brownrigg's bridge, another when discovered astride his ex–Wren secretary, a third with his hand too obviously in the cash box—and the professionals were left to go on making programs.

Wembley had now been completely refurbished as four television studios. The best, One, was a reasonable size, Two and Four slightly smaller, and Three fit only for announcements. There were rumors of plans to build a very large Studio Five—but not yet. The old Granville theatre in Walham Green, clumsily sound-proofed, was Studio Six, and Seven, Eight, and Nine were in the basement of Television House. Although the last was to prove useful for school programs, the other two soon closed down.

In Wembley's Studio One there were four Marconi Mark 3 television cameras, each with a turret of four lenses, ranging from close-up to wide-angle. Three microphones on telescopic booms were mounted on huge Mole-Richardson mobile platforms, enabling the boom operators to see above the rest of the crew and cameras. Wembley was run by Commander Richard Everett, an intelligent and genial exception to the rule that all ex-officers had to be upper-class twits. His comments on productions in the making were often valuable and encouraging.

Designer Michael Yates, who had attended my BBC course in 1952, had set up a strong Art Department, led by Frederic Pusey, a very experienced film production designer (whose son is now equally sought after), with John Clements, ex–BBC, Frank Nerini, whose son also became a fine designer, and Henry Federer. Graphics boasted the brilliant Joe McGrath, later to direct two Peter Sellers films, and Light Entertainment had a crazy young American called Dick Lester who sold the gullible Roland Gillette the idea of *The Dick Lester Show*, a forerunner of his inventions on the Goon Shows and of his work later as director of the Beatles' *A Hard Day's Night, The Three Musketeers*, and other major successes.

In Drama we began to plan the future. Norman Marshall had convinced Gillette we had to have two peak-time drama slots per week—*Play of the Week* at 80 minutes and *Television Playhouse* at 50. He had looked at the 13 Shepperton films and had not been very impressed (though he did put my three straight into the schedules). But trying to put drama onto film at that speed could never match the quality of real movies. So from now on all drama would be *live*.

He realized of course that a live transmission was infinitely more nerve-racking than filming short scenes for actors, director, and crew, but he believed that the feeling of "now or never" would give everyone an extra stimulus. In a way we were lucky that few experienced cameramen wanted to leave the BBC for ITV. The young men we were able to train were eager to try out fresh ideas, and consequently from the beginning ITV dramas looked more dynamic visually than the stodgy group shots still served up at the BBC.

Tania Lieven's inexpensive *The Geranium*, A-R's first live drama, was followed a week later by Henry James's *The Aspern Papers*, directed by John Moxey. My film *A Call on the Widow* was next, on October 6, and was well reviewed. But without another play of my choice ready for immediate production, I was forced to revise an American import, *The End of the Mission* by Roger Hirson, as my first live production from Wembley on November 3. Set in the south of France just after the war, about an ex–GI's search for the member of the Resistance who had betrayed him to the Nazis, it was at least professionally written, and it worked better for our audience once we had turned the hero into a British ex-soldier. With Derek Bond, Selma vaz Diaz, and Zena Marshall, it played well in sets designed by George Haslam, another former film art director.

Five weeks later I directed the old West End comedian Leslie Henson in an amusing piece by Giles Cooper, *The General's Mess*, an "unmilitary episode," with Joan Sims, Jimmy Thompson, and Noel Hood. A typically wry example of Giles's work, it was light and fresh but hardly significant. I knew I had to find something better, somehow.

The A-R was in turmoil. Sales of commercials were less than predicted, and the schedules were being revamped almost daily under pressure from advertisers and management. The Hallé Orchestra concerts and two modestly intelligent discussion programs had been axed. Roland Gillette's position as program controller was rumored to be shaky. Then, quite unmourned, he abruptly left the company on January 17, 1956, and John McMillan, previously general manager of the defunct Kemsley-Winnick, took over. McMillan was born in Sydney, Australia, in 1915 but immigrated to England in 1934 to make programs for commercial station Radio Luxembourg. During the war he commanded the first field radio unit in northwest Europe, which eventually merged into the British Forces Network in occupied Germany. He joined BBC Radio in 1946 as assistant controller, light program, until 1952. After working in American television, he returned to England for the start of ITV.

John McMillan proved to be much easier to talk to than the superficial Gillette, and I was soon able to interest him in two projects I wanted to dramatize and produce. The first was *One*, an American novel of considerable force by David Karp, set in a future society where individual willpower had been reduced to zero, and the second a real-life story that had obsessed me for many years.

Published during the war, Richard Hillary's *The Last Enemy* was a true account of a handsome but arrogant Oxford undergraduate turned fighter pilot in the desperate Battle of Britain. While all his friends and contemporaries had been killed in action, Richard had survived, shot down in flames, terribly burned about the hands and face. Enduring months of plastic surgery, he had slowly discovered real sympathy with his fellow men and women, united in the common struggle against inhuman tyranny. Returning to duty in early 1943, he was killed in a flying accident at age 23. But his book, *The Last Enemy*, lived on as a literate and moving testament to courage and compassion for all time.

The theme—the indestructibility of the human spirit—was the most important I had ever attempted. Richard Hillary was only four years older than me. Coming from a less privileged background, I felt no less a deep and enduring sympathy with the character presented in his book and was determined to do it justice on the screen. McMillan was equally enthusiastic. Both adaptations were immediately commissioned: *One* to John Letts, and *The Last Enemy* to Barbara Harper.

Meanwhile I had been offered the direction of a small film for Rank by a young independent producer, John Temple Smith. It was a cold winter, and Mimi and I needed a new boiler for our house in Radlett. I sought leave from A-R, and the three-week shoot provided us with central heating. *The Hideout* was a typical second feature of the period, about the panic caused in London by an outbreak of anthrax traced to a smuggled consignment of stolen furs. Most of it was shot around the Docks, but John had secured some second-hand sets at Shepperton, so the interiors were played in oddly elegant surroundings, giving the little film, starring Dermot Walsh, Rona Anderson, and Ronald Howard, considerable production value. (Unfortunately this and several other small films I made 40 or more years ago continue to turn up, wraithlike, on late-night television, while none of my better work, transmitted live to disappear forever after one performance, has been preserved.)

On my return to A-R, John Letts's script for *One* was ready and set for transmission on Monday, April 16, (a significant date: my daughter Heather was to have a birthday the following day, becoming "one"). John's treatment of "a foreseeable future" when an apparently caring society brainwashes a nonconformer into mindless acceptance of all-powerful authority (echoing Orwell's *1984* and Koestler's *Darkness at Noon*) was masterly, and was just the chance I needed. I signed two of our best young character actors, Donald Pleasence and Kenneth Griffith, as the dissident professor and his interrogator, and asked George Haslam to design settings both of warm domestic comfort and of contrasting chilling white for the interrogation center.

Admiring Gregg Toland's deep-focus black-and-white photography on *Citizen Kane* and *The Little Foxes*, I began to experiment with lighting director Teddy Shankster, using wide-angle lenses to distort the faces of actors close to the camera while including a background group in unreal perspective. I also wanted a fifth camera on a high rostrum, to look down over the shoulders of Kenneth Griffith and Ronald Howard (framing the shot in foreground) in a small observation room, as they discussed the drugged Donald Pleasence, supine on the floor of a cell 20 feet below them. There was fierce opposition from Engineering, worried about the effect on an image-orthicon camera when tilted more than 45 degrees. We tried, it worked without mishap, and I got the shot I wanted. For other cameras, I chose the most mobile dolly then available, the three-wheeled Debrie. The cameramen were going to be forced to move very fast to pick up each new position accurately throughout the 80-minute drama. (As one observed gloomily, "We're teetering on the edge of the impossible.")

As I planned the complicated production, I felt the benefit of the months of afternoon trial and error in Studio H at Lime Grove. There was no producer nervously second-guessing at my elbow, and rehearsals with Donald, Ken, Ronnie, Raymond Francis, and Mary Jones began in a rare atmosphere of hope as together we discovered each character's emotion and strength.

Camera rehearsal in the studio on Sunday was slow but precise. At eight o'clock on that Monday night I cued the powerful opening bars of Aaron Copland's "Fanfare for the Common Man" and faded up a dark shot of a crowd of people facing away from the camera. Slowly the camera tracked in to a huge close-up of the back of Donald Pleasence's head as a spotlight suddenly hit him and he turned, startled.

"*One*," intoned an off-screen voice. "A story of the foreseeable future"—and we were off into an adventurous hour and a half, punctuated by two short commercial breaks.

As the final captions ended, I faded to black, still unsure how well it had gone. But the phone was already ringing and for the next half hour I spoke to all sorts of people who seemed amazed that it had all been performed live, as so much looked prefilmed.

We had expected minor criticism, but the next day's notices took us by surprise. In the *Daily Telegraph* Richard Sear described "the action of a group of scientists in a hypothetical state confronted with a heretic insisting on his natural qualities of ambition and individuality, and the way they proceed to take his mind to pieces and recreate it was a work of considerable imagination. Peter Graham Scott displayed vivid camerawork and the qualities of a neatly-gauged production."

Kenneth Griffith and Donald Pleasence were widely praised. The *Evening Standard* was even more fulsome. Under the headline MR. SCOTT CUTS LOOSE, television guest critic Robert Henriques began,

> I try to use the word "great" very sparingly. But last night I felt the TV screen had become the medium for a great production. I had watched the play, *One,* on ITA. How did the director, Peter Graham Scott, keep me enthralled for ninety minutes and convince me that a story seen on a small piece of curved glass in Kensington was true? The answer is he obeyed a few well-known rules. He planned the play down to the last detail before he started rehearsing. He told his story in close-ups and in pictures of small groups of people. He used long shots

to locate the events, to create atmosphere and to punc-
tuate mood. In this play *One* a top-class director cut
loose and proved that technical skill and artistic integrity
can make TV a true medium in its own right.

There was even better to come. In the *Guardian*, the normally
curmudgeonly Bernard Levin headed his article, ITV'S FINEST HOUR
(AND A HALF). TRIUMPH OF ONE AFTER SEVEN MONTHS. He continued,

> I toyed on Monday night with the idea of sending a
> telegram to Sir Robert Fraser of the ITA, "All is for-
> given. Come back. We can start afresh. Love." There is
> no getting away from it that Independent Television with
> Monday's production of *One* woke up. Mr. Peter Gra-
> ham Scott's direction was so sure and unfaltering and
> his grip so firm that I can answer for one viewer who
> had the living daylights scared out of him. There were
> some magnificent shots: the silent watchers in their
> eyrie, high above the cell in which Professor Burden,
> played by Donald Pleasence, was being questioned; the
> group of doctors circling the couch on which their vic-
> tim lies unconscious; the naked antiseptic corridor along
> which he is marched for further treatment; the teetering
> camera angle for his drug-induced confession; the rush-
> ing close-up of his fear-crazed appearance as he tries to
> escape from the room in which he is locked with a group
> of lunatics. Visually there was no compromise—nor
> indeed on any other level. The story was compressed,
> but neither simplified nor watered down. The morons
> had to keep up as best they could. Those who stayed the
> course were richly rewarded, not least by fine perfor-
> mances from Mr. Donald Pleasence and Mr. Roy Mal-
> colm. But the greatest reward was surely that provided
> by the author in his ending. For the experiment fails;
> although Burden's mind is emptied of its character and
> an entirely new personality is created for him, there still
> remains the germ of heresy, the spark that makes the
> new man want to be unique in his own way, just as the
> old one wanted to be unique in his. Dictatorship—and
> it is a lesson we would do well to remember—is not
> efficient. The most comforting thing about Mussolini is
> that he did *not* make the trains run on time.

Even the *New Statesman*, with Tom Driberg at his most mag-
isterial, was full of praise. He had "watched it with Mr. Sam

Zimbalist, the director, and Mr. Gore Vidal, a brilliant [sic] young novelist. Both the Americans thought they were watching a film. They were impressed with the smoothness of the transitions between scenes." "Technically," Driberg concluded, "it was the most ambitious production that Associated-Rediffusion and Mr. Peter Graham Scott have yet attempted. We must surely hope that ITV will continue to aim as high as this."

I doubt whether Captain Brownrigg had stayed awake throughout the 80 minutes. Certainly he would have been unaware that we had made a major dramatic statement on the value of personal freedom. But someone must have shown him the opinions in cold print. I was summoned to the bridge, given a small gin and an even smaller raise in salary, but more importantly I was able to argue a sensible budget for *The Last Enemy*.

Meanwhile, however, the treadmill had to be trodden. My next production on June 14 was strictly commercial, an adaptation of *Castle in the Air* by Alan Melville, in which Jack Buchanan had scored some success in the theater, aided by the sharp wit of Coral Browne. Rehearsals were perfunctory. Jack Buchanan spent most of the day on the telephone doing business deals, and only when Coral threatened to leave did he consent to run through scenes. At the last moment he discovered that our studio performance would not have a live audience to watch it. He protested, and the superb Scottish castle Fred Pusey had designed was swiftly cut to fit in an audience. But when the show was transmitted there was very little accompanying laughter, as the audience was unused to seeing television cameras in action and gazed in dumbstruck awe without hearing the jokes.

Four weeks later I was back in the studio with *Rain on the Just* by Peter Watling, about an upper-crust family's fight to save the ancestral home, with Michael Denison, Marie Ney, and Patricia Driscoll. Once again I extended a West End success from its solitary stage setting to give it variety and movement with film inserts. The critics were generally very positive. In the *Observer* Maurice Richardson described the piece as "compulsively viewable, with a quite exceptional performance by Michael Denison as the unpleasantly realistic son." In the *Daily Mail* Peter Black sensed "a strong intelligence at work, pulling together the conflicting characters' qualities—charm, wit, ruthlessness and loneliness—into a closely-knit whole to round off a cleverly judged production."

I now received Barbara Harper's adaptation of *The Last Enemy* and read it with some apprehension. Though excellent in its emotional scenes, it seemed to lack the fine spiritual values I'd discerned in the book. But worse, Barbara had somehow sentimentalized our hero's attitude to his appalling disfigurement in a way I knew, instinctively, Richard Hillary would have contemptuously rejected. So, with Barbara's agreement, I began to rewrite in every spare minute I could find with a fury and energy that astonished me.

There was precious little time left. I had one more play to direct on August 9 before prefilming and rehearsing a large cast in *The Last Enemy* for transmission on Monday, September 10, in Battle of Britain Week.

The intervening production was *Ever Since Paradise*, by J. B. Priestley, Jolly Jack's comic sermon on the perils of love and marriage. With Helen Cherry, Donald Pleasence, and Francis Matthews playing a multitude of characters, I could only hope for the best.

But during the last few busy months ugly rumors had been flying up and down the battleship-gray corridors of Television House. All was not well with Associated-Rediffusion. Despite high ratings for most of our programs and a fair complement of advertising, the costs of the vast administrative body Brownrigg had created meant the company was losing £10,000 ($15,000) a day, £50,000 ($75,000) a week.

We were addressed one gloomy Saturday morning by John McMillan, telling us we had to tighten our belts and cut production costs. As Cliff Owen had predicted a year before, a quarter of the staff was made redundant, including my loyal and untiring studio manager, John Frankau, whom I was able to save only by switching him to a month's temporary attachment to the Sales Department, flogging airtime. (He returned somewhat chastened after his brush with naked commerce.) As a further economy, one of the stranded sea captains, known as "Treacle Boots," suggested that we should rehearse and transmit our plays in only one studio day instead of two, a dangerous experiment unfortunately commenced with *Ever Since Paradise*. Urged to save money, designer John Clements devised a way of projecting stylized cartoon drawings of every one of the many sets, which cut his costs to practically nil but completely inhibited creative camerawork.

Originally planned for 80 minutes, *Ever Since Paradise* I had soon realized would hold up for only 50, and I persuaded Norman to exchange its *Play of the Week* slot for a shorter *Television Playhouse*. There was only one problem. I would have to ask Jack Priestley.

Mimi and our small daughters had moved to a holiday house in Ventnor, Isle of Wight, for July, and I used to join them every weekend. As J. B. Priestley lived in Freshwater, just up the road, I thought it would be easy to call and ask permission to cut his play. The following Saturday I left rehearsal at twelve and caught the car-ferry to the Isle of Wight. After a quick lunch I drove through gathering mist to Freshwater and found his house wreathed in fog at the top of a hill. A heavy but instantly recognizable figure greeted me from the steps and welcomed me in the velvet Yorkshire tones that had enriched his heartening wartime broadcasts.

Ushering me into a fine paneled music room with a minstrels' gallery above, Priestley asked when I proposed to "film" his play. I explained we were already rehearsing for a live television performance. He had unfortunately never heard of Donald Pleasence or Helen Cherry, though he thought he'd seen her husband, Trevor Howard. Indeed he professed little interest in his play's fate on television. He had two things on his mind. First, Ralph Richardson had recently rejected the lead in J. B.'s latest play, preferring to play *Timon of Athens* at London's Old Vic, infuriating a most un–Jolly Jack. "I may not have written a masterpiece," he roared. "But it's got to be better than bloody *Timon of Athens*!"

Then for some reason the old playwright began to harangue me about his latest theory on film production. "You waste too much time shooting sound!" he bellowed. "You should do what the Italians do—shoot it all silent and add the sound afterwards!" I was far too intimidated to suggest that direct sound could capture the actors' original performances in a far better way than any postsynchronization, and in any case I wanted to get back to Mimi before nightfall.

Tea arrived, and with it several members of his family, including his young son, Tom (who was to edit a film for me years later), but as soon as I could decently escape I rose to my feet muttering, "Oh, by the way, we have to cut your play down a bit." Jack Priestley glowered. "*Cut it?*" "To 50 minutes." He thought about it for a minute, then his expression changed. "Cut it all you like, dear boy. It's far too long anyway."

Unfortunately, on our one and only day in the studio the shocking lack of camera rehearsal showed up badly on transmission the same night. Treacle Boots's brilliant suggestion made us look like bungling amateurs. The audience ratings were the worst I had ever had. But there was no time for postmortems. I had exactly four weeks to film and rehearse *The Last Enemy*.

I'd finished the script at night and on weekends, injecting more film sequences and converting as much of Richard Hillary's fine prose as I could into dialogue. I was now word-drunk and had no idea how it would all play. However, when I started casting and heard actors reading the new scenes, I became cautiously optimistic. Hillary's words, when spoken, rang true.

Among the many unknown actors I considered to play Richard Hillary were Michael Bryant, Francis Matthews, and Dinsdale Landen. But in the end they played other pilots and my choice fell on a young man who had been a Rank starlet but had then become a disc jockey in commercial radio. He was now hoping to return to straight acting. His name was Peter Murray.

Peter had just the good looks and arrogance I wanted. But to make sure, I introduced him to the dead author's parents, who were still living in London. The father, Michael Hillary, was a charming Australian who had been a district officer in the Sudan, which gave us something to talk about. His wife, Edwina, was equally welcoming, and as soon as she saw Peter she exclaimed, "But he's exactly like my Richard."

Another key character was Denise, fiancée of Richard's best friend, Peter Pease, who was shot down and killed. In mourning she had visited Richard in the hospital during his long recovery from his burns, and their developing relationship formed the emotional heart of the drama. She was now married and living in Maidenhead, Berkshire, and we spent a pleasant afternoon discussing Richard and the script.

The other important character was Archibald McIndoe, the

brilliant plastic surgeon who had painstakingly rebuilt the hands and faces of so many badly burned airmen at his hospital near East Grinstead, Sussex. He insisted that I must cast very pretty actresses as his nurses. "Always had good-lookers. Did wonders for the boys." With so much goodwill I *had* to get it all right.

I cast John Robinson as McIndoe and Patricia Driscoll as Denise and commenced filming. The organizers of the Maidenhead Regatta allowed us to drape the riverbank with Nazi flags on their Finals day—to the absolute horror of several old officers who hadn't been told what we were up to—so that we could stage the prewar rowing contest in Germany where Richard and his crew, hungover and losing badly, were spat upon from a bridge above by a Nazi stormtrooper, which galvanized them into new life, to row to victory by four lengths.

The Air Ministry lent us its one and only Spitfire fighter for an afternoon of aerobatics, to cut in with archive shots of the real Battle of Britain, and also gave us a scrap cockpit for harrowing close-ups of Richard with flames apparently licking round his face as he struggled to free himself from a jammed cockpit cover. We put a sheet of flameproof glass between Peter and a conflagration of oily rags. He reacted with true terror until the heat became unbearable and he was forced to smash his way out.

For a later sequence, after Richard, shot down, had parachuted into the sea, Peter had to fall into the murky waters of the Thames and lie half submerged as we zoomed into a close-up of his burned face. Unfortunately, with a strong tide running, the harness securing him broke, and he began to be swept away, in danger of drowning in his waterlogged flying suit. But my confident assistant, John Frankau, prepared as always, hurled a lifebelt straight at him and hauled him to safety.

I wanted to start the action very quietly, tracking slowly into Eric Kennington's contemporary portrait of Richard as we heard his voice off-screen, quoting John Donne, "Any man's death diminishes me, because I am involved in mankind…." Then I wanted suddenly to cut to film of the violent aerial battle over Britain's southern coast on that particular day, September 3, 1940, when dark and heavy clouds had cleared to launch Richard and his squadron into the air to kill, or to die, or to suffer fiery agony and months of pain.

Filming with section of Spitfire, August 1956.

As he floated on film, we were to mix to a live close-up of Peter in the studio for which the vision engineers had devised a horrifying ripple effect that seemed to tear at the image of his blackened face and staring eyes, as we slowly mixed into a film sequence of prewar Oxford. Once clear, Peter would be released for the Makeup Department, because apart from the sheer ordeal of a 90-minute live performance he had to undergo continual alterations to his makeup between scenes, starting hideously burned and ending up scarred but presentable. All this was built into the script with short film sequences to allow for cosmetic adjustments. John Frankau and the two stage managers, Peter Yolland and June Epstein, organized the mechanics of the show with sets being dismantled and new ones erected on the run and extras and small parts wheeled in and out of the studio with military precision.

During our first week of rehearsal we were suddenly told that instead of Studio One (which had to have its floor relaid) we would be using the smaller Studio Four. Designer John Clements had to cut down his sets, and the whole operation, plus my camera script, had to be reorganized in a hurry.

As if this wasn't bad enough, even worse news was coming down the engine-room telegraph from Brownrigg's bridge. Associated-Rediffusion was still losing money, not because of a shortage of commercials, but because apart from important dramas, few of the other A-R programs were shown on the whole network, resulting in costly duplication of production effort by all four companies. At last the companies met and agreed on network program-sharing, but too late to recoup earlier losses.

By the end of July 1956, after ten months on the air, A-R reported a loss of nearly £3 million ($4.5 million). John Spencer Wills was invited to lunch by a nervous Neil Cooper Key, a director of his partners—Associated Newspapers, and questioned about A-R's prospects. Knowing precise figures of a considerable upturn in advertising revenue for the winter, Wills was confident of profit by January. However, Cooper Key was unconvinced and offered to sell Associated Newspapers' share in A-R. Wills agreed to buy— at a 25 percent discount. A few days later Wills was invited to meet Key's chairman, Lord Rothermere. "Are you still willing to buy us out?" "Of course," Wills answered quietly. "Done!" said his Lordship.

Wills returned home and suffered a sleepless night. Never had he committed himself so heavily with so little negotiation. But in a few days he had a written agreement, and his parent company, BET, bought the newspapers' shares at 75 percent of the original cost. The word "Associated" was dropped and "Rediffusion TV" was born. The deal was reported to the board during the first week of September 1956, while in cheerful ignorance my cast and crew prepared to go on the air in a few days' time.

Other companies were in financial trouble, too. For although television advertising was proving extremely effective, start-up costs had been greater than anticipated. Associated British had to call on its huge cinema chain for help. The ATV had to find further backing and reorganize the company. But Granada was in truly desperate straits. Having expected to sell advertising to the whole of the north of England from its start in May, the company was in fact only covering Lancashire from one transmitter, and would have to wait until November for the second to be built to include profitable Yorkshire. Sydney Bernstein blamed the ITA, which had promised that both areas would be covered by a single transmitter. But this had proved technically impossible. Aware of Granada's plight, the authority offered a release from paying rental until the second area was covered; but was suddenly told that the company had found another solution.

Once again John Spencer Wills had acted very boldly. He suggested that Rediffusion should in future supply 85 percent of Granada's programs, with the remaining 15 percent made by the northern company but with all costs paid by Rediffusion. For this service, from all advertising revenue Granada received, Rediffusion would take 90 percent of the first £1 million ($1.5 million), 87 percent of the next £3 million, and 85 percent of the rest.

This was a tough deal for the Bernstein brothers to accept, but at least it saved their company from being broken into by outsiders. But it cost them dearly. Over the next three years they would forfeit nearly £7 million ($10.5 million) to Rediffusion. But within a few more years their enormous profits made this historic ransom seem like small change; and ironically enough, Granada was the only one of the four original ITV companies to survive, and it has now become a huge international conglomerate with interests in luxury hotels, motorway service stations, property, office equipment rental, and many other businesses.

Unaware of all this financial juggling, by Friday, September 7, I was enjoying a fairly tidy technical rehearsal of *The Last Enemy* when I was approached by Brian Begg, our publicity officer, white-faced and anxious. He had just seen a smuggled copy of an article set for Sunday's *Express* attacking ITV's "temerity in trying to mount a production of Richard Hillary's Second World War classic *The Last Enemy* on a cheapskate TV budget, risking travesty and an appalling failure."

I went home in turmoil. We were committed to transmit on Monday night, but with this sort of preview the show could be damned before it was even seen. I woke in the small hours to consider the problem again. The story I had set my heart on telling was about to be wrecked by a few sour words from some dyspeptic hack. There had to be some way of stopping publication. Peter Rodd had taught me—always go to the top.

Early that Saturday morning I telephoned the Sunday *Express* office and asked to speak to The Honorable Max Aitken, chief executive of the Express Group. My one hope was that as an ex–RAF pilot, Lord Beaverbrook's son might prove more sympathetic to my production of Hillary's story than his underlings. Amazingly, I was put through and given an appointment for 3:15 that afternoon.

We were planning to rehearse all day, but before 3:00 P.M. I left the action in the capable hands of John Frankau, drove from Kingsway to Fleet Street, entered the shiny black Express building, gave the commissionaire my name, and was shown up in a special elevator. Aitken, seated behind a tycoon-sized desk, looked at me coldly. I began to explain my long-standing ambition to present *The Last Enemy* and the generous help I'd had from the parents, Denise, and McIndoe. Max Aitken listened without emotion, then flipped on an intercom and spoke crisply, "That piece tomorrow about *The Last Enemy*. Kill it." There was a babble of argument from the other end. Aitken flipped the key once more. "I said, 'Kill it.' Give the play a boost. It's a damn good subject." He looked at me. "Will that do?" I started to thank him but was rapidly shown out, back to rehearsal, to be greeted by John Frankau with more bad news.

The vision control ("racks") operators, who balanced the technical quality of each camera, were in dispute with management over recent sackings and had declared an immediate ban on weekend work. Tomorrow, Sunday, was to be our first day in the studio, but without pictures there could scarcely be a camera rehearsal.

I went to see John McMillan, who unusually for a Saturday was in his office. With weary patience he announced that he was postponing the production—indefinitely.

"Forever?"

"Until we settle the dispute."

I argued that we'd never set it up again with the same enthusiasm and the same cast—some of the actors had other jobs—and we were all worked up to concert pitch to perform on Monday night.

"What else can we do?" he asked hopelessly.

What else indeed?

It had taken me exactly four years to reach this point. I was about to realize a life's ambition, a production I believed in, of which we could all be proud. It was for this sort of fulfillment that

I had entered television, accepting all the hard work, the restless nights, the low financial reward. And now it was all to be abandoned, thanks to Captain Brownrigg's inept management and bad labor relations.

But what could I offer as an alternative? I struggled to invent a solution, while McMillan rustled idly through the pages of last week's *Variety*.

Then I found an answer, a fairly desperate scheme that would demand a huge extra effort from the studio crew. I put it to McMillan who, unconvinced, at least allowed me to try it. I hurried back to the rehearsal room to discuss the possibility with a skeptical John Frankau and senior cameraman Geoff Rimmer.

What I proposed was to work all next day, Sunday, in the studio as planned, with full lighting and the cast in costume and makeup, but without the technical operators. Cameramen would have to move dead cameras into place and line up shots roughly by eye. Then by starting an hour earlier than usual on Monday morning, with the full racks crew back on the job, we might still be ready for a run-through in the afternoon and transmission that night.

Geoff was unhappy about dry-plotting the whole 90 minutes unseen but agreed to do his best. In any event, by Sunday evening we had managed to block all 70 scenes, dismantling and erecting sets as cameramen found their way into position—hoping they'd have the right shots next day.

Still dubious, McMillan held on to the original transmission time on Monday. (With nothing to replace it he had little choice!) First Peter Murray had to record his disc jockey show at 8:00 A.M. He arrived at Wembley before 9:30, and we began to watch real shots on the monitors at last. Gradually we checked and replotted every angle, until just after lunch we'd reached the end.

At 3:30 we started a run-through, which in the tradition of all dress rehearsals was truly appalling. With so many stops and starts Vicki had been unable to get an accurate timing. She knew we were allowed 81 minutes but was unsure whether it would run 81 or as much as 83. I rang Presentation. They had a two-minute trailer for the next *Play of the Week* standing by, and if the worst happened they could cut that and let us run over by two minutes—"But not a second more!"

With so much to think about, Peter Murray and I went down to the noisy canteen for the supper break. At 7:30 he was called to Makeup; at ten minutes to eight Vicki and I went up to the control room to await Presentation's countdown. There were all the usual "Good lucks" to cast and crew.

But suddenly I felt a terrible responsibility. I had taken the moving words of a dead hero's testament and cobbled them into dialogue and pictures. If the result in any way cheapened his inspiration it would degrade a fine book before a massive audience.

"Wake up!" Vicki whispered in my ear as the minute hand ticked up to eight o'clock. I cued music, faded up the opening shot, and ran telecine. I watched our Richard Hillary climb into his Spitfire and engage the enemy, saw his plane suddenly engulfed in explosive flame, his struggle to escape from the blazing cockpit, and his parachuting agonizingly into the unwelcoming sea—as we slowly mixed to the rippling, dreamlike studio close-up and heard his voice whisper the first words of the narrative:

> I was going to die.
> I was going to die, and yet I was not afraid.
> I felt only a profound curiosity....

I was transfixed by the action on the screen. Beside me Vicki was calling up each camera angle, and Elsie Grey was cutting to each shot with beautiful precision. In Sound, Sheila Blower mixed music and effects with studio dialogue in perfect synchrony, while in the studio below John Frankau was marshaling his performers into place like an inspired sergeant major. Peter Yolland and June Epstein were resetting props, Teddy Shankster was adjusting lighting as planned, and the narrative moved swiftly on, through the first commercial break into the second act, with the emotional conflict between Denise and Richard achieving a heartrending power we'd never seen in rehearsal. And on, into the third part, to the penultimate scene, as in the book, where Richard, having quarreled with Denise, is in a London pub during an air raid, as the house next door is hit. A rescue worker dashes in asking for help. Richard follows him into the blacked-out night, although with his crippled, clawlike hands he knows he can be of little aid. But he tries, and just manages to heave a broken beam from the body of a dying woman. She looks up into his face, sees his cruel scars, and whispers, "I see they got you, too."

The climax of the book, this was the moment for which I had cast the fine character actress Beatrice Varley. But as Peter tried to lift the beam, laid carefully across her face, it somehow refused to move. He looked around desperately for a moment, too tired to carry on—and suddenly John Frankau leaped into the frame like a demon and hurled it clear. I zoomed in to Beatrice in close-up, she whispered the line, and closed her eyes, slowly dying.

Peter straightened up into the last shot, and back-projection behind him rolled to create the illusion of walking away, as we heard his moving final thoughts.

While at first he had felt only rage at becoming the object of the old woman's pity, slowly he came to realize that "all humanity had been in those six words, 'I see they got you, too.' Her death had been unjust, a crime, a sin against Mankind, Evil itself...." As he walked on through bomb-devastated streets, he gained a new purpose: to *write* of the brave men and women he had served with "who would go on fighting until the ideals for which their comrades had died were stamped forever on the future of civilisation."

The powerful music of Vaughan Williams's *London Symphony* rose in crescendo as I cued the final mix to an aerial shot of wartime London by night, barrage balloons floating over the city in the moonlight, and rolled the end credits, to fade to black at last.

Amazed it had ended so soon, I turned, to see Vicki, her face ashen. "What's wrong?"

She whispered, "We've overrun. It went to 85½ minutes."

"Did they cut us off the air?" (This had happened on ITV a few months before, when a clock-conscious presentation controller had cut the last three minutes of Peter Brook's *Hamlet*.)

I pressed the key for Presentation. "It's all right," a cheerful voice assured me. "We cut the trailer and pushed the commercials back. We're all in tears up here."

As soon as the friendly phone calls stopped, Mimi, Peter, Patricia Driscoll, and I drove to London to hear Michael and Edwina Hillary's verdict. Although the realistic air battle in which Richard had been shot down had been almost unbearable for them to watch, they had felt pride in the undoubted truth and sincerity of their son's message, now presented to a huge new audience. That alone made all our hard work worthwhile.

Next day's papers were amazing. A sensible preview had been substituted in the Sunday edition on Max Aitken's orders, and in three columns in the *Daily Express* under the headline SPITFIRES BURST INTO TV—AND GHOSTS LIVE AGAIN, Robert Cannell wrote, "Sixteen years rolled away last night when television recreated that terrible glorious first Battle of Britain week in the words of one of the immortal Few. Peter Graham Scott's ninety-minute dramatisation of fighter pilot Richard Hillary's *The Last Enemy* evoked for millions moving memories of the days when the blue skies above London were filled with battle and the nights shattered by bombs."

The *Daily Mail* headlined THIS SHOWED US A MAN. "Peter Graham Scott set himself and ITV a frightening task of bringing *The Last Enemy* to the screen last night," Philip Purser began.

> He accomplished it better than I dared hope. The peril lay in the fact that Richard Hillary's book is so much more than just an account of air warfare or plastic surgery. It tells the story of a tremendous interior process, which doesn't necessarily make the most exciting television. But the adaptation, a clear-cut arrangement of the book, didn't shirk it. The air battles were there, in brilliantly edited combat film, the surgical battle was there, and the spiritual battle was there. Technically a triumph, and to sum up, a distinguished tribute to a man who spoke with blazing honesty for his generation.

In the *Telegraph*, Marsland Gander described it as "the most moving play I have seen on either network since Orwell's '1984.' The merits were quite simply those of the book. Alone, of all the many combatants who wrote of their experience in the last war, Richard Hillary found a theme in his own painful acquisition of pity and humanity. The path towards his change of heart was traced with economy, taste and no mean skill."

Even the normally dismissive Maurice Richardson in the *Observer* spoke of "an example of boldness paying off. An excellent adaptation of Richard Hillary's *The Last Enemy*, shirked long ago as too difficult by the BBC. This was one of the best items of the year on any channel."

The *News Chronicle* described it as "an ITV gamble that paid off, in a production which made a courageous attempt to capture the very spirit of the young Battle of Britain pilot's view of life from a hospital bed, giving energetic actor Peter Murray a chance to show he's worth more than appearances in commercials and rowdy stunt programmes."

The extraordinary thing is that after all this praise Peter was not offered another leading part for some months. In the end, with a wife and family to support, he returned to the easier life of a well-paid disc jockey. However, at the year's end, Peter was named "Best TV Actor of 1956" by the *News Chronicle*, which also gave me a "Best TV Play" award. (I received another from the *News of the World*.) But the fact that a play of real quality had commanded a record audience of over 70 percent of those able to receive ITV in London, the Midlands, and Lancashire was not lost on John McMillan. The first Rediffusion production to be telerecorded off-air, it was shown again two years later, when ITV reached 80 percent of the population.

It proved we could dramatize serious themes, the pain and futility of war, spiritual triumph over suffering, and the power of human love, without overt influence in the first year of a "commercial" television service that so many pundits had derided. (Unfortunately its idealistic message, valid in 1956, sounds somewhat hollow in today's materialistic world.)

As prophesied, Rediffusion's financial problems soon disappeared. Within the first months of 1957 each company in the growing network was starting to reap huge profits that made the fears of 1956 seem absurd. But the survival of ITV had hung that first summer on two acts of faith by one individual, John Spencer Wills, in buying out Associated-Newspapers and supporting cash-hungry Granada. Had he not taken those bold steps, Independent Television might have lost its freedom and become a vulgar parody of broadcast commercialism.

In the first year I had directed seven live plays and three television films, nearly all of my choosing, and I had had a hand in most of the scripts. The opportunity for the selection of future subjects should have been unlimited. But I already had an uneasy feeling that our apparent creative freedom was doomed. The brief honeymoon we had enjoyed while the financial experts were too busy structuring new companies would shortly be over, and popularity and audience measurement would become paramount.

The austerity of the immediate postwar period was ending. What few of us realized as we hustled blithely and confidently into the 1960s was that the coming affluence, of which commercial television would be an integral part, would rapidly replace wartime comradeship with a more competitive society often dominated by individual selfishness and a lust for material gain.

4

1956–1962:
The Best Years
of ITV?

Vivid drama—on-screen and off.
I go back to School.

On December 1, 1962, I cleared my desk at Rediffusion and prepared to move to Pinewood. After seven and a half years of continuous production I was to stay away from television for a full 12 months.

Rediffusion, seen by many outsiders as mean spirited and unenterprising, had no less given me sufficient scope to develop as a director, to work with good actors and experiment with words and images—and to build a new house, raise a young family, and consolidate a secure and loving marriage. I had many good friends in the company, but some, like me, felt the time had come to move on.

The independent television system we were leaving was very different from the adventurous and sometimes amateurish broadcasting of the early days. Live transmissions, apart from news and some sports, had been replaced by carefully edited videotape recordings. The all-important weekly ratings were dominated by giveaway game shows and soap operas, which varied in quality from the gritty northern reality of *Coronation Street* to the plodding inanity of *Crossroads*.

Serious documentaries still hovered on the edges of peak-time, but by 1962 original single plays had become almost an extinct species. Profit for the ITV contracting companies was now clearly the first priority. But whatever certain purists (who seldom switched on) complained of, commercial television had become firmly established with the British public, and not even the most dogmatic politician would ever again suggest its closure. Its programs were more popular than anyone in 1955 had dared hope. By the summer of 1957 the ITV audience share was an incredible 73 percent, against the BBC's sad 27 percent.

At first, as if stunned, the corporation did little to change its programs to attract a larger public. Drama remained traditional and studio-bound, and heavy current-affairs programs like *Panorama* still clogged peak-time. But at last, with the end of the 1950s, BBC schedules began to reflect a more urgent search for equality in ratings.

In a perfect world, after the success of *The Last Enemy* I would have liked a few weeks' break to find another major subject. But in the reality of Rediffusion I was back in rehearsal in less than a month with an unimportant drama that did, curiously enough, help to demonstrate how radically our society was changing.

When the play, *HMS* Drake *Will Proceed...*, was transmitted on the evening of November 1, 1956, it was preceded on-air by dramatic film in the nightly ITN news of British warships crammed with troops leaving Cyprus to invade Egypt after Colonel Nasser's defiant nationalization of the Suez Canal. Anthony Eden, superficially an upright and honorable Tory prime minister (held back too long in the wings as understudy to the ailing Winston Churchill), now sick and uncertain himself, had rashly decided to join the French and the Israelis in a perilous war of colonial repossession that neither the United States nor the rest of the world could morally support—a last bellicose gasp of a British Empire that really existed only in memory.

As the news film faded, I cued the opening shots of our minor fiction—coincidentally another destroyer plowing bravely through a hostile sea—and superimposed *HMS* Drake *Will Proceed...,* our title. The play was based on a true-life outbreak of naval sabotage in Malta, climaxing when an aggrieved young seaman struck a visiting admiral. When the ship was ordered to help in the rescue of civilians after a Greek earthquake, the rebel seaman (of course) turned hero.

The navy supplied some very good film, Fred Pusey designed a destroyer engine room, a wardroom, and sick bay, and I'd enjoyed filming the earthquake rescue in Wapping dockland's still uncleared bomb ruins (covered with fuller's earth as Mediterranean dust). But the dialogue, rollicking, true-blue stuff sure to fire the bell-bottomed nostalgia of Brownrigg and Company, seemed pretty feeble in the context of the current bloodshed in Suez.

"Even Peter Graham Scott's brilliant technique," scolded Peter Black in the *Daily Mail*, "couldn't improve such a thin plot."

True enough. But more important was the shocking realization that war between civilized nations, apparently unthinkable after the horrors of Hiroshima and Nagasaki, was all too possible once again. The brief and unsuccessful foray into Suez made us all face the menace of possible annihilation, either through miscalculation or greed. In some minds this generated a "live for today" attitude that brightened the 1960s. Others exerted whatever pressure they could to outlaw nuclear weapons for good. Somehow we survived, though the threat is still with us.

In the pedestrian commerce of independent television the pressure of mounting two dramas a week began to show. Fortunately ATV was now feeding newer plays into the network, and Granada, importing a group of outstanding Canadian directors like Silvio Narrizano and Henry Kaplan, joined by British Cliff Owen and Herbert Wise, added power and pace to the small screen in plays by Arthur Miller and John Osborne.

In the autumn of 1956 Howard Thomas at ABC had also originated *Armchair Theatre* as a regular series of Sunday night events, originally produced by my old friend Dennis Vance, commencing with "The Outsider," by Dorothy Brandon, with Adrienne Corri and David Kossoff. From then on Dennis poured his considerable energy into making one hour of compelling television drama every week (with only one day's camera rehearsal in a converted cinema in Didsbury, Manchester) and was an inspiration to us all.

John McMillan stopped me one day in the corridor to talk about the way broadcast comedy was rapidly changing. Sacred cows dear to the Establishment were regularly being slaughtered on radio in the *Goon Show*—the mocking mimicry of Spike Milligan and Peter Sellers a sardonic forerunner of greater savagery to come in *That Was the Week That Was*, and more recently, *Spitting Image*. Dick Lester had tried to reproduce *Goon Show* humor on television (without too much success), but now, McMillan revealed, Peter Sellers wanted to prove himself as a straight actor and was insisting that I should direct. The only problem was the weak material he suggested. To show his versatility Peter wanted to be seen in not one but two totally different short plays, the first, *Birdwatcher*, a comic country house mystery where an eccentric naturalist unmasks the daughter of the house as a secret jewel-thief, the other, *Snowball*, a bittersweet story of an old storeman in a failing factory defying the attempts of a new manager to improve efficiency (in the end the old man reveals that he owns the works and likes running it the way it is).

Neither play had much substance, but I looked forward to rehearsing with Peter. Thanks to a post–Suez Arab oil embargo, petrol was rationed once again in Britain. Peter bought a tiny, economical bubble-car, and as he lived near Radlett offered to drive me to Kingsway each day. Once, and once only, I endured Peter's hair-raising progress, careering at top speed around and almost under London's trucks and buses, before I settled for the safety of the subway.

Peter's maniac driving was a foretaste of his rehearsal technique. He would plot a scene very quickly, then race through it again, suddenly slamming on the brakes to propose a new, wild idea. The other actors, Lionel Jeffries, Nora Nicholson, and Francis Matthews, all very experienced but unused to such behavior, would pause, take a breath, and try the new idea. Until the next one hit Peter's fevered imagination. And the next. Then whenever he was out of a scene he would start a long and involved telephone conversation, in earshot of the struggling actors. Thus preoccupied he'd miss his next entrance, and the whole cast would wait as he discussed the purchase of some new toy—a camera, a car, anything that took his fancy—until at last we could pick up the scene again.

One day he suggested that *Birdwatcher* should be played in futuristic costumes; the next day he was convinced it would work better in twenties gear, like *The Boyfriend*. In the end his mental roulette wheel slowed to reveal the winner as "Edwardian," just in time for me to reorder the costumes once more.

As we neared a final run-through, Peter suddenly asked me why we always rehearsed *Snowball* first, and not last. "Because we're *playing* it first," I told him.

Peter was baffled, and rightly. *Birdwatcher* was the flimsier of the two plays and should have spun through before the rather more touching *Snowball*. But Peter's "aging" makeup would take at least half an hour to apply. This would be impossible to do in the two and a half minutes we would have between the two plays in live performance. Obviously he hadn't thought of this problem. He stormed up to McMillan's office and demanded that *Snowball* should be done on a different day—or entirely filmed. But it was too late. The double bill had been publicized as a peak-time offering for Boxing Day—only four days ahead. In the end Peter calmed down and agreed to perform the plays in the necessary order.

On Christmas Eve 1956 we had our first camera rehearsal, then after one day's festive break on Christmas Day we assembled with a hungover cast and crew for final rehearsal and live transmission on December 26. Peter had brought in Charles Parker from MGM studios to do his *Snowball* makeup, and the result was superb. The little play became strangely moving in performance. But then Peter had to tear off his factory white coat to reveal his Edwardian knickerbocker suit, wipe his face clean, and become a flippant *Birdwatcher*, just—but only just—making a perspiring first entrance. (Of course, less than two years later all these problems would have been solved by videotape recording, but we didn't know that then!)

But for some reason, in the second play Peter suddenly chose to change all his carefully planned moves on transmission, causing near-panic among the cast and making mincemeat of my carefully plotted camera script. But he undoubtedly gave us a brilliantly funny one-off performance.

Peter Sellers's dramatic debut had been eagerly awaited, but the notices were, as they say, "mixed." Most critics noticed Peter's verve and versatility, comparing him to a young Alec Guinness. His characterization as the old man Snowball was much admired, but it wasn't until some years later that he was able to refine and discipline his inspired talent to achieve the outrageous Inspector Clouseau of *The Pink Panther*, his finest creation. Though we often met subsequently, neither of us had any urge to work together again after this first alarming experience.

The year 1957 dawned for me with feelings of frustration. I had had two "not quite right" productions and needed another success. Fortunately, the American author of *One*, David Karp, had written a second book, *The Day of the Monkey*, about the tensions and violence in a West African country on the eve of gaining independence from British colonial rule. It appealed to me on every level: its topicality (it was destined to be transmitted in the very week that the ex–British Gold Coast became independent Ghana), the lack of bias of its author, and the chance it offered for four black actors—Edric Connor, Lionel Ngakane, Joseph Layode, and Mark Heath.

Edric, a powerful six-footer, had made his name as a singer, and he welcomed the dramatic opportunity as Doctor Luba, leader of the insurgent nationalist movement. Maurice Denham was the fair-minded British governor (personally wanting to prove his worth as an actor after years of "funny voices" on the radio), and Clare Austin, Kenneth Griffith (from *One*), and Campbell Singer completed a strong cast. I embellished shots of an actual West African riot with closer shots of my actors in the thick of it, against the peeling stucco of the old 1924 Wembley Empire Exhibition buildings just behind our television studios. As groups of black extras enthusiastically hurled plastic bricks toward the camera, the riot nearly got out of hand, my frantic cries of "*Cut!*" failing to stop their enjoyment. Then one discovered he had torn his trousers in the melee and demanded compensation, which meant that John Frankau had to dip into his modest fund for payment all around.

Again, the show went well on transmission on February 27, 1957. In the Sunday *Times* Maurice Wiggin commented:

> Best play of the week was ITV's *The Day of the Monkey*, the first time I have known a TV dramatisation of a novel turn out better than the original. The setting was a British colony nearing independence. There was a neat balance of forces—a liberal-minded British Governor beset by Blimps and not quite strong enough to block

them, and a liberal-minded African leader not quite able to control a nationalist movement bossed by a sectarian European Communist. Not at all simple, but Peter Graham Scott's production trapped it neatly with plenty of movement, deft use of film for rioting scenes, and solid acting.

And Peter Black in the *Daily Mail* also approved:

Ten months ago Peter Graham Scott did the cause of ITV drama a power of good by producing David Karp's *One*. The Karp–Scott combination advanced further last night with *The Day of the Monkey*, a genuinely controversial and topical play that will certainly be a contender for a place among 1957's Top Twelve.

The scene was a British Protectorate. The Nationalist Party, plotting for independence, was being run by a white Communist, with the Europeanised Doctor Luba as its national leader. Luba was on terms of personal friendship with Governor Phillips, a decent, humane administrator who lacked the strength of personality to back up his absolute power against the opposition of the most conservative white residents.

Karp's story showed how both men, through the strain of weakness in each, were defeated by the forces of panic and fear. Luba, who wanted his people to have to fight for their independence so that they would value it more, was the first victim of violence. The Governor, Phillips, was beaten up by his own side and finished the play facing an enquiry into his conduct.

The types of folly and wickedness on both sides were persuasively drawn. A first-class television play, and Scott's production and Frederic Pusey's settings made the most of it. Maurice Denham's Governor, Edric Connor's Luba, Kenneth Griffith's Communist, and a viciously accurate sketch of a police chief by Campbell Singer headed an accomplished cast.

The drama had explored much of what I had observed in the Sudan in 1947, the follies and small human successes of an outdated colonial system that had no future in the modern world. Today the play might be dismissed simply as dated agitprop theater, but in 1957 its message impressed many home viewers.

But with four television companies in active drama production (plus the BBC), plays as good as this were becoming harder to find. Rediffusion's Script Department had also been weakened by the departures of Donald Bull to the BBC and Giles Cooper to full-time writing. The most promising script next available for me turned out to be a Viennese comedy, *Evening in Hochsberg*, by the unknown Leslie Boorer, heavily influenced by frothy floss from Molnar and Schnitzler.

Even the story seemed familiar. A gentle town major, reluctant to carry out the order to execute a revolutionary young poet, is visited by the young man's attractive cousin. Deftly and wittily she proposes a scheme to engineer the young man's escape. It would only work with charming and skillful acting, and lavish costumes and sets. I was lucky enough to secure Reece Pemberton as designer, and he brilliantly created the major's palatial rooms, a cathedral interior, and a prison, all within the confines of Wembley's Studio One.

Jeannette Sterke, a dark and lovely young actress who had scored in two of Rudolph Cartier's BBC costume dramas, played the girl, Robin Bailey the major, and a newcomer, Peter Wyngarde, the poet. Thanks to them the performance was light and modestly entertaining, but of little substance.

Rediffusion was now making hefty profits, but my salary had not increased to match. John Temple Smith reappeared to tempt me with two lucrative second-feature films, if I could arrange four weeks off. (I could.) He had the script for one, a murder mystery by Barbara Harper, *Account Rendered*, and a cast including Honor Blackman and Griffith Jones. But he was contracted to Rank to make two, and he wanted to use the same sets for the second film. Could I write something, quickly, that would fill the bill?

I had an idea, and wrote it up in a couple of weekends without too much effort. *The Big Chance* featured a discontented travel clerk who, when a wealthy client cancels a trip to Panama, forges a passport and takes his place. When he arrives at the airport, fog has postponed all flights. He becomes involved with a young girl leaving her rich husband; they spend the night together in a deserted cottage and are suddenly discovered. The girl ruthlessly runs down her pursuing husband in her rented car and goes off to catch her rescheduled flight, while the disillusioned clerk restores the stolen tickets and returns to his own wife.

Adrienne Corri was available as the runaway wife, and I offered the lead to Peter Murray, still hot from *The Last Enemy*. But poor Peter unfortunately caught the mumps the weekend before we were due to start filming, and in a hurry we cast William Russell, star of a *Sir Lancelot* series that had foundered. Corri and Russell worked together splendidly, and Dilys Powell in the Sunday *Times* praised the small film's "good detail, tension and narrative ideas." Nearly 30 years later it was shown on peak-time ITV, and survived.

With the fees from the films, I was able to think about buying a replacement for my aging Morris Minor and a runabout for Mimi. An advertisement in the *Evening News* for a smart, light blue Hillman convertible, almost new, led me to the bachelor chambers of donnish Norman St. John Stevas, who quickly agreed to a deal. Despite any qualms about buying a secondhand car from a politician, I have to record that our bargain from Her Majesty's future Minister for the Arts (now the august Lord St. John of Fawsley) ran happily for some years.

Returning to Rediffusion in the early summer of 1957 I found the same lamentable lack of good scripts. Vyvienne Moynihan, Norman Marshall's redoubtable auburn-haired assistant, had seen my play, *The Breath of Fools*, at Q Theatre and suggested I should adapt it for television. Oddly enough I hadn't considered it. The play had said what I wanted to at that time, but in the intervening two years I had matured a little.

I pulled the script from the bottom of a cupboard and read it again. Some of it was very naive, but overall it still hung together dramatically. There was nothing better on offer, and I'd been given an air date of July 3, exactly four weeks away. I considered all the actors who might play John Hagerman, the domineering director, and remembered Marius Goring, whose strangely tortured good looks had so captivated audiences in the Powell–Pressburger films *The Red Shoes* and *A Matter of Life and Death*.

With no idea whether or not he would act on television, I sent him an uncut script. The following day he phoned. "You've written an interesting play. Tell me, is your director character based on my friend Michael Powell?"

"No—I've never met Michael Powell."

"Good—because if you had I could never have accepted." There was a long pause, then he added casually, "When can we meet?"

We spent the whole of the following day ruthlessly cutting and rewriting. Marius, as I soon discovered, applied his keen intelligence to his own part, and *only* that part, not to the play as a whole. And whereas Peter Sellers or Donald Pleasence had worked instinctively and emotionally to find their characters, Marius built his performance completely intellectually.

My play's tension grew from the spiritual conflict between a young girl's innocent faith and Hagerman's weary cynicism. But, as I soon perceived, Marius was afraid of losing public sympathy by playing a character he saw as "an absolute bastard." In my eyes he was anything but that—simply a man with a strong contempt for innocent belief—but slowly Marius began to water down the director's true acid. Bitter lines like "All actresses are certifiable neurotics" were lost immediately. Speeches that revealed his broken marriage, his hatred of bogus sentimentality and superficial religious ritual all disappeared. At the end of that day Marius had a blander, more sympathetic part to play, and I was the author of *Cinderella*.

And yet—I *wanted* Marius Goring. Even as a whitewashed Hagerman I knew he would give the play power and energy. Most of the minor cast members from Q were free, but unfortunately not Nigel Davenport, who had given the film star seducer exactly the right slimy quality. The original Ann had lost her innocence. Looking for her replacement, I interviewed every aspiring young actress in London, until on the advice of Michael Macowan I chose Susan Wills, then aged 20.

I'd spread the action from the single set of the play into dressing rooms, projection theaters, and even the film set, although, as I had to remind everyone, we were not making a documentary about film production but an emotional drama, a clash of truth and belief. Rehearsals seemed to go well, but on the day before camera-rehearsal Norman Marshall appeared magisterially for a run-through. Susan seemed to shrivel. The performance we had found vanished. I could see how much Norman disliked what he was seeing. At the end he led me aside. "Can you replace the girl?" he demanded.

I explained that she was nervous. "She'd better not be 'nervous' on transmission," he snorted, and stamped red-faced down the corridor.

It was in any case too late to recast. But the fault was not in the actress but in the hasty rewrite that had removed the true cruelty of Hagerman's treatment of the young girl. On transmission I concentrated on careful camerawork, knowing the play had lost its cutting edge. Having given me a year of almost consistently good press, the critics reacted with outrage at my effrontery in presenting my own play. Peter Black described me as "a much-respected and ambitious producer, now the latest to fall flat on his face" in attempting to discuss a serious theme within a simple melodramatic framework.

Bernard Levin, however, admitted the play "was not entirely a waste of time. Thought was definitely required. But it indicated that television directors, no matter how distinguished, should not be allowed to direct their own plays."

The anonymous *Times* reviewer commented that the dramatic and spiritual conflict within the making of a film was "ingenious," but felt the "triumph of religious faith at the end was arbitrary and inconclusive." There was in fact no such "triumph."

Luckily all the scorn was reserved for me. In her debut Susan Wills was complimented on everything from her "nice reserve" to a "maturity of feeling." Marius of course was "splendid" and "exciting." (He knew his own business best!) And that was that.

I directed one more play that summer, Ugo Betti's *Summertime*, with Jeanette Sterke and Douglas Wilmer. I took no chances, giving a pleasant little theatrical piece a standard Alexandra Palace–type production. The critics relented and took pleasure in Jeanette's sparkling charm. Mimi and I drove to the south of France with our young daughters to draw breath.

As expected, Rediffusion had announced annual profits of over £3 million ($4.5 million), more than the first year's loss. The ABC, ATV, and Granada were all healthy profit makers, too. The Independent Television Authority now sought to enlarge the commercial network to include three new areas, central Scotland, South Wales and the West of England, and Southern England.

Though the news of Rediffusion's success encouraged bidders

in Wales and England, there was some difficulty in finding any canny Scots to respond. The only credible consortium to apply was Scottish Television (STV), headed by 67-year-old Roy Thomson, a former car salesman who had built up a chain of low-budget radio stations in Canada and had moved to Edinburgh after buying *The Scotsman* newspaper in 1954. Even Thomson, with James Calcart from Beaverbrook's Glasgow *Evening News* as his managing director, had extreme difficult raising basic finance for the Glasgow station. Sir Alexander King, Scotland's most powerful cinema owner, and many others, declined. However, Lord Balfour of Inchrye and his brother-in-law, John Profumo, were investors; Sir Iain Stewart, the shipbuilder and industrialist, became a director; and Howard & Wyndham, already financially involved in ATV, took up a tenth of the shares and provided its redundant Theatre Royal to convert into a rough-and-ready studio.

Thomson had never wasted money on expensive radio programs. His television strategy was to transmit as much material from the main English network as the ITA would allow. Always a tough negotiator, he wrung the whole of ATV's daily and evening programs (including those bought from the other three companies) for a close-fisted £1 million ($1.5 million), with a similar knockdown deal for news from ITN (Independent Television News). Such programs as Scottish actually made were usually just talking heads against stock backings, and home-movie-standard documentaries. Even their most successful offering, *This Wonderful World*, consisted of bought-in film with linking close-ups of realist veteran John Grierson against a gray flat. No wonder the company was profitable from its first day on the air in August 1957.

From those gushing profits, year after year, Thomson was able to buy the *Times* newspaper from Lord Kemsley (who had doubted commercial television) and build an empire of airways, offshore oil, and popular travel, gaining himself a peerage on the way. Truly, in his oft-quoted words, "television was a licence to print money."

The scene of the next ITV expansion was a geographical hybrid: the unification of South Wales and Cardiff with Bristol and the West of England. The conjunction of two such culturally diverse areas was partly technical. The proposed Cardiff Wenvoe transmitter and the one on the Mendip hills in Somerset would economically cover both regions. But the real reason was more devious. South Wales was more important politically, a Labour stronghold and birthplace of prime ministers. But as it was currently suffering economic depression, a purely Welsh station might not pay its way. Allied to prosperous Bristol it made sense.

Television Wales and West (TWW) was founded by ITV champion Lord Derby, Jack Hylton, whose Rediffusion contract had ended in tears, with Mark Chapman-Walker as managing director, plus a few distinguished Welshmen and rich Bristolians, advised by the ubiquitous lawyer Arnold (later Lord) Goodman. Attempting a network bargain similar to Thomson's, Chapman-Walker was rebuffed by ATV and Rediffusion, but he struck a deal with neighborly Granada, which also sold TWW's advertising airtime.

After delays erecting a South Wales transmitter, Cardiff studios, hastily converted from a farmhouse and adjoining barns in Pontcanna, went on the air as cautiously as STV in Glasgow. Indeed in the first three months the authority had to excuse TWW from making its full quota of 15 percent local programs. In response to local pressure the ITA required one hour per week to be in the Welsh language. "Gwlad y Gan"—"Land of Song"—a musical medley of old favorites, was one welcome outcome. But despite viewer acceptance and considerable financial success after building a modern studio on the outskirts of Bristol, TWW's strictly London-based management gave it a rather uncertain regional identity.

Last of the three new zones to commence transmission in the late 1950s was the rich swathe of farming and commuter country stretching from Dorset in the West to the Channel port of Dover. Covering a larger population (4½ million) than Scottish (3½ million) and Wales and West (3 million), it was also wealthier advertising territory. Unfortunately, with more upper and middle class householders, Southern viewers initially preferred the BBC.

Associated-Newspapers had learned the lesson of its mistimed withdrawal from A-R, and joined by cinema-owning Rank Organization and children's publishers D. C. Thomson (from Dundee, in northern Scotland!), they formed Southern Television, chaired by John Davies (Rank), with General Manager David Wilson (Associated-Newspapers). Again, finance and management were London-based, with no shares distributed in the region. With difficulty the

ITA prevented Wilson from using Rank's Pinewood Studio near London and forced the company to build afresh in Southampton, and later, grudgingly, a shedlike news studio near Dover. However, with energetic ex–BBC employee Roy Rich as program controller and Berkeley Smith, one of Peter Dimmock's ablest producers in charge of outside broadcasts, Southern made valuable network contributions in children's drama and sport after its opening in August 1958.

By then I was involved in a completely different sort of television, which I had never imagined, even in a nightmare — educational programs.

Shortly after ITV started in 1955 the ITA Children's Advisory Committee had first discussed the possibility of including programs for viewing in schools as part of the afternoon schedule. Paul Adorian, Rediffusion's managing director, was attracted by the idea, not because it would explore television's capability, but, cynically, because for each hour of school broadcasting in the afternoon without commercials the company could sell a further six minutes of advertisements in peak-time.

Six minutes a day at more than £1,000 a minute, £30,000 every five-day week, would show an extra profit of another million or so in an academic year. The extra cost of the programs could be recouped by sales to other network companies. This was after all, commercial television.

As early as December 1956 Chairman John Spencer Wills had announced a program of experimental school broadcasts for September 1957 (some months ahead of an educational service the BBC had planned for 1958), and throughout that year I had been vaguely aware of activity in the basement by directors who had not excelled elsewhere. But I was very surprised on my return from holiday in August 1957 to be summoned by Adorian and asked whether I would take over production of the Education Department as "executive producer." So far, apparently, their trial efforts had been disastrous.

I had not met Boris Ford, an ambitious young professor newly appointed as head of education. I knocked on his door, entered, and was pleased to see that he had a black secretary. (In those days black faces were all too rare in television. The young woman was Carmen Munroe, later to establish herself as a very talented actress.)

Boris was affable, and I liked him instantly. He explained that his department had become a dustbin for unusable directors. Rapidly we went through the names; I rejected most of them and called Lloyd Williams to ask for a few new faces: Roger Jenkins, from Bristol Old Vic, wasting his time on advertising magazines; John Frankau, my valued floor manager; and Randall Beattie, cameraman on *The Last Enemy*. The writers list looked more promising. It included Louis Marks, now a top drama producer at the BBC, and Martin Worth, later a stalwart contributor to *The Onedin Line*. I was also introduced to Ford's two producers, Fernau Hall, the ballet critic, and John Lord, an ex-teacher and war hero who subsequently immigrated to the United States, made fine documentaries for NBC, and became one of my greatest lifelong friends until his sad death in 1994.

To my surprise I learned that they had actually been broadcasting five programs a week for two months since May—as an experiment, not publicized to the potential schools. There had been programs on using your eyes in the world around us, appreciating traditional ballads, how to cope with adult life after leaving school, planets, space and the universe, and tolerance and understanding of people of other races. But impressive as this list might appear, the realization had been grim. There had been little use of film, visual aids, or animated diagrams. Usually the time had been wasted in confused chatter from badly chosen and inarticulate people, and the effect had been less valuable than the direct methods of a good teacher. It was obvious we needed film when necessary, better research, and more contact with viewers—the children themselves, not just their teachers.

Together we evolved a new series of programs, with suggested target age groups:

The Farming Year: A weekly report on film, from a typical farm showing the pattern of work right through the year.

Shape in Your Hands: How to begin clay modeling, moving on to pottery, painting,and wood-carving.

The World of Figures: Elementary mathematics made interesting, which John Frankau brought to life with ingenious graphics.

Producing Macbeth: John Lord introducing Shakespeare's play as "a tale of greed, lust and murder," with a final full performance.

So far so good. But it was all very *worthy*. There was nothing to create exceptional interest, popular comment, or argument. So, Boris and I thought again, and argued, and at last came up with an audacious idea, which, if we did it well and in a balanced way, would create an enormous amount of comment and would really attract the attention of the general public.

For nearly two years ITV had lived off advertising. Most of the commercials shown had been balanced and informative about useful products, socially beneficial, raising the standards of living. But some had made impossible claims for their wares. In those days, for instance, cigarette commercials were still allowed, suggesting not only that smoking was a mildly pleasant occupation, but that it was a positive, manly way of becoming a grown-up—a dangerous suggestion to impressionable children to form a habit that might seriously damage their health. In our program we would simply show the powerful persuasive arguments that might be used and ask our audience to *Judge for Yourselves*, in a hard look at modern advertising.

We would have to maintain impartiality by inviting advertisers and their agents onto the program to argue their case against whatever points we made, but I still thought the program would cause people to think—no more than that—about some of the untruths propagated by unscrupulous salesmen.

The first scripts for *Judge for Yourselves* were duly written. Criticism of advertising was if anything muted and rather general, leaving scope for reasonable answers. However, I thought it wise to send them to Rediffusion's newly appointed advertising sales manager (recruited from Ford Motors—oddly enough the man who had offered me a job two years before). His reaction was explosive. What the hell were we *doing*? Did we want to turn children who would grow up to be adult viewers *against* commercials, for God's sake?

Patiently I tried to explain that we were only endeavoring to show the difference between good, effective advertising and untruthful hype. But I might as well have been denying the Ascension of Christ in the Middle Ages. Shouting "Bloody sabotage!" he rushed off to see McMillan.

Management closed ranks swiftly. Changes were demanded.

The rather earnest but thoughtful scripts were filetted to show that advertising was really the economic backbone of Western prosperity, and we went into production.

Paul Massie, a young Canadian actor who had recently starred in Anthony Asquith's film *Orders to Kill*, was our link man, but somehow he made some of the claims for advertising sound patronizing and cynical. There was more rumbling from Adorian and McMillan, but far worse trouble from a different quarter. Rediffusion had appointed a number of professional educational advisers who had read and approved the first script but had not seen the altered version before it went on the air. They were furious at the lack of consultation and threatened to withdraw from the whole scheme.

This would never do. The programs were worth money. I was sent for by Adorian. Did I realize the reaction these programs would get from our bread and butter customers—the advertisers?

Not if they were intelligent enough to see what we were really saying, I argued. We *were* commercial television, but we were also a public service. The job of our educational programs was to enlighten our young viewers in challenging ways, and surely responsible advertisers, confident of their own products, would respect our impartiality in advising skepticism of others' specious propaganda.

Adorian didn't agree. As an employee of Rediffusion, I was formally instructed to follow company policy. Educational guru Sir John Wolfenden was brought in to placate the educational advisers. Boris Ford resigned (to become director of studies at Bristol University). In the future McMillan would vet all scripts from early stages. (In fact I continued to supervise production for the first year or so, until at the beginning of 1959 Enid Love was enticed from the BBC to become Rediffusion's second head of Education.)

Judge for Yourselves slowly expired. The ATV and Scottish, which had taken the school broadcasts for the same sound business bonus of six extra minutes of commercials a day, tactfully suggested that they should be more involved in production. Granada, which had not been interested, also wanted to coproduce. By 1960 all four companies were sharing the task of making five hours a week for a national network.

But our efforts had been noted by the ITA, which rapidly

tightened the rules against untruthful claims in commercials, and a few years later Prime Minister Harold Wilson used our scholastic experiments as an argument for introducing television's Open University, one of the outstanding educational innovations of modern times. So the clash of Adorian's commercialism and our creative energy had beneficial results in the end, though not without pain for us all.

Apart from viewing daily rushes from *The Farming Year*, and enjoying John Lord's *Macbeth* series, skillfully directed by Roger Jenkins (who followed this success with *Hamlet* and *Twelfth Night*), I had little to do but watch each half-hour program transmitted (live) twice to cope with different school timetables (and to double the extra commercial time allowed every evening!).

That year Norman Marshall had been persuaded to award a "Rediffusion Prize for Best Original Play" at Cheltenham Festival. On the first occasion it was won by Geoffrey Scanlon, a young RAF officer with *Shadows*, based on the life of John Logie Baird, the unsuccessful television pioneer whose biography Michael Mills and I had shied away from recreating five years before. This lucky coincidence gave me (who had after all benefited more than most from the realization of Baird's dream) the chance of making a graceful tribute to a man who had known more frustration than fulfillment. Unlike Michael's unfortunate effort, the new script was well researched and very moving, the story of a brilliant eccentric who had the right idea at the right time but simply lacked the technological ability to achieve a profitable result. It had far too many scene changes, and Baird's early business ventures—patent everlasting socks, jam-making in the West Indies—were treated farcically, but with a certain amount of polish from Barbara Harper it rapidly became workable.

Schools TV programs ended with the term in November 1957, so Norman set me a transmission date of December 18. Not liking the title *Shadows*, I renamed the play *A Voice in Vision*. Michael Gwynn, looking quite like Baird in his lean and hungry years, was to play the lead; Leslie Phillips his lifelong friend "Mephy" (or "Mephistopheles"); and Gwen Watford his wife; with Jean Anderson, Stratford Johns, Alan Cuthbertson, and Ewen Solon in strong support.

Once more we carefully constructed a copy of the original

"televisor" and gathered together all the assorted junk of the inventor's workshop. When he first transmitted a picture of a ventriloquist's dummy's head from one shabby room to another (by wire), in Frith Street, Soho, Baird had rushed into an adjoining office, grabbed a typist, hauled her into a darkened room, slammed the door, and commanded her to look toward a small screen. As the red, glowing image of the dummy's head, eyes staring madly, had suddenly appeared, the terrified girl had uttered a piercing scream and run for her life. For this scene it was vital to find an actress without inhibitions. Muriel Cole, Rediffusion's statuesque casting director, known as the "Duchess of Wembley," produced a young girl currently working behind a counter in Boots, the chemists, who had written in for an audition. She had large expressive eyes, untidy hair, and protruding teeth and was very nervous.

I asked her, "Can you scream?"

"I—I think so."

"Then *scream*. Loud as you like."

The girl filled her lungs and suddenly let rip with a great howl of anguish that brought people rushing in from neighboring offices to see what I was doing to her. When order was restored, I asked her name.

"Jackson."

"Have you a first name?" She told me. Thus, shrieking, Glenda Jackson made her first professional appearance.

It was good to be back in rehearsal after all the politicking in schools, particularly with Leslie Phillips, who had been a boyhood friend at Italia Conti's Stage School. Now that our families lived close together in Hertfordshire we saw a lot of each other socially.

This time I was able to get Baird's ramshackle machines working properly. We even achieved a fuzzy orange picture on the neon tube with our 22-line mechanical scanner. Michael Gwynn and Gwen Watford brought a delicate poignancy to the tragic inventor's muddled career of endless arguments and demonstrations to skeptical engineers at the BBC and to financiers, who swung from enthusiasm to gloom at the first setback.

The scene of his lonely death in 1946, after the triumphant reopening transmission of the Victory Parade by other men using a rival television system, was one of the most moving I can remember.

During the final performance I felt a weird sense of contact with this strange man, John Logie Baird, whose erratic enthusiasm had sparked off much of the research that had made popular television come alive.

The critics were oddly divided. Raymond Bowers in the *Mirror* raved, "The most moving play of the year"; Philip Purser in the *Chronicle* liked "a straightforward tale of setbacks and disappointments"; Marsland Gander in the *Telegraph* praised "an absorbing story of fanatical devotion to an idea"; but Peter Black in the *Mail* was disappointed, "except for the two moments when Baird transmitted his first television picture, and the sad day in 1937 when he learnt that the BBC had finally rejected his system."

In the *Guardian* Bernard Levin wrote us all a stern reproof: "If John Baird could see the use being made of the miraculous machine born of his suffering, would he still think it all worthwhile? 'I Love Lucy,' 'Highway Patrol,' 'Mark Saber' — imbecile panel games, sweaty comedians, mindless pap — the great tide of trash that rolls relentlessly from ITV week after week. Did Baird have a vision of the richness his invention could add to the lives of millions? Where in this pre-digested cretin-fodder is there any hint of gold among the dross?"

Where indeed? Levin at least *watched* our work, but he reflected the current intellectual view that ITV was strictly for morons. True, serious documentaries had already been pushed out of peak-time, apart from soft current affairs like Rediffusion's *This Week*, which still lacked a strong editor. But ITV drama remained well ahead of the BBC. In 1958, Sydney Newman, an expansive Canadian with a flair for encouraging new writers, arrived to take over ABC's Sunday night *Armchair Theatre*, and commissioned Alun Owen, Clive Exton, and Mordecai Richler to write their first television plays for directors like Ted Kotcheff, Charles Jarrott, John Nelson Burton, Philip Saville, and Patrick Dromgoole. At Rediffusion the revitalized Script Department was discovering new writers like Stanley Miller, Paul Jones, and Paul Lee, and bought the first works of Harold Pinter for Joan Kemp-Welch's stylish treatment.

But plays were firmly scheduled between giveaways like *People Are Funny*, where members of the public volunteered for on-screen humiliation under the idiot grin of Derek Roy, and the appalling Carroll Levis amateur talent show—another exercise in contempt for human dignity. After only two years, popular television was straining too hard to reach the lowest common level.

I glimpsed the roughhouse atmosphere in which ITV network schedules were concocted when, early in 1958, Lloyd Williams fell ill and I was made assistant program controller for three months, attending planning meetings with Lew Grade, Cecil Bernstein, Howard Thomas, and Company, to hear the amazing street-market trade-offs being done with programs caringly produced with true passion, convincing me I had no future away from production.

On Good Friday 1958 I directed a 50-minute piece, *2000 Minus 60*, adapted from an Australian radio play by James Workman. Set in the future, in the last hour of the present century, it depicted the efforts of a group of scientists trying to divert a lethal runaway nuclear rocket aiming for London, creating a powerful sense of imminent disaster. I enjoyed devising the special effects, seen on monitors, of various weapons being unsuccessfully fired at the rocket, and was well served by a cast that included Charles Lloyd Pack, John Robinson, and June Thorburn. But the characters were paper-thin, and it was poor stuff compared with some of my earlier work.

In May John McMillan, conscious that Rediffusion had neglected good music and the Hallé Orchestra for some time, asked me to set up a program of operatic excerpts with Sir John Barbirolli. We asked pianist Joseph Cooper, an attractive and knowledgeable presenter, to introduce the items, three popular duets from *La Bohème, Carmen*, and *Madama Butterfly*, and contracted Richard Lewis, Victoria Elliott, Veronica Dunne, and Marina de Gabarain to sing them.

Barbirolli wanted to start with a bang—the full orchestra fortissimo in Wagner's overture for *Lohengrin*, "The Ride of the Valkyries." Then he needed something sweet and soft to lead into *Bohème*. I suggested "The Humming Chorus" from *Madama Butterfly*, but Sir John couldn't face the thought of endless close-ups of tight-lipped northern lady singers relentlessly humming away. But with cameraman Adrian Cooper I spent a sunny afternoon filming backlit, romantically moving exotic flowers reflected in water to evoke a mood, and Barbirolli loved our "truly inspired interpretation." Transmitted at ten o'clock one June night from the ABC Didsbury studio near Manchester (home of the Hallé Orchestra), after only one rehearsal for plotting cameras, staging all the moves, and checking costumes and makeup, the 50-minute show attracted a larger audience than expected. But alas, no one in authority seemed to notice that pop culture could work on ITV.

McMillan was seized with another "creative" idea. Now that Rediffusion was well into profit, he proposed that the third anniversary of our opening night in September should be celebrated with a two-hour special of six playlets set in different European capitals, entitled (without apology to D. H. Lawrence) *Women in Love.*

I was instructed to go with Casting executive Weston Drury to Paris, Madrid, Rome, Munich, Vienna, and Stockholm, spending no more than two days in each, to find a young and glamorous actress and an appropriate story for every city. The trip was an exciting prospect, but the task of finding good actresses needed far more research.

In Paris we drew a blank. Neither of the girls I'd heard about was interested. In Madrid we saw a brilliant lead in a musical, Maria-Jesus Cuadra, and signed her, ignoring her very broken English. In Rome we picked an Italian starlet, Scilla Gabel, and discovered a French girl, Yvonne Monlaur. In Munich we attended a television rehearsal and found Annette Grau. In Vienna Bill Drury met his old friend Yul Brynner, who introduced us to Frances Martin, and at Stockholm's Royal Theatre we were impressed with Anne-Marie Gyllenspetz. All I had to do now was find six 17-minute playlets.

Bridget Boland came in with a charming idea: a British ex-officer returns to the Roman trattoria where a young woman had sheltered him during the war and falls in love with her daughter. Philip Guard delivered a witty comedy set in the Austrian Tyrol. Michael Ashe gave us a tough Munich police thriller—a girl on the run after killing her lover. Robert Rietty wrote a bittersweet piece about a prostitute in the barrio in Barcelona comforting a guitarist, unaware that he is losing his sight, and Charles Terrot conceived a delightful farce set on a yacht on the Riviera.

Only the Swedish script had to be found. Over lunch, Michael

Meyer, the distinguished and witty translator of Ibsen and Strindberg, told me a ridiculous story of his first visit to Uppsala when he was very young, and he attempted to captivate a beautiful girl without knowing a word of her language. *Song Without Words* was born— a play without dialogue, which I decided to direct myself.

For the other plays, I had star directors like Joan Kemp-Welch and Julian Amyes, plus Robert Tronson, Tania Lieven, and Ronald Marriott, and strong casts including Sean Connery (before his world fame as James Bond), Daniel Massey, Terence Morgan, John Fraser, Moray Watson, and Graham Crowden. Hollywood's George Sanders would introduce each story on the night of September 22, 1958.

It was impossible to produce all six plays live on one night from Wembley Studios, but Rediffusion had just become the first British television company to invest in the recently unveiled AMPEX system of video-recording on two-inch magnetic tape. Four of the plays (including the Swedish one, which was mostly filmed in Stockholm) were made in advance, the first dramas ever to be recorded on video-tape in Britain. The other two were slotted in live from the studio on that night.

However, despite all the advance publicity, the special theme song, and the huge audience we attracted (even the good notices the little Swedish piece attracted for "originality"), I realized I had fallen into the trap of producing trivia almost on the level of the painful game shows and end-of-the-pier comics that so offended Bernard Levin.

Where could I find better material? A careful search of the Script Department yielded nothing much. Then on the BBC's *Panorama* I saw a drunken Irish playwright—Brendan Behan— whose *The Quare Fella*, a slice of life in Dublin's Mountjoy Jail on the eve of an execution (based on his own experience) had recently finished a run at Joan Littlewood's Stratford East Theatre Royal.

In 1958 both Britain and Eire still maintained capital punishment for murder, although there was considerable debate about its possible abolition. The power and compassion of Behan's play, showing the effect of a death sentence on the other incarcerated criminals, was deeply relevant, and its wider showing to the growing television audience would be a major event.

Without much hope I contacted Behan's agent and found out

that though the film rights had been sold, the television rights were still available. (This would never happen these days, when film and television rights are sold as a package.) I found out the maximum Rediffusion would ever pay for rights to a play, had Vicki type out a short letter of agreement, visited the bank, and arranged to meet Brendan in a pub near Kingsway.

A typical Brendan Behan evening ensued. Songs, some bawdy, some sad and sincere, a lot of bottom-pinching for any passing female, and a river of booze. Some hours into the entertainment I mentioned the television rights of *The Quare Fella*. Brendan opened his good eye. "How much?"

I told him (twice as much as the company had ever paid before!). He belched. "In cash," I added.

Both eyes opened. "Now?"

"Right here." I got him to sign two copies of the letter on the bar counter and handed over the wad.

Next day his agent was on the phone at dawn, swearing "sharp practice," "improper conduct," and the rest. But I had Brendan's agreement. The only thing I didn't have was copy of the actual play. However, Alan Simpson of the Pike Theatre in Dublin helpfully produced a tattered, scrawled-over script, and I was in business. Many of the actors who had appeared in Alan Simpson's original Pike production (before the more famous one at the Abbey) were available in London, including Wilfrid Brambell, Dermot Kelly, Liam Gaffney, Brian O'Higgins, Neil McCarthy, and Charlie Roberts.

On stage the action had been confined to a section of the cell block, and a small exterior where the condemned man's grave was being dug. The intended victim of the hangman was never seen, only talked about. I asked Frederic Pusey to design the biggest set Studio One would hold—a huge, two-story cell block with catwalk and bridge, and a barred gate at the end leading to an exterior exercise yard, flanked by the outer wall of the cell block, with one barred window, enabling the camera to creep up and glimpse the condemned man for an instant, at the beginning and end of each act.

I was given permission to film the opening-title background at Wandsworth Prison in South London, a crane shot starting at the locked prison gate, climbing higher and ever higher, until, over the top of the wall, we could see the gloomy shapes of the Victorian cell blocks inside. Unfortunately no one thought of warning the prisoners at exercise within the precincts. As the crane bearing the cameraman and me loomed up over the high wall, first one, then several reacted, cheering us on, thinking it must be some daring escape bid and ruining the shot. They were hustled inside, and we made a second attempt, this time lurching over the wall to reveal a deserted exercise yard and cells beyond.

We were also allowed inside Pentonville Prison to record a small group of trusty prisoners marching up and down the echoing stone chambers and the clang of the iron gates slamming shut behind them (tactfully dropping packets of cigarettes for the lads wherever we went).

Although Rediffusion had now proved the value of videotape, *The Quare Fella* was to be performed live on November 5, 1958, for there was still a superstitious mistrust of the new device, and in any case Brownrigg had banned any cutting of tapes, as he considered a £50 roll of reusable videotape worth more than production perfection!

Rehearsals had gone well, and we went on the air with confidence. The first act ran through smoothly, though we seemed to have added half a minute of running time. Toward the end of the second act, with six prisoners gathered around the open grave, betting their Sunday bacon rasher on whether the guilty man would be "topped" or not, we began a series of fast close-ups of individual reactions. Some of the cuts only lasted half a line. I had four cameras and six actors. Therefore cameras One and Two had to change to a different close-up of another actor after each of their cuts was taken.

Suddenly camera Two went blank. The actors, unaware, carried on at normal speed. I called, "Three-shot, Three!" and punched up his camera as Three rapidly found a group of prisoners. Then I noticed Four's picture, which I needed next, start to wobble as well. Camera One was on the wrong side of the group to help. Elsie Grey whispered, "Five?" Five was the spare camera, perched on a rostrum at the other end of the studio. Without instructions the operator on Five zoomed in to hold a high shot of the group round the grave—but with a Fisher sound boom right across the shot.

The Control Room door suddenly crashed open. "Oh *look*!" Joyce Brownrigg's fluting voice trilled. "I think they're on the air!"

"For Christ's sake be quiet!" I shouted, then to the sound man below, "Lift the boom, quickly!" The operator cleared the shot just as we cut to Five. My whole sequence of close-ups was lost, but we were still on the air—and no one would have noticed the changes.

Four's picture came back, Two was pulled away, and with a little rejigging we were able to finish the sequence on close-ups as planned and run into the fade-out to the act-end commercial break, against the raucous, cocktail parroting of Captain and Mrs. Brownrigg and friends, watching the below-stairs staff perform their duties. As the commercials appeared, Brownrigg glared in my direction.

"We had a problem," I muttered. "Two cameras went down."

"You should have been prepared," Brownrigg admonished, before leading his gossipy little party away, Joyce Brownrigg gaily commenting, "They *do* get awfully temperamental, don't they?"

Vicki urgently warned me that we were now one minute over length, so I quickly had to tell the floor manager to warn the actors that the first scene of Act Three would have to be cut completely. Unfortunately, losing this little scene between two sympathetic warders, although not affecting the plot, lost the best moment of Liam Gaffney's part. But before anyone could argue, we were on the air again and sailed through to the end titles without any more technical problems. The next day Peter Black praised "a production that brought out the play's qualities, the enormous enjoyment of character expressed with true pity for humanity's self-inflicted cruelty." Maurice Wiggin in the Sunday *Times* admired "the weird language, every word stamped with the token of sincerity, creating its own strange poetry." The *Times* noted "performances that did full justice to the avalanching fecundity of the writing." Kenneth Young in the *Telegraph* sensed "the feeling of barbarism inherent in the death penalty, shown with an insinuating power denied to more obvious anti-capital-punishment propaganda."

Once again, in a dramatic context, we had potently focused attention on a major contemporary issue. Many letters came in from people who had never before considered the brutalizing effect of capital punishment on a condemned man's fellow-prisoners, or on those deputed to take his life.

McMillan was delighted, on a more mundane level. *The Quare Fella* achieved an audience-rating of 68 percent, against the BBC's 32 percent—a remarkable feat for a play in Irish dialect full of unfamiliar slang. Of course Brownrigg never referred to his truncated studio visit, but Chairman John Spencer Wills sent me a personal note of congratulation from the Rediffusion board "in the hope that it will spur the Drama Department to even greater efforts!"

My newly appointed agent, John Redway, took a much more practical view, telling me I was wasting my time at Rediffusion when I could make much more money as a feature film director. Maybe, but I liked the choice of subjects and freedom of action in television. However, our third child was on the way and we needed a larger home. Mimi and I found a delightful woodland site on the edge of a Surrey golf course, and with architect brother-in-law Kenneth Reeve Young we started planning the house we hoped to build. To please John and Barclays Bank I took leave from Rediffusion to direct a couple of low-budget features: *The Headless Ghost*, which exploited the comedy talents of Clive Revill and Richard Lyon; and *Breakout*, a near-documentary about a prison break scripted by the then-unknown Peter Barnes, with Lee Paterson and a young Billie Whitelaw in the leads, made for Rank and Julian Wintle, who had just reopened Beaconsfield Studios in Buckinghamshire with ambitious plans.

While I was away, in January 1959, a further program company had been added to ITV coverage: Tyne-Tees TV, serving nearly 3 million more viewers in northeast England around Newcastle, headed by local industrialist Sir Richard Pease and solicitor Claude Darling, with vaudeville producers George and Alfred Black adding theatrical flavor. But like Scottish, Tyne-Tees didn't waste much money on local programs, relying heavily on the network Big Four's offerings for surefire profits. It wasn't until 20 years later that the company attempted to raise its profile and became a source of original programs, with a trickle of children's and popular adult drama, as well as rock music series like *The Tube*.

Back at Rediffusion at the beginning of 1959 my problem was still finding original scripts, so I turned to adapting novels. I secured the rights to Storm Jameson's *A Cup of Tea for Mr. Thorgill*, with its theme of a Communist cell in an Oxford college, and quite ruthlessly adapted it as more of a thriller, retitled *The Face of Treason*, for a fine cast, including Adrienne Corri, Andrew Cruickshank, William Russell, and Robert Harris.

Patrick Gibbs in the *Telegraph* headlined A PLOT THAT EXCITES THE INTELLECT—"and also good to watch because of a whole gallery of interesting character studies played by some of London's finest actors." Peter Black was dubious about relying on adaptations from novels to fill the play vacuum, but Richard Sear in the *Sketch* congratulated us on an "imaginative piece of television."

Five weeks later I broadcast *Family on Trial*, a play sent to me by John Wiles (who had won a prize similar to mine in the 1955 Q Theatre play competition) about the dramatic effect on an apparently normal, middle-class family of their young son's suicide at school. For the first time I had the pleasure of working with truly gifted actress Judi Dench, then barely out of drama school, playing the daughter, who acts as the conscience of the whole guilt-ridden family, with stalwarts Andrew Cruickshank and Bernard Lee in support.

Working with a well-plotted script and with actors as good as these made every day of rehearsal a pleasure, every minute a chance to try out a new idea or to consider anyone else's suggestions for interpreting the author's intention.

The play went well on transmission (still live). The *Times*, under the headline A GRIPPING EVENING'S VIEWING, found it "tightly-plotted, well served by a distinguished cast, confidently directed." Lyn Lockwood in the *Telegraph* described "a sincerely written and absorbingly characterized tragedy of a disunited family, excellently performed by Bernard Lee, Andrew Cruickshank and Judi Dench." But once more Peter Black was uneasy, calling the drama "wildly theatrical" (which it certainly was not!) "but gripping and well-acted."

Undeterred, I had to find another play for July. I decided on a recently published novel set in India during the Second World War, *The Mark of the Warrior*, by the then unknown Paul Scott who, I discovered, had a semi-managerial job in publishing and wasn't at all keen on television. He accepted lunch. We found we had much in common. His near-autobiographical novel of the tensions, jealousy,

Bernard Lee, Judi Dench, Andrew Cruickshank, Helen Christie in *Family on Trial*, **1959.**

and eventual violence among British Army officer-cadets in an Indian jungle barracks was within my own experience. At last he agreed to adapt it himself.

The script, neatly typed, arrived four weeks later, and whereas Miss Storm Jameson had cheerfully confessed she "hadn't the first idea" how to adapt her novel, Paul Scott had compressed and dramatized all the ideas in his book with brilliant economy. ("I *am* an editor," he admitted diffidently.) I cast Robert Harris as Major Craig, survivor of the terrible retreat from Burma, posted to an officer-training unit where he meets Cadet John Ramsay (Paul Massie). Craig knows the secret of Ramsay's brother's death in action, for which he feels personally responsible. He encourages Ramsay's harsh treatment of his Indian soldiers, resulting in Ramsay's murder by an Indian lieutenant he had driven too far. We filmed the jungle scenes in the tangled woods just below the skeleton of our new house, and the last battle across a Burmese river was fought through the foaming waters of the weir at Old Windsor.

I was allowed to tape one sequence in a set that couldn't be squeezed into Wembley Studio, but otherwise the production was as usual transmitted live. Once again we had a popular success.

Lyn Lockwood in the *Telegraph* admired "a worthwhile production with well-directed jungle scenes and fine performances from Robert Harris, Paul Massie and Ewen Solon," and Richard Sear in the *Daily Sketch* found it "a first-class production with realistic action scenes giving a ring of truth." But the *Times* raised the old bogey of "whether adaptations from novels made good television."

They were certainly popular. In 1959 the single play was still riding high in the ratings. *The Face of Treason, Family on Trial,* and *The Mark of the Warrior* were all in the week's Top Ten, while the BBC still floundered in the dusty theatrical library with played-out Pinero. The corporation was also missing the chance of using some of the talented crop of new young actors—Michael Bryant, Judi Dench, Dinsdale Landen, Glenda Jackson, Patrick Wymark, Anne Stallybrass, Frank Finlay, Richard Pasco, Diana Rigg, and John Thaw—whom I was lucky enough to direct at the beginning of impressive dramatic careers.

I was also anxious to work with Paul Scott again, but he was rather vague about it. It was only when I met him at some publisher's party that he confessed he hadn't thought his television play good enough because it left out so much of the novel's essential characterization. Years later his novel *The Chinese Love Pavilion* was optioned for a film and never made, but it wasn't until *The Jewel in the Crown*, adapted for television by another hand after Paul's tragic early death, that he became recognized as a dazzling and original writer.

I had one more script ready to go, my adaptation of Robin Jenkins's novel *The Changeling*, which I retitled *The Boy from the Gorbals*. I went to Glasgow to pick 15-year-old Hamish Wilson to play the lead as a petty thief from a bad home who comes under the influence of his desperate-to-do-good schoolmaster. Hamish has since become a highly respected director, and his natural ability already shown alongside some uninhibited Glaswegian actors like James Copeland, Robert James, and Madeleine Christie. Filming was completed near Dunoon on the west coast and in the slums of the Gorbals (which were rapidly being demolished all around us). The live transmission passed smoothly, and for some reason the play was number one in the week's Top Ten, ahead of *Sunday Night at the London Palladium* and all the giveaway shows.

"Hamish is a find!" the *Daily Mirror* trumpeted, leading a chorus of praise for the boy and the play ("a gem; a delight to watch; Rediffusion can be proud"), all overlooking the fact that once again it derived from a contemporary novel!

The network was about to expand again with the addition of Anglia TV (the Eastern Midlands, about 2½ million more viewers) and Ulster TV, (Northern Ireland, 1½ million). John Woolf, the distinguished film producer (*Oliver!, Room at the Top*, etc.), with Laurence Scott of the *Guardian* newspaper, Aubrey (later Lord) Buxton, theater-owner Donald Albery, and Norfolk's Marquess Townshend formed the Anglia board, and John asked Brownrigg if I could be released to become their head of Drama (at of course a much higher salary) to enable them to produce eight plays a year. Characteristically, the gallant captain refused, but he allowed them to "borrow" me to produce and direct their opening night play in Wembley Studios.

The chosen script, *The Violent Years*, by Ladislas Fodor, which I suspect was an unmade film, was told in flashback from the cell of a man accused of murder as he waits for the jury's verdict. Starting in the Austrian Tyrol in 1914, where Julia (Hildegarde Neff) meets Misha, a young composer (Laurence Harvey), the story ran through various complications of a forced marriage and an illegitimate son who grows up to be a second Laurence Harvey and, in the United States, accidentally kills a man he finds molesting his mother. It was melodramatic hokum, but attractively served. Poulticed with layers of Mendelssohn's Violin Concerto and a cast who deserved better, including Gwen Frangcon-Davies, Joss Ackland, Renee Ray, and Anthony Newlands, Anglia hoped for a big popular success.

I had known Larry Harvey as a struggling young actor.

Bisexual, he had shamelessly exploited lovers as diverse as middle-aged comedienne Hermione Baddeley and a well-known film financier's son to further his career. He was now married to actress Margaret Leighton (today a rich publisher's widow), and for a brief period they owned 16 acres of woodland adjoining our new house and threatened to build and become our neighbors!

Having recently scored a huge international success in John Braine's *Room at the Top*, Larry was now a star to be reckoned with but was still just as pleasant professionally. We enjoyed a brief weekend in the Swiss Alps filming a few background shots, and rehearsed and tape recorded *The Violent Years* at a leisurely pace of one half-hour act per day.

Unfortunately, Larry hadn't been told about Brownrigg's "no editing" rule, and when we were within minutes of completing recording a good take of the complicated first act, Larry made a minor fluff, stopped dead, turned to the camera, and said, "Okay, Peter. Can we cut it here?"

The floor manager started to explain that at Rediffusion we always went back to the beginning and did the whole lot again to "save the tape"—but Larry wasn't having any of that. He called John Woolf, and within a few minutes I received a red-hot signal from the bridge, "You may cut the tape for the Anglia play. But don't make it a habit."

Broadcast on October 27, 1959, with a suitable fanfare as Anglia's first offering, *The Violent Years* received the sort of critical reception I had feared, but because of its stars, its lavish settings, and its soap opera values it was well up in the Top Ten. Anglia was satisfied, but later it produced many more distinguished plays for ITV before settling down to an annual stream of *Tales of the Unexpected*. Anglia also created *Survival*, the outstanding wildlife series from Aubrey Buxton, besides excellent local programs, gaining considerable prestige other companies might well envy.

A few nights later, Ulster TV, headed by my old friend William McQuitty, distinguished documentary filmmaker, writer, photographer, and Egyptologist, and Brum Henderson (destined to become ITV's longest-serving managing director), transmitted their first programs. Though hampered by smaller revenue, Ulster encouraged the spread of adult education by pioneering two forerunners of the Open University, *Midnight Oil* and *The Enquiring Mind*, as well as having one of the most original local news bulletins reflecting the special character and culture of the region.

The five remaining areas, Devon, Cornwall, the Borders of England and Scotland, the Channel Islands, and North Wales, covering the last 4 million viewers, didn't open until 1961 and 1962, but their effect on network programs was minimal. Rediffusion, ATV, ABC, and Granada continued to provide shows that delivered big audiences. The minnows were content to count the money.

Domestically Mimi and I were busy. Our first son, Robin, had been born at the beginning of production of *The Violent Years*. During the brilliant summer of 1959 our new house had been taking shape, but was inevitably costing far more than expected. John Redway proposed a lucrative scheme for me to take six months off from Rediffusion to direct three films and seven television films for Lew Grade on the run.

The first film was adapted from a harrowing BBC documentary about an unmarried mother, *A Woman Alone*, by Colin Morris. Bought by the American producer Irving Allen (later a partner in the James Bond movies), it had been rewritten as a sentimental comedy for Anthony Newley and Bernie Winters, with songs by Lionel Bart, of *Oliver!* fame. The unmarried mother was Anne Aubrey (nearer and dearer to Irving Allen than any of us cared to be!), with Newley and Winters as a couple of comic laundrymen in close confinement. Redway insisted that this film, made at MGM in Cinemascope, would help me up the ladder to bigger things.

It didn't, but two low-budget films I made at the time for Julian Wintle, *Devil's Bait*, with Jane Hylton, Gordon Jackson, and Dermot Kelly, and *The Big Day*, with Donald Pleasence and Andrée Melly, both with tight, well-written scripts, attracted the right sort of attention.

In January 1960, in the middle of all this furious activity, we moved into our new house with small daughters and baby son. Captain Brownrigg and wife Joyce, who lived nearby, invited themselves to tea to inspect married quarters. After his second cup of Lapsang Souchong, having surveyed the whole property, Brownrigg looked at me thoughtfully and made a remark that was to affect my whole future. "Pity we let you off to make all those films. We're

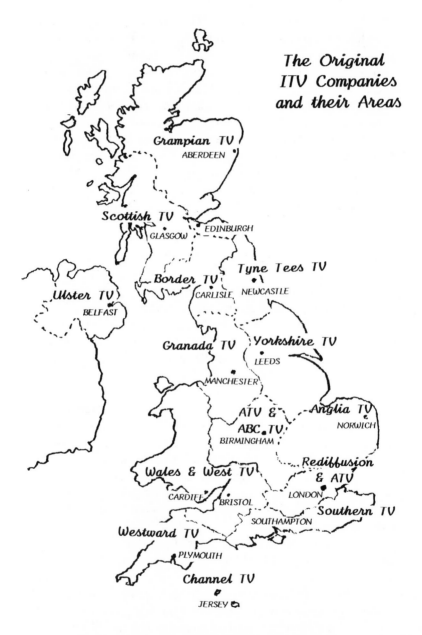

The Original
ITV Companies
and their Areas

Grampian TV
ABERDEEN

Scottish TV
GLASGOW   EDINBURGH

Tyne Tees TV
NEWCASTLE

Border TV
CARLISLE

Ulster TV
BELFAST

Granada TV
MANCHESTER

Yorkshire TV
LEEDS

ATV &
ABC TV
BIRMINGHAM

Anglia TV
NORWICH

Wales & West TV
CARDIFF   BRISTOL

Rediffusion
& ATV
LONDON

Southern TV
SOUTHAMPTON

Westward TV
PLYMOUTH

Channel TV
JERSEY

Transmission areas of the original ITV Companies.

never going to pay you enough to live in this sort of style." (At that time Rediffusion's profits were approaching £8 million [$12 million] a year!)

Reeling slightly, I returned to Kingsway in the spring to find that Norman Marshall had been replaced as head of drama by the witty but waspish Peter Willes, causing Peter Cotes to return to the theater. I thus became senior drama producer.

But good scripts were still as rare as ever. Peter Watling, author of my 1956 hit *Rain on the Just*, delivered an original television play, *A Moment in the Sun*, about a middle-aged businessman's fling on the Spanish Costa Brava with a 19-year-old and his inevitable disillusion and return to his wife. Written with feeling and insight, though slight in theme, it played well with Griffith Jones, Guy Middleton, and Christina Gregg. Ron Grainer wrote a charming theme song, Reece Pemberton designed pretty sets, and the *Times* gave Peter a flattering author's notice. The *Telegraph* called it "one of the most appealing dramas to appear on television for a long time"—but it was really too tenuous for me to have bothered with.

Seeking more substance, I adapted yet another novel, *The Darkness Outside* by George Johnston, an Australian who lived on the Greek island of Hydra. Set in the Iraqi desert, the story tells of a party of archaeologists cut off from civilization by the failure of their radio, who are on the point of a major discovery, the climax of many years of patient excavation. They are suddenly thrown into confusion by the appearance of a wild old Englishman who staggers into their camp shouting frenziedly about "a horde" that has overrun Europe. Is he sane—or simply driven delirious by the sun? The tightly knit group, united by a common purpose, begins to disintegrate. Some argue that they should drive to the nearest point of civilization, nearly two days away. But the leader of the expedition, Purcell, aware of the imminent rains that will ruin their dig, urges them to stay and complete their task. The action erupts into violence, and ends in tragedy and disillusion.

The characters were well observed, and Marius Goring, Virginia Maskell, Jack Hedley, Patricia Driscoll, and Anthony Newlands made the most of them. (Marius's suggestion that we should "have a look at the script together" was firmly resisted. The script was played as written.)

For the part of the old Englishman I decided to gamble. Wilfrid Lawson was one of the finest actors of his generation, with a particularly distinctive voice; his Alfred Doolittle in the prewar film of Shaw's *Pygmalion* a definitive performance. But like many masculine actors who secretly despise the whole business of dressing up and painting their faces, Wilfrid had become rather a drunk, considered unemployable. I met him when he was playing a small part in a play directed by Joseph Losey. There was something insane about his feverish eyes that made him exactly right for the old man. Peter Willes disagreed. *The Darkness Outside* was, as usual, to be performed live. Suppose Wilfrid was so paralytic that the whole show stopped? I assured Peter that whatever happened we would carry on—live television always did. (A few months before, in an *Armchair Theatre* directed by Ted Kotcheff, an actor had actually died of a heart attack on transmission. Luckily the play was about a small group of nuclear survivors in a shelter. The actor who had to approach the collapsed figure thought he had merely fainted and filled in with "Wake-up-old-man" free speech until Ted cut to the next scene. None of the cast was told. The body was removed during the next commercial break, the survivors vamped the missing man's lines, and viewers were none the wiser.)

But I had reason to remember Willes's warning when we went filming. The opening shots of the old man stumbling through the desert had to be shot in the sandy wastes of a local gravel-digging pit. Wilfrid arrived late, but he seemed to be sober so we started, although the weather was dull and cloudy. At lunchtime, unfortunately he disappeared, and on the first take in the afternoon he began to stagger, finally falling flat on his face in the sand. With difficulty we raised him to his feet, but it was obvious that there would be no more filming for Wilfrid that day. The next morning, however, he turned up bright as a button, apologized for "feeling a bit sick," and as the sun shone brightly almost made me feel he'd done us a good turn!

When rehearsals began, he made no effort to befriend the rest of the cast. On the third day Marius arrived with a heavyweight BBC script under his arm and announced that he'd just been offered the lead in Zuckmeyer's *The Devil's General*. The other actors were suitably impressed. Suddenly Wilfrid's organ-pipe voice rang out from a far corner, "*The Devil's General*, Marius? You couldn't touch it!"

Marius marched furiously over to confront the old man. "*Mister Lawson*. Do you consider yourself a better judge of acting than the British Broadcasting Corporation and their finest producer, Mr. Rudolph Cartier?"

Wilfrid was unabashed. "You haven't got the balls, Marius. The only man to play that part is Trevor Howard." He paused. "Or possibly *me*, perhaps."

Marius turned on his heel. War was now open between them. But it added considerable bite to their performances. Not for the first time I learned the value of personal antipathy in the strange craft of ensemble acting. But rumors of Wilfrid's "difficult" behavior were spreading. Willes urged me to recast. I refused, but as a compromise I offered to engage an understudy and rehearse him secretly. If Wilfrid appeared at all shaky in the studio I would make a rapid substitution.

But Wilfrid had learned his lesson—or his agent had warned him. On transmission day he seemed quiet and abnormally well behaved. As we broke for supper I asked, "Coming for a quick drink, Wilfrid?" He stared at me and shook his head reprovingly like a temperance preacher. "Never touch a drop before the show, my boy."

I tottered away, unable to believe it. On transmission the cast soon realized Wilfrid was on top form. Marius Goring, blazing with hatred for the scruffy old actor, rapidly responded to Lawson's amazing performance as it developed and blossomed in a way never rehearsed. Together with Jack Hedley and Patricia Driscoll they all lifted the play from mild melodrama to high passion.

The *Times* forgot its strictures on novel adaptations. With the headline THOUGHTFUL PLAY'S CHALLENGE it praised "notable acting, impressive settings by Frederic Pusey, and direction of grim urgency." The *Telegraph* called it "a spine-chilling 90 minutes with a well-written thriller." The rest of the papers were equally enthusiastic.

Peter Willes had now instituted a weekly private entertainment known as the "Friday Script Meeting" at which the readers and I would consider the latest heap of recently submitted new plays. Choosing to read from some ultrarealist piece with an inspiring title like *Piss in the Sink*, Peter would enact all the parts, particularly the females, and reduce us all to helpless pulp. But very little producible was unearthed despite the newfound freedom of the 1960s, though not even the most sordid matter was shirked by our unsolicited authors. "Is there," Peter would groan, "*any* unpleasant disease or disgusting sexual perversion to which we *haven't* been dramatically exposed?"

Hardly. But I did turn up a play by a milk deliveryman, Mike Watts, based on present-day prison experience, skillfully balanced between low comedy and moving tragedy. *The Pot-Carriers* showed a first offender, Rainbow, becoming the confidant of a cocksure "trusty," Redband, who reveals all the inside racketeering possible within the prison kitchen. The dialogue was extraordinary, a mixture of prison slang and near-poetry. I urged Peter to buy the play and looked forward eagerly to its realization.

Ronald Fraser played Redband, and David McCallum (before he went to Hollywood to become *The Man from Uncle*), Rainbow. Martin Wyldeck and Andrew Crawford headed a cast of reliable working-class actors.

After *All Correct Sir* and *The Quare Fella* I was practically an old prison hand. Frederic Pusey designed a huge prison kitchen and yet another cell block. Mike Watts's dialogue was so refreshingly original and the characters so well observed that rehearsals passed all too quickly. Once more all 90 minutes were performed "live" with a minimum of technical problems.

The dramatic structure was as loose and episodic as Brendan Behan's play, and I had expected fairly lukewarm notices. But instead the critics praised Mike Watts lavishly for the freshness of his observation. "Sign him up," sang Maurice Richardson in the *Observer*. "Richly promising, he writes with a light sure touch." In the Sunday *Times* Maurice Wiggin found the play "compulsively viewable, with brilliant acting topped by a splendid performance by Ronald Fraser. Anyone who can write such dialogue should have a future." The *Times* felt we had "captured the complexity of prison's emotional climate, and the ready camaraderie of shared adversity," while the *Telegraph* agreed that "both characters and atmosphere had a genuine ring about them, and the leavening of enforced humour held one fascinated from start to finish."

Once again viewers' letters showed how much serious thought could be stimulated by a sincere play. It was as if I had taken millions of people on a close inspection of a typical, crumbling, ugly, Victorian-designed British prison, to experience and share my own personal revulsion for the inhuman three-men-to-a-cell overcrowding, the revolting lack of sanitation or bathing facilities, the denial not only of freedom and useful work, but even of regular clean laundry. Other correspondents were appalled at the social damage caused by such poor facilities for education and retraining, inevitably turning prisons into breeding grounds for further vice and crime, with inmates dragging out a bored half life of illicit drugs, homosexuality, and the occasional outburst of mindless violence. As with *The Quare Fella* and *The Last Enemy*, dramatic truth had really hit home.

The following day, Bob Lennard, casting director for Associated British Pictures, called. He had recommended that they buy the play for enhancement into a feature film for me to direct. Unaware of this, Peter Willes summoned Mike Watts and gave him a three-play contract. In due course he delivered, and I directed two of the plays the following year, but though quite skillful neither had the dramatic force of *The Pot-Carriers*.

However, despite this achievement a belief had grown in ITV management that single plays didn't carry the same guarantee of big audiences as drama series and serials. ATV had already had a ratings success with *Emergency Ward Ten*. Rediffusion began to police the airwaves with *No Hiding Place*, and Granada had started to gain a huge following on Mondays and Wednesdays with *Coronation Street* (commencing locally in 1960, fully networked from May 1961).

John McMillan, of whom we had once hoped so much, now dazzled by the glittering prize of high ratings, had bought A. J. Cronin's prewar medical drama *The Citadel*, and insisted that I should produce it. John Frankau had made all sorts of television since his schools debut but was keen to get back to drama. We agreed that he would direct eight of the nine episodes and I would handle the middle one. McMillan and Willes were difficult to please over a choice of leading actor to play the dour young Scottish doctor based on Cronin himself. In the end, with our filming date looming, we settled on Eric Lander, who had built a solid reputation as the homely Detective Sergeant Baxter in *No Hiding Place*, and we completed the main cast with Zena Walker as his wife and Noel Harrison as the doctor friend—the part his father, Rex Harrison, had created in the old Robert Donat film for MGM.

South Wales presented its wettest face when we arrived in the Rhondda Valley to film the opening scenes near Pontypridd. On the last day a shivering Zena Walker was just too cold and wet to act, so we rewrote the scene for the warmth of the studio.

It was a pleasure to be able to relax and watch John Frankau work. His casting was impeccable, his rehearsals well organized, and his camerawork sure. We transmitted over Christmas 1960 and into 1961, presenting McMillan with the regular high ratings he needed.

But real-life drama suddenly demanded my attention. Way back in 1956 a group of us had formed the "Guild of Television Producers"—not a labor union but an association for meeting and discussing technical and creative developments. By 1960, when I was elected chairman, we had swollen to over 200 members, and we decided to amalgamate with the British Film Academy (eventually becoming the British Academy of Film and TV Arts—BAFTA).

Dennis Vance, my one-time actor friend in Italy, begetter of ABC's *Armchair Theatre*, a founding member of the guild, had had rather a rocky passage since leaving ABC, both professionally and domestically, culminating in a stormy affair with a young female director. He visited us one Saturday, looking bloated and hungover, with a woeful tale of crossed love. The following Monday the BBC News announced that a "Dennis William Vance, an 'ITV Producer,' had been arrested for stabbing a girl at Teddington Studios."

I summoned the guild council, and we decided to mount a defense fund. I hurried to Brixton Prison, where Dennis was remanded, to give him the news. His usually ruddy face was chalk-white, his manner, as he sat hunched in unfamiliar blue prison fatigues, rather offhand, as if he'd been tranquilized.

In those days visitors faced the inmate in a small wooden cubicle, separated by a thick pane of glass, edged with a narrow frame of wire mesh. It was impossible to touch, or even to hear properly, as he whispered his version of what had happened. He had been to see the girl in her studio office the previous afternoon, hoping for reconciliation. There'd been another row, Dennis had picked up a paperknife, the girl had panicked and grappled with him, and in the confused struggle she had sustained a wound in the chest. I'd already contacted the girl's doctor, and was able to reassure Dennis that the wound was not too serious, though she was badly shocked.

I asked if he had a lawyer. He nodded. I should have realized that a survivor of three divorces would certainly have a legal adviser. But Dennis needed serious help. With the aid of Andrew Miller-Jones, a distinguished pioneer producer and pillar of the guild, I was able to contact a barrister who specialized in cases where psychiatric evidence was necessary. Dennis was clearly mentally disturbed. The strain of trying to work on two productions, one BBC, one ITV, plus the emotional upheaval had tipped him over the edge.

For the next few days I worked through a list of executives, producers, and actors, seeking donations. The response was a mixture of philanthropy and Pharisee. The BBC to a man (and woman) closed ranks. Dennis's problem was, they insisted, nothing to do with them. Others were (thankfully) more helpful. A top executive at the *Times* newspaper made a large gift. Diana Dors, whom I didn't know, simply said, "Put me down for 500, love," and a check arrived the next day. Others, friends and enemies, varied between puritanical horror and real generosity. In the end, Dennis's defense was paid for by large and small sums from cameramen, makeup girls, production assistants, and typists.

Dennis duly appeared in dock and was charged with causing actual bodily harm. Our Queen's Counsel produced overwhelming psychiatric evidence of the mental stress involved in producing original television week in, week out, year after year, complicated by broken marriages and other problems. Found guilty, Dennis was put on probation for three years; he spent a short time in the hospital to calm down, and within a few months was back in production, as riotously alive as ever. Sadly, the girl he wounded changed her job and dropped out of sight.

Back to normality at Rediffusion, the best effort Willes's script unit could find was a tattered melodrama, *Doctor Everyman's Hour* by Leslie Reade, the story of a brilliant but arrogant surgeon, Hugo

Conradi, who demands that a large hospital bequest secured by his efforts should be used solely for his research rather than for more beds. A friendly colleague opposes him, Conradi admits to an affair with the colleague's wife, a patient dies on the operating table, and Conradi is accused of negligence. All good stuff, worthy of *Emergency Ward Ten*.

With the fine German actor Albert Lieven as Conradi and Adrienne Corri as the unfaithful wife, it worked on its own melodramatic level, but I knew we were scraping the bottom of the barrel. But Glenda Jackson, still unknown, played a tiny part as a juror. No one had any idea of her future as an international star (and later as a minister in a reforming British government), but she was clearly a committed actress. I kept a camera on her during the long court inquiry, snatching cuts of her reactions throughout, which considerably heightened the scene's tension and impact.

John McMillan had another creative flush and decided we should dramatize a series of Algernon Blackwood's *Tales of Mystery*. In the early days of BBC television, these had been read to the camera by a hammy old thespian, Bransby Williams, to fill an undemanding quarter of an hour. But most of the short (some very short) stories had little substance, simply a one-line surprise at the end.

I managed to interest Giles Cooper, Philip Broadley, and Barbara Harper enough to have them choose a theme from any story they liked and virtually write their own original half-hour Gothic mystery around it. With John Laurie introducing each story as the eerie Algernon Blackwood, some fine casts, direction by John Frankau, and dramatic visual and sound effects, we again scored in the ratings, causing McMillan to demand a further 13 episodes the following year.

My next single play, *A Different Drum* by Frederick Aiken, was simpler but more deeply felt. An eccentric and unpopular schoolmaster discovers that one of his pupils could become a talented organist, given proper tuition. But the boy is also a star footballer, causing conflict with the sports-mad headmaster, and confusing the boy and his parents. In the end music is defeated, and football scores.

Eric Portman played the schoolmaster (echoing his success in Terence Rattigan's *The Browning Version*), Joyce Heron his wife,

Douglas Wilmer the head, a young Cavan Kendall the boy, and Jean Alexander (soon to gain national fame as Hilda Ogden in *Coronation Street*) his mother. The sincerity of the writing shone through fine performances. Unfortunately, I could never persuade Frederick Aiken, a successful schoolmaster, to write another play.

The critics responded as hoped. "A first play of more than ordinary merit," stated Peter Black enthusiastically. "Remarkable skill and sensitivity," droned the *Times*. "A fine story told with irony and truth," observed Richard Sear in the *Sketch*.

My next, *I, Having Dreamt, Awake*, by John Symonds, another first play, was a curious mixture of Pinter and Alan Ayckbourn about a middle-aged gas fitter whose complacency is exploded by the arrival of his brother from the United States, who, apparently a millionaire, insists on moving their ailing mother into a very expensive nursing home. The gas man's wife is very impressed and plans to run away with the brother-in-law, but suddenly he is revealed as a none-too-successful confidence trickster, and he runs for it, leaving the dreaming gas fitter to pick up the bills. A modest actor, Timothy Bateson, scored a critical triumph as the antihero, along with Jasmine Dee as the wife, Dudley Foster as the brother, and Janet Thompson as the daughter. Writing in the *Observer*, the distinguished Philip Toynbee complimented my "invention and ingenuity" and used the little play as stick to beat the BBC: "in recent months the ITV channel has been giving us better dramatic entertainment than its rival."

I was about to take another short break from ITV. John Temple Smith and I had reworked Russell Thorndyke's *Doctor Syn* into a new screenplay for Hammer Films as *Captain Clegg* (in the United States, *Night Creatures*, where it still appears all too frequently on late-night television). And Associated British had completed its "enhanced" film script for *The Pot-Carriers* (giving Redband a wife and Rainbow a tearful girlfriend) and was eager to go.

I also needed time away from Rediffusion to consider my future. Though Peter Willes had encouraged Harold Pinter to write two or three plays for Joan Kemp-Welch to direct, basically he mistrusted new, ambitious writers with something positive to say. In any case, single plays were now considered to be losing the popularity fight against soap opera.

Finally there was the financial problem. Rediffusion paid far less than any other ITV company. As senior drama producer I was still getting little more on the Admiralty-inspired low pay scale than the dullest new director in the basement. Brownrigg argued that I mustn't be paid more than Willes. But the needs of a fruity old bachelor were far less than mine with a growing family to educate.

With a couple of films in a few months I could quadruple my Rediffusion pay. Under my contract I had to give one year's notice, which I duly gave from the beginning of December 1961. Permission was granted for me to do the Hammer film in October and November, but not for *The Pot-Carriers* immediately afterwards. At last I wearily offered to pay Rediffusion one-quarter of my whole *Pot-Carriers* fee for a further two months' release, which Brownrigg, presiding over a company coining millions, grimly accepted.

Captain Clegg, or *Night Creatures*, starring Peter Cushing, Oliver Reed, Patrick Allen, and Yvonne Romain, a rollicking adventure among the ghostly smugglers of Romney Marshes, was briskly shot at Bray Studios and in the surrounding countryside. Besides being Peter Cushing's own favorite performance, it was a huge success when sold to Universal in the United States.

The film of *The Pot-Carriers*, again with Ronald Fraser, but with Paul Massie in the David McCallum part and a much improved cast, was also well received. Robert Jones's realistic sets and Erwin Hillier's stark black-and-white photography created a powerful atmosphere.

I returned to Rediffusion for my last year, 1962, to find that the actors were striking for higher fees from ITV. When at last the dispute was settled in May, I directed three more plays as the months sped by toward my release. At last, Brownrigg had relented. Plays were no longer broadcast live but recorded without breaks the day before transmission. Editing, however, was still forbidden.

Murder in Shorthand, with Oliver Reed and Justine Lord, was a well-constructed thriller that Peter Willes and the critics rated higher than I did. ("Gripping whodunit, excellent cast," the *Telegraph*; "Ingenious," the Sunday *Times*; "Back with a Winner," the *Mirror*, and so forth.) Frankau and I then launched 13 more *Tales of Mystery*, which proved McMillan right about ratings, finally achieving number three in the weekly Top Ten.

With Mimi, premiere of *The Pot-Carriers*, London Pavilion, 1962.

The Second Chef, recorded in August and transmitted in October, was Mike Watts's second play, set in a roadside café, where a casually employed dishwasher slowly reveals to the owner's wife that he is on the run, under suspicion for a child's murder. The woman, half in love, believes his protestation of innocence, and they begin a secret affair. Slowly the café owner discovers the awful truth of the young man's true guilt.

With Oliver Reed (then a sober young man), Jane Hylton as the wife, and Ronnie Barker (a straight actor, not yet half of *The Two Ronnies*) as a truck driver, Mike showed that he could deliver a highly effective mixture of powerful emotion and low comedy. But his next, my very last production for Rediffusion (and for technical reasons transmitted live from the studio), was a disappointing potboiler, *The Pinkness of It All*, a comedy about a pair of scruffy professional gamblers trying to pull off a big betting coup to send a niece home to Australia to get married. Ronnie Barker, Sam Kydd, and Wanda Ventham did their noble best, but my farewell to Rediffusion ended on a muted note.

I had been with the company for nearly eight years, since its beginning, and had produced or directed 35 full-length dramas and 29 series episodes, and had participated in an adventurous pioneering experiment in school programs. Every one of those plays began as someone's unique inspiration. Each had to be designed and cast, music to be selected, actors rehearsed, a technical script of hundreds of angles laboriously written, and cameras carefully plotted in the studio, until the finished result was proudly presented to the public—and then lost forever.

Rediffusion was a company of opposites. At the beginning John Spencer Wills and Paul Adorian had simply believed in vigorous commercial competition with the BBC. Below them a rigid administration completely failed to understand the richness and complexity of imaginative thought required to make good programs, or to value the worth of the creative people they employed. Even John McMillan, who had begun so well, had fallen victim to the lure of the second-rate in his pursuit of ratings.

The past decade had heralded the new prosperity and greater social freedom that grew during the 1960s. Television was involved in those changes, though sometimes more as chorus than initiator, as young hairdressers and dressmakers, made rich by teenagers' newfound purchasing power, became opinionated "personalities," and four Beatles in pudding-basin haircuts twanged out the electric guitar catchphrase "All you need is love!"

But there was very little real love in commercial television, only a quest for profit. Neither religious leaders nor politicians had the wit or popular contact to deliver a more inspiring message, and dutiful close-ups of the devout intoning meaningless hymns were no substitute for moral and spiritual inspiration from above.

So, cabinet ministers droned out their well-rehearsed clichés, missing the golden chance of speaking directly and personally to viewers in their own living rooms. The ITA failed to guide the television companies with any sense of public duty, and helped by cheap imports, commercial television came to rely more and more on those old box-office standbys, sex and sadism, vice and violence. Four-letter words slipped into everyday speech, school discipline slackened, and a permissive age dawned, with television a handy culprit for professional pessimists deploring society's newfound "blasphemy, sedition and filth," failing to recognize it as simply part of a self-generating liberty.

In response to well-publicized complaints, changes were mooted, prompted by thoughtful people of greater stature than the angry few. In 1960 a government committee under Sir Harry Pilkington began once more to study British broadcasting and consider its future, its main spokesman Professor Richard Hoggart, a popular historian but a fervent opponent of commercial television.

Their report, when finally published in June 1962, detonated a frenzied reaction from all the ITV companies, particularly Rediffusion, for despite all the innovations since 1955 the report agreed with Bernard Levin's sour judgment that ITV was "a great tide of mindless trash, of idiot panel games, smutty comedians and little else." (All our combined efforts to provide quality drama might as well have happened on another planet!) Their bleak recommendation was totally to restructure the whole system. The Independent Television Authority should plan its own future program schedules, commission independent producers on merit, and sell all the advertising itself.

This was clearly unworkable. But Rediffusion should have

taken more heed. While the BBC was applauded for its professionalism as a national broadcasting service, the report deplored its having to lower its quality standards to compete with ITV. The corporation's reward, no less, was the promise of a second channel to oppose ITV more effectively.

If Rediffusion had had a more perceptive management they might immediately have poured some of the company's overflowing profits into better-quality programs, including music and drama. They did not. Single plays became fewer, and junk giveaway shows, plodding policemen, and terrible comedians remained the staple fare of London ITV, until, in 1967, when program contracts came up for renewal, Rediffusion and TWW were the only companies to have their franchises canceled.

Rediffusion shareholders didn't suffer, however. The London weekday contract was awarded to a new company, Thames TV, a merger of ABC and Rediffusion sharing profits equally, but with 51 percent of voting shares held by ABC and management and program choice in the able hands of Howard Thomas and his team. Although Brownrigg had retired, it was a deadly vote of no confidence in John McMillan's program judgment. After a year or so running ITV Sport, he vanished from the scene.

Peter Black in the *Mail* contended that "all this upheaval added nothing significant to programmes in number, quality or regional flavour"—but that was too harsh. Under Jeremy Isaacs, Thames flourished, making important series like the powerful *World at War*, and major advances in drama with Verity Lambert, even though the old weekly magic of *Armchair Theatre* was never recaptured.

Rediffusion's staff gained an unfair reward, being handsomely paid off before reporting the next day by union agreement to either Thames or the new London weekend contractor. Wembley Studios, scene of so much hectic activity night after night, was sold and became a film studio again. Television House in Kingsway was also disposed of and now houses the Registry of Births and Deaths, with nothing to show of the genesis and burial within 13 years of a once-proud and energetic television company.

5

1959–1964: International Promise and a Second BBC-TV

*"Danger Man," "The Avengers"—and
the BBC gets another channel.*

From before the Coronation, the traditionally unadventurous British film industry had always treated the growing popularity of television with a mixture of disdain for its cruder production quality tinged with anger at its perceived ability to erode the cinema audience. But from the early 1950s films made especially for television began to fill empty studios and provide a steady source of work for unemployed film technicians.

Even before ITV, Hannah Weinstein, a fearless American, commenced a series called *Robin Hood*, starring Hollywood has-been Richard Greene, which ran to 143 episodes. Filmed in polystyrene dungeons and a studio forest where no leaf ever stirred, it nevertheless sold all over the world and jolted Lew Grade into making film series for ATV of *The Elusive Pimpernel, Charlie Chan*, and *William Tell*, none of which matched *Robin Hood* in international success.

The producer of *William Tell*, Ralph Smart, whom I had met in Italy, called me in the summer of 1959 when I was having a good run of live television plays at Rediffusion and invited me to lunch. He was planning a new film series for Lew Grade about a NATO secret agent, *Danger Man* (retitled *Secret Agent* in the United States) to star the highly regarded Patrick McGoohan. Born in the States of Irish stock, McGoohan had played *King Lear* at Sheffield at age 23. I had seen him recently as Starbuck in Orson Welles's slapdash stage production of *Moby Dick* and as a neurotic clergyman in *Serious Charge*.

I read a couple of the first scripts, which weren't bad within their limits. The formula demanded that John Drake (Danger Man) should arrive in a Middle Eastern/South American/North Bulgarian town to find that his agent has been arrested/kidnapped/murdered. He meets a frightened girl—who can't tell him why she's scared. A mysterious stranger attacks him and fails (end of Part One). In Part Two he meets/thinks he sees/doesn't meet his agent and discovers The Plot. In the last five minutes he has a fist fight/scuffle/chase and saves the world for freedom once again. All in 25 minutes flat.

It sounded fun. I would learn more about how to film and edit fights and action sequences. So, in the six months I had negotiated to be away from Rediffusion, between the Anthony Newley film and the Donald Pleasence one, John Redway was able to fit in seven episodes for me practically one after another.

Brian Clemens, who wrote many of the scripts, and Ian Stuart Black, originator and story editor, were sharp professionals ready to rewrite when and where necessary, and we were able to cast good actors like Warren Mitchell, Patrick Wymark, John le Mesurier, Charles Gray, and Maxine Audley. But I found Patrick McGoohan a demanding leading man to work with, frequently challenging my visual concept of a scene (though often allowing himself to be convinced).

But in the time available, getting proper coverage of five minutes of screen time a day without argument was eight full hours of hard work. Everything was meant to be shot inside the stages at MGM, Elstree, a large and prestigious studio (now, alas, demolished and used as a council refuse dump). As a boy I had fantasized my future life of ease as a director at MGM—of swimming pools, sunshine, luscious starlets. Well, I'd made it—working day shifts at the coalface (coal mine)!

Because the studio had a vast stock of old feature film sets, scripts had to be tailored to fit whatever was available. A meeting between Drake and his furtive associate would suddenly be arranged in a nunnery chapel, or a Hapsburg ballroom—because it was there. Every story had to have one garden/forest/jungle studio exterior because MGM had a famous gardener's greenhouse full of exotic plants. (Minimal real exteriors were covered by a second unit with doubles by the brilliant unknown John Schlesinger—who could complain?)

Used as I was to the comparative leisure of television rehearsals, with time for discussion and development of each scene, it was a harsh discipline to have to preplan actors' moves like chess pieces and shoot the first time. The next week's script never appeared before the penultimate Friday afternoon. After a weekend of telephone calls, Patrick would sometimes arrive on Monday morning to confront us with a completely rewritten script. But it *was* usually much better.

For the first time I had a named place in the MGM car park. One day Lew Grade came charging on the set shouting, "Here, someone's left an old banger in your parking space!"

I explained that as my smart convertible was in for service I was borrowing my wife's slightly battered prewar Morris Eight. "Can't have that!" Lew roared. "This is MGM! Think of your image—*my image!* I'll see you have a Rolls Royce and chauffeur tomorrow!" (Of course, no Rolls ever arrived, but it impressed the unit.) The crew was in fact superb. With Brendan Stafford lighting and Jack Lowin operating, the films were attractive visually, and when shown again on Channel Four *25 years later*, they withstood close examination. But it was possible for me to survive at that pace for only a few weeks.

During my last three years at Rediffusion I took short leaves to direct more television films: four episodes of *Sir Francis Drake*, with a nearly-made-it ex–Rank star, Terence Morgan, as Drake; Jean Kent as Queen Elizabeth, and Howard Lang and a very young Michael Crawford as a pair of Drake's sailors. Because the series was produced by Anthony Bushell, Laurence Olivier's associate on *Hamlet*, scripts were more literate than usual.

Lew then persuaded me to make a pilot for a series doomed from the start. Its title, *Mr. Riviera*, told all—a bottom-drawer script and a blown-out lead. We had a pleasant week filming at sea and in Monte Carlo, but the result sank without trace. I also made four episodes of MGM's *Zero One* (Danger Man as airline investigator, saved by the leading presence of Nigel Patrick, a truly brilliant comedy actor). So much for television films. As Joseph Losey once told me, "It's not hard for a director to make money—if he's prepared to pay the price."

When I left Rediffusion in December 1962 I soon had the prospect of three feature films. Julian Wintle had been a friend for many years and was now a producer of some integrity, having backed Lindsay Anderson and Karel Reisz on their first film, *This Sporting Life*, J. Lee-Thompson on *Tiger Bay*, and John Guillermin for Peter Sellers's first international success, *Waltz of the Toreadors*. Julian was also a remarkably brave human being, having inherited hemophilia, a blood disease that caused him daily pain that would have defeated a lesser man. Yet he lived a life of outward charm and personal courage, sustained by marriage to a talented writer, Anne Francis, and two sons, Christopher and Justin.

He had already penciled me in for several episodes of a proposed new television series, *The Human Jungle* (with Herbert Lom as a psychiatrist), when a problem arose on his current feature film, *Bitter Harvest*, from a script by Ted Willis for Rank. Peter Cotes was directing at Pinewood, but after two weeks Julian was unhappy with his slow pace and rather old-fashioned style. Within days of leaving Rediffusion I was urgently summoned to dinner and asked to take over.

This was very embarrassing. I admired Peter's work in the theater, and he had helped me into Rediffusion. I had no wish to push him out of a job. But Julian assured me production had stopped, Peter had already stood down, and if I refused he could easily find another director. Under pressure I agreed to read the script. Ted had turned a prewar novel of a young Welsh girl going wrong, ending her life in booze and drugs, into a sharply observed parable for the so-called Swinging Sixties which needed fast presentation to make it live. The next day I saw Peter Cotes's rushes. I am sure he was sincerely seeking some deep meaning in a lightweight script, but the result on the screen was simply ponderous. Julian pressed me for an answer. Out of respect for his judgment I accepted and prepared to shoot the following day, a decision I soon regretted. Cotes's set designs seemed square and unoriginal, and I would never have cast some of his chosen actors. In particular, Janet Munro's attempt to portray a 17-year-old virgin with a real-life broken marriage and countless lovers behind her, stretched credibility too far, and John Stride, Franco Zeffirelli's Romeo, was too attractive for the clumsy laborer hopelessly in love with a heartless young girl seeking fame. Many of the other actors were Peter's theatrical friends, not the type of realistic players I was used to. Ironically the film was shot on the very stage at Pinewood where, at 14, I had watched Alfred Hitchcock and been inspired to become a director.

It was, no less, my first chance to try modern style on a big budget film. I experimented with a hand-held camera at a wild theatrical party, spinning it around among the guests while the elders of Pinewood muttered about "this madman from TV." John Davies, the Rank Organization's chief executive, having heard rumors, came onto the set one afternoon and questioned me about my "previous experience" as if talking to a beginner. I mentioned a few award-winners like *The Last Enemy* and *The Quare Fella*. Davies had never heard of any of them. I said they had been enjoyed by millions on television. "Ah, *television*," he sneered, before turning to go. "Well, we won't hold that against you!" Needless to say, I shot the best parts of the film on location near Cardiff, away from Pinewood's unreal sets.

To my surprise, *Bitter Harvest* was well received, and Janet Munro, soon to meet a tragic end herself, was complimented on a sincere and moving performance. But although Peter Cotes had been paid his full director's fee, he felt his professional status had been hurt. He sued Rank and Julian Wintle for "substantial damages." For several days Julian climbed the stairs to the law courts and anguished while the case dragged on, until it was finally dismissed.

My next film came from Associated British. Charlie Drake, a boisterous comedian from television who combined on-screen pathos with off-screen arrogance, had asked for me after seeing *The Pot-Carriers*. The script for *The Cracksman*, by Lew Schwartz, was an amusing tale of a master locksmith led into a life of crime by a smooth-talking con man. It gave Charlie plenty of opportunity for knockabout comedy routines, from the opening, as he cycled eagerly through London's night streets with a replacement key to open the jammed gates of the Tower of London, recklessly smashing right through the great portal to emerge from the moat covered with water weed, but still keen to oblige. Then there was a later trip through a nauseating prison sewer in an escape bid, and a nightclub routine where he ruins a balloon dancer's act by bursting vital balloons— all good clean fun.

This time I had an art director, Anthony Masters, whom I liked; a cameraman, Harry Waxman, I admired; and my own handpicked cast, including George Sanders, Dennis Price, Ronnie Barker, Finlay Currie, Patrick Cargill, Geoffrey Keen, and Nyree Dawn Porter. We shot through the unusually snowy months of February and March 1963, and the film was happily finished with little delay. When it opened at London's Warner Cinema, Penelope Gilliat in the *Observer* headlined the story MASTERY OF CHARLIE DRAKE over eulogistic praise for his clowning quality, and most of the critics followed her lead. At the box office it was the most successful film Charlie ever made. (Unfortunately his next, which I was also to direct, was his worst.)

Our second son, Martin, was born on June 6, 1963. I was already busy on a third feature, *Father Came Too*, for Rank, a sequel to Ken Annakin's successful *The Fast Lady*, with Julie Christie and Stanley Baxter. This time the same couple, now married, undergo the tribulations of trying to convert an old ruined cottage into their dream house; their efforts constantly thwarted by interfering father-in-law James Robertson Justice. The basic idea seemed so hackneyed that I suggested making the ruin an old railway station and adding in a "ghost train" subplot. But neither producer Julian Wintle (again) nor writer Jack Davies would buy it, though it might have improved the resulting film. Thus, *Father Came Too* ended up as a ragbag of "Carry On" comic postcard gags, nobly suffered by Stanley Baxter, Sally Smith (in place of Julie Christie, snapped up by Hollywood), Leslie Phillips, Ronnie Barker, Terry Scott, Philip Locke, and Timothy Bateson.

As soon as this was finished, Julian had another script he wanted me to develop, *The Innocent Gunman*, by John Dighton, which he planned for Peter Sellers. I agreed to read it, but secretly

I was dissatisfied with sort of film I was being offered, and indeed with the whole big studio concept, which shackled the action to plain interior sets rather than finding interesting real locations.

There were also vital differences for a director between television and film. In television I was virtually master, molding the performance in rehearsal, and directing the cameras' precise composition from the images I could see on a monitor. In films I had always to rely on the unseen skill of an operator. But this was not the main difference. In television I was the main creator, delivering the show as I had conceived it straight to the public. In films, because of the higher cost and greater risk, the producer (even one as sympathetic and friendly as Julian Wintle) usually felt he had to impose his own judgment on the final work, particularly during the editing. This meant (I had to admit) that my heart was still in the comparative freedom of television, and I began to look around for a new opportunity.

The BBC production quality had remained high during the first years of ITV, with *Panorama*, a well-argued weekly analysis of topical affairs; *Sports Night*, a thorough coverage; *World Theatre*, conservative but well acted; Denis Mitchell's prison documentaries, and light entertainment that included Benny Hill, Tony Hancock, and Billy Cotton's band show, all contributing to the varied mix. But the hard fact remained that throughout the late 1950s the BBC's audience share remained at 30 percent to ITV's 70 percent. Morale among talented producers sagged. They believed they were delivering good programs that should have been an important part of society's daily culture, but viewers were simply not being attracted. Publicity was poor. The *Radio Times*, the BBC's program magazine, was a drab, gray bore. BBC presenters seemed upper class and remote, and on-screen promotion of forthcoming programs was practically nonexistent. But by 1960, when Hugh Carleton Greene, brother of novelist Graham, was appointed director-general, the BBC was being forced to consider ways of regaining a sizable audience without necessarily abandoning quality, and Greene at once recognized this as his chief priority.

The BBC's independence of finance and politics was worthless, Greene realized, unless it gave its producers complete freedom of action, and he knew more than most about the value of freedom. As a newspaper correspondent in Germany before the war, he had watched the rise of the Nazis, hating "the intolerance and degradation of character caused by loss of individual liberty and expression." For two years after the Nazi defeat he had reconstructed the shattered German radio network, insisting on democratic independence, completely excluding political parties from any control over what was transmitted—an independence hitherto unknown in German broadcasting.

He had then traveled to Malaya to build a psychological warfare organization to combat the persuasive efforts of Chinese Communist insurgents, who were gaining considerable support in outlying towns and villages. Again he was successful, raising civilian morale and encouraging guerrillas to surrender. Similarly, when he took over the BBC his first task was to restore the spirits of the program-makers, by freeing them to "trust their own judgment on what should be shown, only referring serious doubts upwards."

In those days it was revolutionary actually to trust producers to know what they were doing as responsible members of society. Greene's inspiration spread through all departments. Icy, upper-class female announcers disappeared. *Tonight*, under Donald Baverstock and Alasdair Milne, became a lively opening to the evening's viewing. David Attenborough's *Zoo Quest* presented an intimate look at wildlife in remote parts of the world as never before. *Monitor*, guided by Huw Wheldon, ranged over popular art, from Turner to Andy Warhol, and gave chances to directors like John Schlesinger and Ken Russell. My other old 1952 classmate Michael Peacock took over the nightly news, turning it from a pallid, cinema-type newsreel into an informed source of real information, allowing personable news-readers to present well-considered judgment on the events of the day. Peter Watkins delivered a powerful re-creation of the 1746 Battle of Culloden, the final humiliating defeat of the Highland Scots by the Hanoverian king of England, showing the murderous cost of pitting emotional nationalism against superior military force. Drama series of quality appeared, like Andrew Osborn's creation of Simenon's *Maigret*, with tough portrayals of Parisian taxi drivers, whores, and pimps, plus *Z-Cars*, by John McGrath, Troy Kennedy Martin, and Allan Prior, a hard slice of Liverpool action, showing that the soft soap if ITV's *No Hiding Place* was doomed. In comedy, where cash-rich ITV could outbid it for any star comedian, the BBC commissioned unknown writers to write situation comedies for good actors, evolving successes like *Steptoe and Son*, with Harry H. Corbett and Wilfrid Brambell as a couple of argumentative junkmen, *Till Death Do Us Part*, with Warren Mitchell as a loud-mouthed Cockney bigot, and *Dad's Army*, an affectionate sendup of the wartime home guard.

Hugh Greene's influence also produced a late Saturday night show unlike anything that had been seen before, Ned Sherrin's *That Was the Week That Was*, an irreverent look at the preceding seven days in songs and sketches, pricking the balloon of political pomposity, satirizing hitherto taboo subjects—royalty, religion, sex, racism, and extreme patriotism—with speed and wit, turning the unknown David Frost into a household name and provoking an outcry from cabinet ministers, churchmen, pompous news editors, and the ITV companies that envied its rapid ascent to 10 million viewers.

By their originality these programs were slowly recovering an audience from an ITV already becoming tired and repetitive. In addition, the BBC's second channel was in active preparation under Michael Peacock, fresh from his success with the news. His idea was to give each night a special theme. Sundays would be for major plays; Mondays, variety and music; Tuesdays, adult education; Wednesdays, repeats of earlier successes; Thursdays, hobbies and minority interests; Fridays, drama series; and Saturdays, classic serials.

The BBC2's launch was also planned to promote the replacement of old 405-line pictures with higher-definition 625-lines (requiring viewers to buy new sets), which would in the future become the sole transmission system of both BBC1 and ITV, starting first in London and rapidly spreading north and west. But the first night, April 24, 1964, became a total disaster when a massive power cut blacked out half the capital. However, Peacock thus managed to generate a great deal of extra publicity, and the opening the following evening proceeded without a hitch.

Unfortunately his "different theme every day" didn't attract much of an audience. Manufacturers complained bitterly that the highbrow tone wasn't selling new 625-line sets. After just a few weeks, Michael was shifted sideways to become controller of BBC1 and my other classmate David Attenborough took over BBC2. Together they evolved a contrapuntal scheduling system that put a popular American Western on BBC2 against *Panorama* on BBC1 and ensured that through the evening BBC as a whole offered an entertaining choice that challenged the attractions of ITV.

My own interest had been kindled by the appointment of Sydney Newman, who had made ABC's *Armchair Theatre* compulsive viewing for over five years, as BBC's head of drama, promising a *Play of the Week* of equal power. Newman understood that television was for a huge audience, most of whom would never set foot in a theater "even if you gave them free beer." He demanded writers and directors who could grab viewers' interest right from the first minute, with plays of contemporary truth in a rapidly changing society.

I didn't know Newman, but my friend John Elliot had been promoted from producer to executive for the Saturday night play. John had briefly been my assistant when I was a film editor, but he had prospered in the BBC, having written and produced the award-winning *War in the Air* series, and directed three of his own original television plays. He immediately offered me a December production but had very few scripts ready: a routine piece about a harassed suburban housewife, and a scrappy musical comedy that needed work on the script, about a zany young man in love with a television star.

I took up the challenge of the second, signed Leonard Rossiter to play a manic game-show presenter, along with Sally Smith and Tony Tanner. *It's All Lovely*, by production assistant David Proudfoot, gave us a surprise hit for Christmas 1963.

Working at the BBC in the 1960s was quite different from the Lime Grove make-do-and-mend setup I had left eight years before. Production had moved into the new Television Centre at White City, with eight well-equipped studios extending like the spokes of a wheel around the hub of a circular office block, and superbly trained crews ready to respond to any director's creative ideas.

At the beginning of 1964, James McTaggart, one of Sydney Newman's new producers, asked me to direct Ted Willis's saga *The Four Seasons of Rosie Carr*. As this wasn't planned until April, I spent a few more weeks at Pinewood trying to make something of the *Innocent Gunman* script, until finally Peter Sellers said "No."

I had never been to the United States. Now I had time. My flight to New York was delayed and diverted to Gander, Newfoundland. Director Otto Preminger was among the waiting passengers. I introduced myself, and he offered me several very useful introductions in Hollywood.

In the austere years in Britain just after the war, America had appeared to us as a land of abundance, of huge cars, rolling wheatfields, luscious fruit, sunshine, and vast wealth. My first sight of New York, the broken-down outskirts, garbage-strewn gutters, rusty fire escapes and filthy taxis, was a savage shock. But slowly I began to explore the city and enjoy its sheer vitality and its treasures: the Guggenheim, the Frick, the Whitney, the Museum of Modern Art, the Cloisters, the Metropolitan—even Coney Island. On Broadway I saw James A. Jones in *The Great White Hope*, and Alec Guinness as a most unlikely Dylan Thomas in a play by John Brinnin. I visited Radio City and watched NBC's version of *That Was the Week That Was* from the control room. I met Bob Markell, who was producing *The Defenders* in a surprisingly cramped studio, and pitched a few of my own ideas.

Naively, with three competing American networks and public service television, I had expected a certain interest in the serious dramas we were making in Britain. But after some years of excellent live drama production in New York, the heavy money appeared to have moved to Hollywood into filmed series and television movies.

I was soon welcomed in Beverly Hills. Laurence Harvey, now making *Butterfield 8* with Elizabeth Taylor, had bought a house in Laurel Way with impressive views over Bel Air. Ingo Preminger, producer brother of Otto, opened many more doors for me. Peggy Robertson, Alfred Hitchcock's assistant, whom Mimi and I knew from Elstree, took me to Universal where I met George Santoro. I agreed to direct an episode of *Court Martial*, with Bradford Dillman and Darren McGavin, when it started at Pinewood.

Peter Sellers was also in town, but sadly he was having a pacemaker fitted at the Cedars of Lebanon Hospital, and he hardly recognized me when I called.

I visited MGM, Paramount, Fox, and Desilu. *Secret Agent* (*Danger Man*) was still being shown, and people seemed to know about my other work over the years. My American agent nearly persuaded me to stay in a friendly warm environment and make some money. But I really had no choice. My roots, our house, and growing family were all in England, where the incentive of making drama of real value and relevance still remained. With regret I left the sunshine and comfort of the Beverly Hills Hotel for the gray certainty of Shepherd's Bush, the BBC, and *The Four Seasons of Rosie Carr.*

Ted Willis, one of the innovators of film and television writing, creator of the film *The Blue Lamp* (its television offspring *Dixon of Dock Green*) and many other fine plays, once claimed that the four plays in his *Rosie Carr* were his best ever. Certainly this story of a Cockney woman (based on Ted's own mother) at four stages of her life—from the early twentieth century to the present (1964)— was powerfully written, much stronger than his superficial film script for *Bitter Harvest*. In rehearsal, with a cast including June Barry (as young Rosie), Jane Hylton (Rosie at ages 35, 50, and 75), and James Bolam, we discovered many tender and true moments.

The first episode discovered Rosie as a very new Edwardian barmaid in London's East End befriending an earnest young socialist nearly dying from hunger (James Bolam) but rejecting his marriage proposal in favor of a flashy street trader, Tommo (Kenneth J. Warren, a hefty Australian). With rollicking barrel organ music from Tom Springfield and lively cameo performances, the show began with gusto.

In the second play Tommo has returned from the First World War, wounded and unemployed. Rosie struggles to make ends meet working in a laundry, laughs off the amorous advances of the owner, and saves enough to send her firstborn son, Eddie, to Australia.

In the third, during the prewar Munich crisis, Rosie sees her daughters married off, supports the republican workers in their losing fight against fascism in Spain, and is finally widowed.

In the fourth, set in 1964, she has become an interfering grandmother, meddling in her daughters' marriages and generally making a nuisance of herself, until at last she is packed off to spend her declining years with her son, Eddie, in Australia.

Tom Springfield wrote evocative music for each play, and Evan Hercules designed sets that brilliantly recreated the different periods. The *Times* and the *Telegraph* both praised "excellent performances," and *Variety* added that it was "directed by Peter Graham Scott with style and panache." The series built a huge Saturday night following and was repeated on BBC2 a few months later.

Offers were now pouring in. In three weeks, without a break, I was in the ATV studios recording *Memory of October*, an ingenious black comedy by Leon Griffiths about two eccentric Hungarian refugees incompetently planning the murder of a minister visiting Britain from their old country. With Warren Mitchell and Kenneth Griffith as the plotters and Alfred Lynch as a hopeless assassin, it promised to be interesting.

Warren, now a household name as Alf Garnett in *Till Death Us Do Part*, was going through a "method-acting" phase, and he asked me how he was supposed to find a Hungarian accent. Solemnly the next day I presented him with a complete Linguaphone course in Hungarian, and as far as I know he worked at it doggedly to find his curious accent. I also employed a stray Hungarian as a coach, whose favorite phrase sounded something like "gudonyaspor!" Finally curious, I asked him what this Hungarian word meant in English. He astonished us all by explaining he'd picked it up in Australia—*"Good on you sport!"*

Unlike the word-perfect Warren, Ken Griffith arrived at rehearsal not knowing a line, prepared to learn it on the hoof. This offended perfectionist Warren. I realized that the friction between them helped the play and did nothing to calm Warren down. Unfortunately, on our last day Warren took us all for lunch at his favorite Indian restaurant and insisted on ordering for us all. Naturally Kenneth wanted something quite different. The row that erupted between them made any question of an afternoon run-through unthinkable. Dislike had turned to positive hatred.

By the time we recorded, tempers had cooled, but there was still enough raw aggression between them to give both performances an angry edge. Perhaps this was the reason *Memory of October* won Leon Griffiths the Writers' Guild "Best Original Play Award" for 1964.

I was now asked by ABC to direct two episodes of a new series,

Redcap, about a military policeman, starring John Thaw, already amazingly mature at 22. Both scripts were excellent. The first, by playwright Richard Harris, set in Aden, provided good opportunities for Leonard Rossiter as a psychopathic sergeant and Ian McShane as a cynical recruit. The second, by Troy Kennedy Martin, set in Cyprus, was an interesting early example of Troy's tense but gripping style.

No sooner were these finished than Julian Wintle called me to say that he was about to start producing an enhanced series of *The Avengers* on film. Developed from a modest *Police Surgeon*, it was already a successful taped crime-busting fantasy for ABC, with a suave, well-tailored Patrick Macnee and Honor Blackman in black leather, flooring their assailants with brisk judo.

Howard Thomas grasped the opportunity of matching Lew Grade's international triumphs by raising the budget for filming, with Patrick unchanged but adding a new blonde grappling partner. I started shooting the first episode in Hunstanton, Norfolk, a mystery set in a remote village whose inhabitants are terrorized by paramilitary forces emerging from tunnels under an unused airfield. After a few days it was obvious that the blonde was taking herself and the piece far too seriously, discovering "synergy with Ingmar Bergman's *Seventh Seal* within the basic concept" instead of vigorously exploiting the script's real wit and originality. Back in the studio Patrick Macnee became more and more reserved, getting no reaction to his genuinely funny jokes. We finished on schedule feeling very subdued.

Wolf Rilla commenced shooting episode two, while Howard, Julian, and I viewed the first rough-cut of episode one. As the lights came up at the end no one spoke. At last Howard broke the silence. Production would stop. The girl was wrong and would be replaced.

For the next few days we combed the agents' files looking for new contenders. Emma Peel had to be every man's (and every woman's) ideal: sexually irresistible, witty, modern, and independent, able to defend herself or—with the right man—to enjoy mutual conquest. After a week we had 24 possibles.

From Monday morning I filmed tests of four women per day in three typical scenes, with Patrick gamely speaking the same lines and making the same moves with as much charm from first to last.

Every day Howard, Julian, and I would review the previous day's hopefuls in increasing gloom. Perhaps the girl we needed didn't exist.

I knew one of two of the actresses from earlier shows. One was a girl I'd met resting under a piano at a Christmas party. Tired of lining up the same old moving shots, I decided to shoot her test all in one big close-up, with Patrick speaking the lines offscreen. The girl responded well, but I was afraid I'd spoiled her chance. I caught her leaving the studio and apologized.

"Don't worry," she smiled. "You must be out of your skull with it all. I'm not that keen anyway." But Howard and Julian saw something different about her, and thus Diana Rigg was cast as Emma Peel, and *The Avengers* became a long-running hit all over the world.

As winter turned to New Year's, 1965, I directed three episodes of the early series: *Murder Market*, Diana Rigg's first appearance, with Patrick Cargill and John Woodvine, about a bogus marriage bureau in a real business of contract murder; *Master Minds*, with Macnee and Emma Peel joining a course for superintellectuals being secretly hypnotized to act as urban terrorists; and *A Sense of History*, with Patrick Mower, Robin Phillips, and Jacqueline Pearce as undergraduates caught up in a strange blood-cult determined to wipe out dull students.

Julian wanted more, but I had set up *The Campaign* with the BBC, a novel by Gillian Freeman I had found about a young, high-pressure salesman descending on a small country town as a fund-raiser for the local church, and his devastating effect on the kind and sincere vicar, his daughter, his wife, and the local parishioners. I enjoyed its powerful clash of spiritual belief and commercial greed, and persuaded Gillian to adapt it herself.

Back at the now familiar Television Centre with a script full of substance, I cast David Buck as the young salesman, Philip Latham as the vicar, Isobel Black as his daughter, and, as an elderly parishioner, veteran Dame Fay Compton, whom I hadn't seen since I was a boy actor in *The Winter's Tale* at the Open Air Theatre 28 years before. The play was as satisfying as anything I'd ever done, making its spiritual point far more economically than I had in *The Breath of Fools* eight years before. I also met, as my studio manager, an amusing young man called Tim Vignoles, who was to become an important part of our future. It was Tim who persuaded his friend Dudley Moore to bring an electric organ and his trio to dub a wonderfully effective score for me.

But in that spring of 1965 I was beginning to take stock. I was now past 40, with a delightful wife and growing family, a house we'd designed ourselves, doing a job I loved in a growing industry. In the last year I'd had a popular success with *Rosie Carr*, won an award with Leon Griffiths, started a major international series, and directed a play of my choice. And yet I wasn't satisfied.

I'd had the best years of live television drama. Now, with tape recording, the old gut-wrenching but tremendously exciting challenge of delivering 90 minutes of complicated and polished studio production was over—and would never return. Popular television now demanded series, not single plays, and fine writers like Troy Kennedy Martin and John Hopkins were regularly producing good work there.

What, then, was I looking for now?" The ambition that had driven me into television, the urge to communicate, to present in visuals and words my individual expression of life as it is—or as it might be—was not being fully satisfied.

Some of the work I had done had been worthwhile, some gimmicky and cheap. I needed some vehicle, a contemporary theme that would present me with more of a challenge than the material currently available.

Which, by coincidence, was exactly what I was about to find.

6

1965–1968:
Oil on Dramatic Waters

Mogul, The Troubleshooters, *and a*
trip to Scotland for BBC2.

With the end of the Second World War and the creation of a welfare state, offering basic provision for the sick, elderly, and unemployed, Britain's rigid class system of inherited privilege for the few began to crumble. Working-class young men and women, educated beyond their parents' imagination, started to mirror contemporary life in fiction and other media.

Conscription, two years of enforced military service for all fit males of 18, ended at last in 1962. During the so-called peace, virtual schoolboys had been exposed to harsh discipline and bloody warfare in Korea, Malaysia, Cyprus, and Suez, but had found comradeship despite the foul language, and with the shock of military incompetence discovered that their brains were better than those of their traditional masters.

It was now fashionable to be cynical about our rulers. But the absurd popular entertainment of the Profumo spy scandal (when a British defense minister lied in the House of Commons, denying his affair with a call girl known to the Soviet naval attaché) probably had less impact than John Osborne's plays *Look Back in Anger* and *The Entertainer*, which showed the vanishing British Empire to be as irrelevant to modern times as a tired old music hall comic. Freedom of thought and sexual behavior was now accepted, along with new design, new satire, and a whole disposable culture. This heightened awareness of unfulfilled possibilities made me search for something better in television.

In the spring of 1965, John Elliot and his wife, Elizabeth, came to dinner. It was a quiet but pleasant evening with old friends—until John began to unfold the gloomy story of his past year. I hadn't realized, despite his three plays, that he wanted more than anything to concentrate on becoming a serious writer, but shortly after our collaboration at Christmas 1963 he had taken the plunge, resigned from the security of the BBC after 15 years, and launched himself into the cold world as a freelance author.

Above all he had one obsession: to create a television drama series about big business. The ATV already had *The Power Game*, well scripted but completely studio bound, but John had a wider concept of a world enterprise involved in the production and marketing of that essential aid to modern living: oil.

At that time neither oil nor gas had been discovered in Britain's North Sea. Like most of Europe, we relied on supplies from Nigeria and the Middle East. John had made good progress with British Petroleum and Shell for filming their worldwide operations and using their own considerable library footage. But it was the great variety of characters he wanted to explore. In his own words:

> My new series will combine, in a single flourish, oil-based adventure with the intrigues of the Executive Suite.
>
> Oilmen have formed themselves into the most romantic community of our time. They take coffee with sheiks, and pump ten thousand gallons into an aircraft as casually as you put five into your car. They are explorers, tearing about noisily in huge vehicles, and silent office-workers, rapt before their ledgers. Some die in swamps of mysterious diseases, some are scientists, some politicians, some engineers and some are very rich. They are all members of a fascinating kingdom within our society.
>
> Oilmen spend their lives in attendance on an invisible spirit. A few actually *see* it, perhaps slopped over the back bumper of a customer's car, or in a sudden terrible blaze bursting from a bore-hole. Much of the time oil moves in its mysterious way through miles of

underground pipeline and in the bellies of monstrous floating tankers that convey it to its final destiny, the moment of explosion to create power and heat and speed in most of our machinery, giving reason and wealth to the vast industry of oil—which must be seen as one of the most romantic and exciting regions of dramatic entertainment ever explored.

It's high-octane, top-grade up-to-the-minute television magic, and it's available here and now, ready to go....

But the trouble was that the BBC, which had let him leave with a commission for the first script and a vaguer promise for a series of 13, was *not* ready. He had toured oil installations in Germany, Syria, Nigeria, and Libya and come back fired with inspiration for four scripts and ideas for many more. But the BBC head of drama series, an ex-writer himself of dour aspect, was not enthusiastic. "We have to wait," he said. After months of frustration, in which John had had to eke out a living writing hack documentaries, a new head of series was fortunately appointed. Andrew Osborn was an extroverted ex-actor who had developed as a superb television producer. He immediately saw the potential and pushed John's series into the schedules for transmission in the summer of 1965.

But there were further holdups. A producer and story editor were assigned, but they disliked John's elegant realism and wanted more muck and guts. John's title, *Mogul*, was arbitrarily changed to the weaker *Delta*, "to avoid confusion with an existing oil company." After unhappy weeks of argument, the producer and his editor left for another company. Another producer appeared, waxed enthusiastic, and then suddenly vanished to a better job in Australia. After 15 hungry months, poor John was high and dry once more, with the BBC nervously considering cancellation.

"Why not produce it yourself?" Mimi asked. John shook his head. That would mean admitting the failure of his bid to become a full-time writer. I read the enticing words in John's format. Dazzling images raced through my mind—the dancing flare at the top of a drilling rig, racing cars at Le Mans, massive tankers battling through storms, sleek aircraft, speedboats—plus the amazing clash of characters, smooth businessmen and oil-stained roustabouts, slick salesmen and cautious scientists—here was a sudden chance to make a brilliant television series unlike any other yet made.

John caught my eye. "I suppose—*you* couldn't … ?

I smiled. I *could*. A couple of directing commitments might easily be postponed. The following morning John took me to the Television Centre to meet Andrew Osborn, already dictating a letter finally killing the project.

I pleaded and promised. Andrew, always an enthusiast, relented. Within a few days I was in a producer's office at White City with new story editor Tony Read suggesting ideas for the five or more scripts out of 13 that John would have no chance of writing. There was no time to lose. Recording was to start in June, less than three months ahead. We had to find a cast and four lively directors, design sets, and pre-film in Malta, in Libya, and on a North Sea oil rig.

First we had to change the title back again. *Delta* was pussyfoot. It had to be *Mogul*, powerful and impressive. (John was delighted.) Above all I had to find a new style. It was no use my dreaming of a series with more impact than ever before if I couldn't see it in my own mind.

The show had to move fast. Oil was about movement, pressure, speed. Scenes would have to start in the middle where the meat was without actors drifting through doors, and cut straight to the next on the last word of the climax. I needed dynamic camera angles. Television cameramen were getting awfully lazy, offering up loose head-and-shoulder shots (easier to hold in focus) when asked for tight close-ups. On *Mogul* we would insist on tight shots and more camera movement.

I designed a crude logo—a mountainous, slab-shaped *M* with the word *Mogul* underneath—to be used everywhere, in studio sets, on the front of every script, in the *Radio Times* billing, and made up in various sizes printed on adhesive plastic to be stuck over genuine oil company logos on petrol tankers, pumps, and oilmen's helmets anywhere we filmed. (Soon *Mogul* stickers became a badge of pride on our crews' car windshields.)

Using Tom Springfield's specially composed jazz saxophone theme and some of the most spectacular of the oil companies' shots— a sudden gush of oil from the earth, a spurt of flame, fast-moving boats, cars, and planes intercut with the ubiquitous *Mogul* sign—I created a rapid opening title sequence like a 30-second ITV commercial.

John wanted to start the series with his original script about an attempted takeover in Germany, which explained the company setup. But oilmen were already drilling in the North Sea, and although no oil or gas had yet been found, there was bound to be a strike soon. Our first director, Michael Hayes, and I persuaded John to set his first story around a marine drilling rig, an industrial espionage thriller investigating which one of three Mogul men leaked vital information about the first North Sea discovery, with added action-adventure as the oil rig "blows out" and has to be capped in a fearful storm. The filming of this climax presented a difficulty. Neither British Petroleum (BP) nor Esso would let any film crew aboard their North Sea platforms, and although British Petroleum had a training rig on land at Eakring, Northamptonshire, they refused to cooperate, as, in their opinion, "blow-outs simply don't occur these days."

However, we were able to persuade them in time. Meanwhile, Tony Read had found other writers: Canadian John Lucarotti, who had worked in oil, had a fine grasp of technical matters, and would over the years develop special adventures in rocket research, powerboat races, and even the Arctic wastes, and James Mitchell, whose knowledge of shipyards gave us another running theme on the problems of building oil rigs and tankers. From *Z-Cars* we borrowed Kenneth Ware to write a comedy about an aggressive female publicist, and I brought in *Pot-Carriers'* Mike Watts for a human drama on a long-distance tanker and an amusing piece on *Mogul*'s "Driver of the Year."

Next came casting. We didn't need stars. For our ruthless managing director, Bryan Stead, we all agreed on Geoffrey Keen, a fine character actor usually wasted in every rank from corporal to brigadier in gung-ho British war films. His more compassionate chief accountant, Willy Izard, was a natural for Philip Latham's calm dignity, and for the "troubleshooter," Thornton, ready to quell an industrial dispute, cap a blazing well, or settle a boardroom punch-up, we chose rugged Australian Ray Barrett. Barry Foster and Ronald Hines were also featured in the first series, but with too many regular characters they failed to last.

We should have had a strong female lead, but in those days in the oil business, men were dominant. We gave Thornton a troublesome wife, but she and he were divorced by the end of the second series. It was not until the thirteenth episode in that first year that we created Jane Webb, played by Philippa Gail, an outspoken assistant to Managing Director Stead, to show his human side.

We needed to film a sequence with tankers in a Mediterranean port for Mike Watts's script, and desert scenes for two of John Elliot's episodes, "Young Turk," about competitive dealing with a sheik and the problems of an aging executive, and "Out of Range," where Willy Izard's son, attached to a desert survey party, gets lost.

Tim Vignoles, whom I had procured from the BBC Plays Department (despite bureaucratic resistance) because his father had been a Shell Oil managing director, was rapidly dispatched to Libya to organize a week's filming. He returned within a few days having secured at nominal cost a complete Shell Oil geological team, including three Land Rovers, drivers, and a cook, ready to go.

With cameraman Peter Hamilton, I paused at Malta to shoot the tanker scenes, then flew on to Tripoli. Libya was then still ruled by King Idris, but small American and British air bases remained. We had been warned about Libyan Customs. They duly impounded our camera and sound gear as we arrived, causing the first of many delays.

Our party, Peter and his assistant, two sound men, Tim, director Max Varnel (whose father Marcel had directed Gracie Fields and George Formby in the 1930s), and two actors, Percy Herbert and Terence Edmond, had been booked by Tim into the Del Mahari, a seedy establishment on the Tripoli seafront built as a brothel for Mussolini's officers when Libya was occupied by Italy before the war. The rooms were tiny, but it was cheap and cheerful, much favored by oilmen for the afternoon feast of nightclub dancers rehearsing on the roof. (One of them, Eileen, a delightful 17-year-old, in time became Mrs. Tim Vignoles.)

It took us a day to prise our equipment from Customs, and while Max started shooting in Tripoli streets, Tim went to borrow a practical (and illegal) rifle we needed for a desert shoot-out. I went to recce a "sea of sand" Max had heard of nearby that would save us from traveling at least a couple of hundred miles south to the real Sahara. The suggested location turned out to be a limited and useless patch of featureless dunes, but at least Tim returned with an old Lee-Enfield rifle wrapped in a blanket.

The next morning actor Terence Edmond discovered that his luggage had been shipped off from the hotel lobby with a crowd of departing tourists. We all contributed necessary shirts and underpants to see him through the week and finally set off south, driving up onto a plateau about a hundred miles inland to the town of Garian, where the Italians had tried to build a colonial settlement, now crumbling and vandalized. The one and only hotel boasted no electricity, with buckets of water delivered at dawn in mockery of the ornate brass taps in the cracked basins. A further hundred miles or so south, we were told, parched scrubland would turn into real desert.

We left our bags and drove on. Sure enough, after the oasis of Misda, the true desert, vast and pitiless, stretched before us. We shot until dusk's sudden appearance and returned to the discomfort of Garian. Dinner that night, and every night, was a peppery couscous ("Rice pudden and bird droppings," as Max called it), before ascending to iron bedsteads and the all-night braying of donkeys, wildly barking dogs, and doleful Arabic arias.

The muezzin's call to prayer roused us at five, and we were off down the rutted track to the desert once more. Lunch packed by the hotel was a slab of dry bread and greasy goat cheese, a few dates, and grimy bottles of local cola, brought to near boiling by the hundred-degree heat. Bon vivant Tim had a word with our Shell cook. The following day, very early, he bought a young live sheep in Garian market, which traveled fearfully to the location in the back of a Land Rover, was slaughtered and skinned without ceremony in the desert, and transformed by the cook into a delicious soup and roast lamb barbecued on the truck's radiator grill laid over hot embers in the sand. For the first time we enjoyed chops branded "Land Rover" in reverse, both sides.

The discomfort of the heat and flies made for speed in shooting. No one wanted to linger. We completed nine script pages for the two episodes in three days, sped back to Tripoli, rescued Terence's lost luggage, and were able to put down for a night in Rome.

Peter Sellers, now more or less recovered, was filming at

Cinecitta, and invited Max and me to dinner with his new wife, Britt Ekland. For no good reason we were joined by a morose Italian astrologist who persisted in forecasting a sad future for the happy couple.

Back in London at the end of May, I had to spend two weeks away from *Mogul*, at Pinewood, fulfilling the commitment made to George Santoro at Universal in California the year before, to direct an episode of *Court Martial*. The script was efficient, undemanding, and bloodless, typical of the Hollywood television I didn't want to spend my life on. There was plenty to organize at White City when I surfaced. In two weeks we were to start recording a 50-minute episode every week for three months, not at the Television Centre but at the less well-equipped Riverside Studios, notorious for its bad sound-proofing and a leaking roof.

John had delivered the second draft of his North Sea opener, "Kelly's Eye." Michael Hayes and cameraman Tony Imi had returned from Eakring with a superbly staged oil rig blowout, courtesy of the combined hoses and manpower of three local fire brigades. Director Bill Slater was casting the second story, "Young Turk," designed to establish Barry Foster as a young working-class negotiator in the Middle East upsetting not only the local old Mogul manager but also the sheik he had been sent to placate. David Proudfoot had already signed Judi Dench and Edward Woodward for the third, "Safety Man," exploring the domestic havoc of a deserted husband and safety officer at a huge oil refinery, who crazily threatens to blow up the whole plant on the day of a royal visit unless his wife can be contacted and made to return. And Max Varnel was filling the smaller parts for his episode, "Out of Range."

A few days later Michael's principal actors assembled in the usual dank and gloomy army drill hall for the read-through before rehearsals began on episode one. They were formally introduced, eyeing each other like new boys at school. I welcomed everybody and explained I wanted a fast, punchy show that would startle somnolent viewers into really watching what was happening on the screen—a producer's pep talk followed by total silence.

Then they began to read. Most actors mutter their lines at a first reading, but Geoffrey and Philip were almost inaudible. The smaller parts were gabbled through by Michael and a female assistant.

Scenes I had high hopes for sounded flat and trite, but I knew it would all come to life in rehearsal.

But John was more pessimistic. As the actors departed for lunch, he insisted on going through every line of the script, suggesting cuts, and it was only with great difficulty that Tony and I prevented him from massacring his brainchild before it had drawn breath. Then, after four days' hard work, Michael had his last run-through for us in the bleak drill hall. I could see that Ray Barrett had already created a strong troubleshooting character in Thornton, but I still felt Geoffrey and Philip were saving energy in their scenes together. I muttered the usual encouragement to all the actors, privately told Michael of my worries, and left the hall feeling rather discouraged. After all my grandiose pronouncements on our being "dynamic" and "refreshing," the show as a whole still lacked passion.

The next day we moved into Riverside "Studios," a depressing gray warehouse on the sludge-filled banks of the Thames at Hammersmith. The sets were late arriving, and were only half erected by the time Michael had to start plotting cameras at 2:00 P.M. Derek Dodd, the designer, was still chasing up missing props as, to the crash of loud hammering, Michael tried to achieve his first shots. Bewildered actors forgot lines and had to be coaxed back into correct positions. But as soon as I saw the first graded pictures, I realized that lighting director Nigel Wright was making it all look too soft and pretty. I drew him aside and explained I wanted hard, sharp black-and-white images, like the best fine-grain film. Nigel sighed, tore up his notes, and started to give *Mogul* the tougher look it demanded. Michael was now contriving some excellent shots. My spirits started to rise again, even though by the scheduled break at 10:00 P.M. he hadn't reached the end of the script.

He quickly caught up the following morning and staged a "stagger-through" after lunch. I was now worried about the soft quality of the telecine sequences. The technical manager blamed the outdated Riverside telecine machines. The operators tried again, but I was suddenly aware that we were only making a summer replacement for *Z-Cars*.

After a short tea break, Michael began his final dress rehearsal, our last chance to see the whole show before recording. We had only

90 minutes to record a 50-minute episode, so there would be precious little time for retakes. At the end of what seemed an incredibly dreary performance, John and I grabbed Michael for notes for the cast.

At eight o'clock, after half an hour's "lineup," when cameras were finally matched, I slipped into Michael's seat to record the standard opening, superimposing titles precisely on the right shots of the fast-cut film. Because it established the style, I had to do it myself, but sitting in the familiar chair released much of my first-night tension. Then Michael took over, running his first film sequence: the oil rig, dim and mysterious, far out at sea, a drunken figure falling out of a taxi to scramble for the departing rig-ferry, and in daylight Thornton's car arriving at the shabby port office. "Cue him," Michael directed. Then the vision mixer punched up camera one. Ray Barrett as Thornton, sent from the head office to investigate the serious leak of information about the first gas discovery, entered the studio office. The show rolled on, faster and better than in any rehearsal. In short, sharp scenes, the suspicion, the conflicts, the laughter, and the bitterness, revealed the industrial spy as Thornton's old tool-pusher friend—and then the oil rig blew out on film.

Thornton's old mate reacted like a hero, scalding his hands on burning valves to shut off the gush of oil, saving the rig. Thornton duly made a full report to Managing Director Stead, but was brutally told that whatever his personal feelings, his old friend must still be fired for disloyalty.

Suddenly it was over as Tom Springfield's epic theme hammered through the end titles, and we were all into the pub, not sure of what we'd made. It had seemed realistic, fast moving, and entertaining, but we'd have to wait three weeks for transmission and the verdict of our uncommitted audience.

Early the next morning, and for the next 12 Fridays, it was back to the drill hall for the read-through of episode two, "Young Turk." Bill Slater was an entirely different director from Michael Hayes, smooth and diplomatic where Michael was touchy and instinctive. The new members of his cast were excellent, and it seemed to read well. Encouraged, I returned to the Television Centre to check the edited film on Max Varnel's "Out of Range," and to help David

Proudfoot prepare episode four. I'd taken a gamble on David. He had never directed anything to date, but he'd written my Christmas effort two years before and had assembled a splendid cast in addition to Edward Woodward as the neurotic safety officer and Judi Dench as a sympathetic secretary. He had already seen "Kelly's Eye" and understood what I meant by "style."

Our tight schedule meant rehearsing on Saturday as well as Monday and Tuesday before going to the studio on Wednesday and Thursday. Often Ray Barrett had to be detached for filming on Monday (and sometimes even on Tuesday too) while the others carried on without him. So while episode two was in rehearsal, David filmed Ray in the climax of four at the BP refinery in the Isle of Grain, Kent.

Bill moved into Riverside for camera rehearsal at midday on Wednesday. I was busy with Tony Read on scripts five, six, seven, and eight when abruptly summoned to the studios by an irate John Elliot. I quickly saw why. The *Mogul* style had been completely lost. John's harsh, vibrant script was being played like gentle drawing-room comedy against a Somerset Maugham set of potted palms, Edwardian bric-a-brac, and a whirling punkah fan, whereas a modern oil company manager's house would be contemporary and functional.

Bill Slater and his designer listened patiently while John spluttered his complaints. They agreed that the basic flats forming the set could be hurriedly repainted, the museum piece props swept away, modern furniture drawn from BBC stores, and the manager's wife's costumes transformed from E. M. Forster to Mary Quant. Despite all this, the play was at last recorded the following day without a hitch, and was extremely moving when the old manager at last accepted that his gentle, prewar diplomacy had no place in *Mogul*'s aggressive oil world.

"Out of Range" followed swiftly. The Libyan open vistas gave us an added dimension, but Max Varnel's studio work was competent rather than adventurous. However, Philip Latham, as the bereaved accountant Izard, who lost his son in a needless accident, was subtle and moving, restoring all my faith in him.

In rehearsal "Safety Man" promised to be the best so far, and David lived up to all my expectations, handling the tender and delicate scenes between Judi and Edward with masterly skill on the final recording. Morale was riding high. The night before, Wednesday, July 7, 1965, "Kelly's Eye" had been transmitted, well over 18 months since John Elliot had set off round the world in search of a series.

The critics were gratifying. Under the headline THE MOGUL SIGN MEANS HAPPY VIEWING, Kenneth Eastaugh of the *Daily Mirror* wrote, "A new series about oilmen gushed on to BBC1 last night. Bubbling with getaway people and blaring music, scenery streaked with speed as determined young men walked along glistening corridors of power. Thornton, played by Ray Barrett, an operations manager marked for the boardroom, is a virile tough man's man who has fought his way up from Alaska to Arabia—a winning role."

Julian Holland in the *Mail* called it "the spickest spannest glossiest, sheeniest series TV has ever known." The *Sketch* raved, OFF TO A RATTLING GOOD START: "Scenes replaced each other with the speed of tracer bullets. It looked expensive, directed and produced with real flair."

Only Marsland Gander in the *Telegraph* grumbled. TALK BLURS NORTH SEA OIL STORY: "After watching this first effort I felt only moderately enthusiastic despite the vast effort involved." (He changed his mind later and became a valuable supporter.)

The oil companies expressed cautious approval. But the audience was disappointingly low—about 2 million less than the well-established *Z-Cars* regularly achieved in the same slot. It didn't build much more either, as we painstakingly rewrote, cast, designed, rehearsed, and recorded a new episode every week. As we'd hoped, "Safety Man" was well received ("Strike a Light, This Was Powerful Stuff!" commented Michael Wale in the *Sun*), and Mike Watts's two episodes, "Tosh and Nora" and "Driver of the Year," were original and well directed. Michael Hayes and John Elliot collaborated on the only script I really disliked, "Meet Miss Mogul," a flippant beauty contest trifle featuring Suzy Kendall as a petrol pump girl on the make. David Hemmings played a sharp fashion photographer, and was spotted by Italian director Antonioni to star in his film *Blow-Up*, but the series was not enhanced.

Bill Slater brought out the full drama of racial conflict and intermarriage in the West African "Wildcat," but then left to take leave. With the departure of Max Varnel as well, I was able to bring in two survivors from Rediffusion, John Frankau and Roger Jenkins. Frankau directed "The Schloss Belt," John Elliot's determined rewrite of his once-rejected first Germany story, which at least gave us a quick trip to Hamburg. Roger shot James Mitchell's "A Job for Willy," about a shipyard foreman who pushes his own son too far on a *Mogul* tanker contract. Both episodes produced increased audiences, followed by "Stoneface," our first from John Lucarotti, featuring the problems of an overstressed native Canadian-Indian drilling supervisor in the Arctic, with some of the most beautiful film (courtesy of BP) we had seen so far, and Ken Ware's "The Way It Crumbles," a PR/motor racing squabble well directed by Shaun Sutton.

The run was almost over. John Elliot and I had argued the merits of each story in what had hurriedly developed into a very variable series. We agreed the final episode should bring our three protagonists, Thornton, Stead, and Izard, together and mainly explore Stead's character, showing him as not just a powerful, profit-hungry *Mogul* apparatchik, but as an unfit and lonely middle-aged widower whose professional life was his only interest.

At last, rather late, John created "Borrowed Time," in which Stead collapses while inspecting a pipeline in the Middle East, and temporary secretary Jane Webb, unglamorous but sympathetic, is sent out to look after him. Together they start a slow journey home and in Jane's company Stead's impatience and preoccupation with power slowly drain away. Their innocent relationship becomes warm and affectionate. Back in London, Stead has a boardroom showdown with Lister, a fellow director determined to oust him and take his job. Stead discovers that Lister and Jane once had an affair. He moved smartly back into action and skillfully outwits the usurper, and *Mogul* claims his affection once more.

It was the quietest and least spectacular script we had had. There were no blowouts, fast cars, or blazing oil rigs. The emphasis was on the interplay of skillfully observed characters. John Frankau had already proved to be our most subtle director. He took the script and in John's words "turned base metal into gold." As Stead, Geoffrey Keen, who had done little but thump a desk in the series so far, gave us his performance of the year against the waspish Douglas Wilmer as Lister, and we saw an unexpectedly effective and emotional debut by Philippa Gail as Jane Webb.

When this episode ended the series in September, our audience, though better, was still well short of *Z-Cars*'s best. However, *Mogul* had made an impact. Purser in the Sunday *Telegraph*, Wiggin in the Sunday *Times*, and Richardson in the *Observer* all applauded our efforts. The sheer size and vitality of the subjects, with locations stretching from Alaska to Africa, had impressed many viewers. Our final "Appreciation Index" from BBC Research was a much-better-than-average 81, and the report ended with the simple quote "More please."

But there were no encouraging words from above at Television Centre. Indeed, Controller Michael Peacock (who often flavored his comments with ill-chosen slang) was heard to refer to *Mogul* as "a summer dog." Perhaps all the *Mogul* signs and the big *M* stickers we had plastered over so many petrol pumps and oil installations were doomed to molder away in the prop store.

In any case Andrew Osborn had other plans. He offered me a three-year contract, and though I hadn't been thinking of a long stay at the BBC he also offered another enticing project. British education was undergoing a dramatic change. Whereas up to then, at age 11 children were separated by ability into attendance at grammar schools or other less demanding establishments. Now every child would go to a "comprehensive school" catering for all levels of scholarship.

Sinclair Aitken, education officer at BBC Glasgow, and a story editor, George Byatt, had fired Andrew with the idea of a series based on the troubles and triumphs of a typical comprehensive in a Scottish "new town." I immediately saw that the plots could be real and raw—of family hatred, child abuse, unemployment, and sexual frustration, all the conflicts and rough humor of a cold and deprived society, at that time practically ignored by the mandarins of Whitehall.

I flew up to Glasgow and liked Sinclair and George, but BBC Scotland filled me with trepidation. The attitudes and even the equipment seemed years out of date. The only dramas they had so far attempted were slow-paced serials and dull Bridie plays photographed in reverential long-shot. How on earth could they possibly cope with 26 weekly hours with the pace and action I would demand?

Sydney Newman, head of drama, was also up visiting. We were invited to lunch with the controller, BBC Scotland. I had not packed a formal suit, and Sydney was equally casually dressed in a red shirt and brilliant neck scarf. We were ushered into the presence of a gloomy man in a funeral director's outfit of black coat and striped trousers, who positively recoiled at our raffish appearance.

An ancient waitress in cap and apron hovered like a ghost from the 1920s. Sydney and I had discovered the nectar of the country the night before and waited to be offered some more rare malt whiskey. Our host slowly unlocked a cupboard. "I think this is a special occasion," he murmured as he unfestively produced a small bottle of grocer's shop cider.

Conversation as we munched our lukewarm shepherd's pie and turnips was difficult, but there was one issue I wanted to raise. I wasn't satisfied with the lunch arrangements for my leading actors in the studio on recording days. The only canteen I'd seen always had a long waiting line of chattering clerks and typists. I suggested we might have a separate table with waitress service for my principals, to ease the strain of their 12-hour day. The controller looked shocked. "We don't have any of that elitist nonsense here. Why, we had Dame Peggy Ashcroft in that queue once."

"But she wasn't doing an hour of drama every week."

He looked puzzled. "A whole *hour?*"

"Every week. Like *Mogul*. You've seen that, haven't you?"

He smiled a smile of superior wisdom. "Oh, I'm far too busy to sit and watch *programs*."

But despite him, I found the right person to ask, and when we started recording, my actors had their own small, private dining room with a waitress. I had also found a great deal of unfulfilled talent in Glasgow—actors bored with underuse, writers dying to write, cameramen, editors, set designers, makeup and costume supervisors—all looking for a better chance.

On our bumpy flight home I told Sydney of my hopes for the show. (I was, alas, not feeling my best after a typical Glasgow celebration the night before.) Sydney slapped me on the knee. "You can do it, Pete," he said confidently. "If anyone can, you can." Unfortunately, at that precise moment the plane gave a frightful lurch, and I had to grab for the paper sickbag and lose my breakfast.

"Goddammit!" Sydney roared. "The only time I throw you a compliment you throw up!"

In London (recovered), I persuaded Tony Read to join the project, and we commissioned the first script from playwright David Turner (whose *Semi-Detached*, starring Laurence Olivier, was currently running in London), and others from Scottish writers Tom Wright, Jack Gerson, Bill Craig, Jack Ronder, Ian Kennedy Martin, and from old hands James Mitchell and Ray Jenkins. We found a young Scots story editor, Fiona McConnell, to assist Tony, and returned to Scotland for an extensive tour around comprehensive schools in Glasgow, and Kirkcaldy in Fife. With the aid of Director of Education Dr. Douglas McIntosh, we met a variety of teachers, all of whom had original ideas for stories.

Our series centered around housemaster Ian Craig, happily married with a young son at the school, but we lacked an arresting title. One day I said something to Tony about "this man Craig," and he stopped me. "That's our title," he exclaimed.

This Man Craig it became. While in Scotland I saw as many actors as possible. John Cairney, playing Robbie Burns in a one-man show at the Edinburgh Festival, was a natural for the lead. Ellen McIntosh became his wife, Brian Pettifer his son, the splendid Leonard Maguire the headmaster, and a young Royal Shakespeare actress I saw at Pitlochry, Joan Alcorn, another teacher. For supporting parts we drew on the huge reserve of fine Scottish actors like Andrew Keir, John Grieve, Isla Blair, Alex McCrindle, James Grant, Stuart Mungall, Helena Gloag, and many others.

The initial resentment at the "impossible demands of this Englishman" (even one with an ancient Lowland name) rapidly disappeared, and I received real cooperation everywhere. The main problem, after finding new rehearsal venues, creating film cutting rooms where there were none, and so on, was in finding child actors, as there were no stage schools in all of Scotland. For David Turner's first episode, which I was going to direct, I needed a particularly wide-eyed 12-year-old girl, and I found no one suitable in Glasgow. In the end my search took me northeast to a Saturday morning drama club in Aberdeen to find the ideal—Margaret Greig, who, never having seen a film camera or television studio before, was soon shivering in the wind-lashed shipyards in Govan playing her first scenes like a veteran.

The other parts and the crowded studio classrooms were soon filled with eager volunteers, who were not allowed to forget they were schoolchildren first and television actors second—no truancy was allowed. When, after rehearsing in a freezing mission hall in Renfrew, the production came into the studio, I could feel the mounting enthusiasm, which paid off in a first-class technical performance all around. The story of Rosie, a one-parent child driven to near-suicide by harsh treatment from one particular mistress, rang movingly true, and when shown on BBC2 in January 1966 the series was welcomed as an original event. "This Man Craig's remarkable virtue," wrote Peter Black in the *Mail*, "is the total conviction with which it sets up its situations and characters. It was like watching a living slab of Scotland."

But the treadmill of weekly series offered no rest on laurels. Ian McNaughton, later the brilliant innovator of *Monty Python's Flying Circus*, came up to direct a few episodes, as well as young and untried Moira Armstrong, who already showed the original eye and skill with actors that were to win her awards later. John Frankau and Roger Jenkins also made the journey north. The unknown boys and girls playing leading parts displayed considerable sensitivity on camera, and *This Man Craig* went on to become part of the Scottish cultural scene in that bitterly cold winter.

Tim Vignoles arrived to tell me he was leaving the BBC to sell programs around Europe for Hollywood's MCA. Bubbling with good news, John Elliot announced that Michael Peacock had been won over by people's enthusiasm and had at last slotted a further 26 *Mogul*s for 1966, to begin recording in March. But this meant I would have to leave *Craig* immediately, just as we were getting into our stride.

Andy Osborn found another producer to take over, and *This Man Craig* carried on for 52 episodes over the next two years. The Glasgow team seemed unmoved by my imminent departure, and on a wet Friday night, as soon as Moira had finished recording our fourth episode, I said a few hasty "good lucks" and taxied alone to the airport.

At the booking desk I was asked to wait, and was allowed to walk out to the plane only when all the other passengers had been seated. As I hurried up the aircraft steps, a crowd emerged from the shadows—practically everyone who had worked on *Craig*—singing the old plaintive lament for Bonnie Prince Charlie, "Will Ye No Come Back Again?" at the tops of their voices. It was ridiculous—but oddly moving.

John and Tony were already discussing new script ideas for *Mogul*—26 whole hours to fill seemed an awfully large vacuum. Peacock had insisted, despite John's heated opposition, on a change of title, from *Mogul* to *The Troubleshooters*—and that's how it stayed for the next six years, 172 episodes in all. We knew our characters and had found our form. Now we could build. We created a new executive, Alec Stewart, ruthless and smooth, secretly waiting for Stead's job, and brought in Robert Hardy from the Royal Shakespeare to play him. Deborah Stanford was to play his equally ambitious but more humane wife, Ros. Philippa Gail would stay as Stead's assistant, and Justine Lord would continue for a short time as Thornton's dissatisfied wife. At last our women had some real character.

Our conflicts could now be set anywhere in the world, in Saigon or New York, Cairo or Copenhagen, the clashes and triumphs were directed by Stead from the London office—a unique opportunity for a dramatic reflection of contemporary life in mid–1960s Britain. There was no shortage of writers eager to participate. Besides John Elliot and Tony Read, we retained John Lucarotti for worldwide action, James Mitchell for industrial flare-ups, and Ken Ware for slick forays into the marketing scene.

Ian Kennedy Martin, terse and perceptive, Vincent Tilsley, cynical observer of human folly, and John Gould, informed sophisticate, all came in with good ideas. In David Weir we found someone who could write wittily and with authority about the devious machinations of business and government. To him we owed the best of the new Alec Stewart episodes, particularly when we transferred the ambitious executive to the United States.

There was no question of our slumming in Riverside again. The show was to be recorded from TC3 in the Television Centre—for me always the happiest studio. We had the pick of directors too:

Producer: a BBC image. *The Troubleshooters.*

John Frankau, Roger Jenkins, David Proudfoot, Terence Dudley, and, for the opening story, Moira Armstrong. But I still needed an energetic director for Lucarotti's action-packed scripts.

A young man in his early twenties came to see me one morning carrying a telerecording of a couple of episodes of some soap opera he'd directed in Canada. The lighting was poor, the script worse, the acting abysmal—but there was something arresting about the lively camerawork. Thus James Gatward became our principal action director, and as he gained experience he became more adventurous and technically innovative, frequently upsetting conservative BBC engineers. He was the first director at the corporation to pioneer EDITEK video-editing, and frequently used 16mm film (rather than the usual 35mm) to shoot in tight corners. Twenty-five years later he showed the same enterprise when chief executive of TVS, the major ITV company for southern England, from 1982 to 1991.

While I had been braving the ice and slush of Glasgow, John Elliot had slipped off to sunny Trinidad and had come back with three good scripts set in the Caribbean. The first pushed Thornton into an offshore drilling operation threatened by political corruption, while his wife dallied with a flashy deep-sea diver; the second, an interesting study of the young fiancée of a *Mogul* geologist who loses her memory during the riotous pre–Lenten Carnival in Trinidad; the third, an adventure in exploration in the jungles of Venezuela.

But how could we make them? By dredging up background shots from film libraries? A horrible thought. But if we shot a sequence on a real Trinidad oil rig with everybody wearing *Mogul* helmets, had a double for our heroine running in and out of the actual Carnival, and set other key shots in a tropical location, a special trip could be made worthwhile. John Elliot agreed. In fact he had already contacted Sydney Hill, of the two-man Trinidad National Film Unit.

I tried the idea on Andy Osborn, but he was locked, as usual, in a financial crisis on some other program and gave me a loud "No!" The next day I persisted, setting out all the positive gains to the show, and ground out a grudging agreement. I could go for a maximum of one week, taking a BBC camera and film but no help. The Carnival costume worn by the double would have to be bought in Trinidad and brought home for studio work. It wasn't much, but it was enough.

The 13-hour economy flight finally arrived at Piaco Airport, Port of Spain, Trinidad, in blue, plush warmth. From the darkness a huge man with a great smile grabbed my hand. "I'm Sydney. This is my assistant, Aziz." His diminutive companion, coffee colored beside Sydney's ebony, nodded cheerfully. Rapidly Sydney arranged with customs that we'd pick up all the equipment the following day. To the welcoming peals of steel bands rehearsing for the big event, we drove through the suburbs to the old-fashioned but comfortable Queen's Hotel. Although it was about 4:00 A.M. London time, Sydney briskly got down to business, spelling out the problems. He had never used a 35mm Arriflex camera before but would try. I asked, "Could Aziz load the film magazines?"

Sydney frowned. I hastily agreed that I would learn to carry out this essential task myself. (I had watched assistants do it many times.) I produced my shot list, which had grown with scriptwriters' enthusiasm from a few sequences to over 150 shots.

"All in seven days?" Sydney gasped.

"That's all I'm allowed," I replied.

"*Man!*"

We worked out a plan. On day one we would retrieve the camera from customs and shoot Sydney's old blue Cortina (which could easily be matched in England) bearing a large *Mogul* sign on either side, driving through Port of Spain streets and in other scenic settings around the island. On day two we would drive 50 miles south to the BP Trinmar base at Point Fortin, take the company helicopter out to the rigs, and shoot everything we could find of drilling at sea (with the men wearing *Mogul* helmets). Day three we would finish on the rig and drive back to Port of Spain. Day four I would fly alone (for economy) early to Tobago to film establishing shots and back-projection material at the luxury hotel at Crown Point. On day five (Sunday) we could use members of the local subaqua club as doubles for the various diving sequences. Days six and seven would be Carnival Time. But, Sydney interrupted, I did realize, didn't I, that he would not be available to shoot on the second Carnival Day as he had to act as a judge for the costume prize? I blanched, and said we'd meet that problem when we came to it.

The next morning, once we had regained our camera, I struggled to load the magazines in a stifling bathroom, fingers fumbling unfamiliarly with sharp-edged film shielded from light inside a black cotton changing bag. I then set off with my crew to complete day one, more or less according to plan. Port of Spain was a bustling city of eager, shouting crowds, every face an amazing alternative of African, Spanish, Indian, French, Chinese, or British origin, laughing and arguing as we moved among them recording the lively scene.

As the day grew hotter, we drove on out of town toward the northern mountains and spectacular Maracas Falls, passing through swamp and forest and straggling villages of paint-peeling shacks, suddenly discovering white plantation houses set in green lawns among shady trees. By dusk we had more than enough traveling shots of the blue Ford in many locations, and a whole library of establishing tropical vistas.

With Sydney's firm promise to be at the helicopter pad at Point Fortin by 9:15 the next morning, I picked up a small, beat-up, rented Simca and drove 50 miles south in gathering darkness to the point, where BP had built a magnificent employees' residential compound of family bungalows nestling among palm trees, surrounded by a high wire fence. I drove up the security barrier, and after a certain amount of telephoning was welcomed into the rest house. At 9:00 A.M. sharp the following morning I found the helicopter pad and awaited my team as BP's own passengers climbed aboard. At 9:10 the pilot began to look worried, at 9:15 he started the engines, and at 9:20 he took off, minus one embarrassed BBC producer.

Just after 10:30 the Cortina roared down the dusty road and an unrepentant Sydney rolled out. "Man, what a night!" (Carnival time had begun early.) We managed to call the rig by radio, and the helicopter made an unscheduled flight back and out again to the drilling platform, standing high and ugly on enormous iron legs above the churning sea.

I'd made the first *Mogul* series without setting foot on an oil rig. The reality in size and clanging noise was overpowering. I shouted an explanation of what I hoped to shoot to a dubious manager, deafened by the generator's heavy regular throbbing and the clash of huge metal tubes swinging down to be screwed into the long line of pipe that would soon swiftly rotate the drilling bit at the other end, gouging at the earth's crust hundreds of feet beneath the ocean.

The crew of roustabouts and roughnecks, some American, a few British, but mostly Trinidadian, cheerfully donned *Mogul* helmets from the Shepherd's Bush prop store and carried on with their jobs as Sydney and Aziz clambered about the rig, getting a harvest of superb background shots that were still being used three years later. We lunched royally in the deafening crew dining room, then carried on shooting until the light faded. The next day we borrowed the helicopter and took some of the first-ever aerial shots of marine rigs stretching across the broad ocean like flaring, futuristic scarecrows all the way to Venezuela.

On day four in an ancient Viking I flew the short hop to Tobago, begging permission to shoot "a few scenic shots" at Crown Point. As I puttered around the beachside terrace and pool, shooting backgrounds that would later be back-projected behind our actors in Ealing Studios, the $200-a-day guests must have been unaware of their roles as extras in our first episode.

Thanks to Sydney's persuasive powers, the next day the sub-aqua club turned out in force. I picked doubles for Thornton, his wife, and her diver/lover. They were all slightly surprised when I explained I would have to buy their costumes off their bodies after filming to match the continuity with our London actors, but once that was settled we captured some beautiful images around the coral beach.

The following morning I was awakened well before first light by the insistent, plangent rhythm of hundreds of steel drums. Trinidad was *en fete*, "playing mas" (masquerade). Each village had its own bands, all in competition throughout the year to produce the biggest, most glittering and outrageous costumes for the great procession that tripped and sambaed through the capital all day and all night to arrive at last on the second day before the judges in the stands at Queen's Park Stadium.

Sydney had arranged for us to film one of the best bands in Port of Spain. There was a slight hitch when their leader named his fee, as I was hoping to buy some of their costumes as well. At last, with pauper's eloquence I persuaded him to accept slightly less for the lot, parted with most of my BBC cash-float, and the group was ours, ready to shoot.

Except for one problem. Sydney had just discovered that he had to start judging the Carnival costumes somewhat earlier—in fact immediately. Which left Aziz and me. I had never operated an Arriflex camera or judged the exposure for a movie shot. ("No help" had been Andy's order. How right he was.) At last I had three magazines loaded, lasting about four minutes each.

I guessed the exposure, lined up the scene where our doubled heroine in Carnival costume runs through the traffic in Port of Spain's main street, switched on the camera, and cued her to go. Dodging buses, mopeds, and speeding cars, her huge headdress tottering high above her head, the girl made her perilous way through the throng. We tried a second shot, which was okay, then a third—and the magazine jammed in the camera. Reload and carry on. Again, and again the mag jammed. With my last roll we finished the sequence. As the temperature rose rapidly and I struggled to reload three magazines in the back of the cramped Simca, I began to realize how hard camera assistants have to work. But somehow we completed all I had hoped to film.

The second day of Carnival was even noisier and busier, an open-air steam bath of packed gyrating bodies in extravagant glittering finery, gaudy and loud with bright color. I kept on pointing the camera, filming whatever came by, reloading and shooting again until the sun mercifully settled behind the palms. At the hotel I sank into a bath, hoping our bandleader would remember to collect and deliver the chosen costumes when his exhausted members finally finished dancing.

I sorted the heap of camera gear Aziz had carried in, carefully cleaning each lens and slotting it into its velvet-lined compartment, wiping layers of rich red dust from the camera. Then I set about unloading the magazines for the last time, sealing the undeveloped film in cans. One of the mags was firmly jammed. I went downstairs in search of a screwdriver, but obtaining anything so mundane among the great mass of sweating, delirious humanity singing and swaying through the lobby was impossible. It was already eight o'clock. I'd been invited to dinner at the Queen's Club by the local BP manager and was going to be late.

I made some sense with the hall porter, and he disappeared for a long time, finally emerging with a sort of flattened meat skewer. Better than nothing? I wondered. I went back and tried to force the jammed film from the roller with the nearly useless tool. Then Sydney arrived, brandishing a ten-page form I had to fill in to re-export the camera and film from Trinidad. While I puzzled through lists of equipment and code numbers, he volunteered to collect the costumes.

I had nearly finished the form by 10:00, when Sydney reappeared, crestfallen. The bandleader had changed his mind and wanted his original fee plus more for the costumes. I had no money and no means of getting more that night. At last Sydney offered to negotiate and let me add the extra to his fee which would (eventually) be paid by the BBC from London.

I slowly repacked all the gear and the forms and my own luggage. At 11:00 Sydney triumphantly entered with an armful of soiled and tattered costumes. Boxes were found, and the sad, secondhand finery stowed away. At 11:45 I set out wearily for the Queen's Club, to arrive like Cinderella in reverse as midnight struck and the bars slammed shut for Lent, leaving one would-be reveler parched and frustrated.

Early the next morning my luggage, battered cardboard boxes of costumes, camera cases, tripods, and all filled a second taxi. The plane took off late and made an unscheduled stop at Barbados, which gave me a chance to say hello to Dennis Vance, newly sun-tanned, who had (temporarily) surmounted all his domestic problems and been appointed general manager of Barbados TV. (But alas not for long!) I reached the London Airport at last, snapped up the only available porter, and finally made the Television Centre amid a mountain of rough cargo.

"Enjoy your holiday?" Andrew Osborn greeted me breezily. I smiled weakly. The film was processed, and Moira stitched all the invaluable material into her Ealing-shot scenes so effortlessly that one critic jealously inquired, "Where is the BBC getting all the money for lengthy Caribbean locations with actors and large crews?"

Our second episode, "Birdstrike," by John Lucarotti, examined the problem of sudden power failure in passenger planes caused by flocks of birds being sucked into jet engines during takeoff. John Frankau was in rehearsal with the regulars, plus Adrienne Corri and Peter Copley, when we were abruptly informed by management that our studio was being requisitioned for a pre-election interview with Prime Minister Harold Wilson, and I would have to choose which provincial studio to record in, from Glasgow, Manchester, or Bristol.

I chose Bristol because it was nearer home, and made my first acquaintance with a city I was soon to know well. The BBC studio in Whiteladies Road, though fairly well equipped, was half the size of our regular TC3 at Television Centre. Therefore I had to split the episode in two, shoot on four sets only, and then strike and build the other sets to complete the show two days later. The whole process was costly, confusing to the actors, and time-wasting on our tight weekly turnaround, and I was furious to see later that the Wilson interview was simply a two-handed affair that could have been made in a small hospitality room with black drapes!

However, this was not the reason our opening two or three episodes were not greeted with the unanimous enthusiasm that had encouraged our first series. The trouble was that we were now seen as an established success, to be sneered at rather than cheered.

But the greater public had discovered the show at last, appreciating the fact that we were able dramatically to explore any social or political issue of the day. Our writers were delivering more meaningful scripts. Tilsley planted a terrorist bomb on a *Mogul* tanker, John Elliot examined corruption in war-torn Vietnam, and Ken Ware investigated the cracking-up of the famous son of a legendary racing driver taking on the challenge of the world water speed record, and forced by his sponsors to make his attempt in hazardous wind and weather, leading to tragedy.

Donald Campbell, a recent holder of the world water speed record (and son of one-time world motor speed record-holder Malcolm Campbell), publicly objected to this story and appeared on television to challenge our veracity. Tragically, he died almost one year later in a water speed record attempt, having started out in difficult conditions under similar unreasonable pressure from his backers.

Thus *Mogul* began to gain a reputation for uncannily accurate prediction. A big Alaskan oil strike was predated by one of our episodes. When Rhodesia (now Zimbabwe) was subjected to an international fuel blockade because of its failure to institute a proper democratic voting system for all citizens, black and white, we truthfully showed a way that certain companies were shipping in huge amounts of oil despite the ban. The organized escape from Eastern Europe of a top scientist about to be executed as a spy was suggested by one of our stories weeks before news broke of an actual, very similar rescue. Saddest of all was the coincidence of an episode that began with the crash of a British Vanguard at London Airport. The main news, which immediately preceded our weekly episode of *The Troubleshooters,* opened with a real-life crash almost identical to the one we had staged and filmed weeks before.

I rang Andy Osborn immediately, and although it was impossible to arrange a substitute program, he managed to get a short explanatory announcement before our episode. Nevertheless, many people wrote in to complain of what they saw as an error of taste.

However, *The Troubleshooters* continued to be the BBC's top drama series, and all concerned proudly applied their own particular skill. Good scripts flowed in, always authentic, contemporary, and thought provoking, whether set in Australia, Africa, Canada, or the Far East, and our team of actors and directors grew in confidence until all 26 programs had been completed.

In November, at the annual ball of the Society of Film & Television Arts (soon renamed the British Academy of Film & TV— BAFTA), I was handed the prestigious award for Best TV Drama Series by Lord Louis Mountbatten. But I was even more thrilled by a note from my old mentor Huw Wheldon, now controller of television programs:

> Dear Peter,
> You have made a lot of friends with *The Troubleshooters* and, I am sure, enlarged the circle of those who admire your work and the energy you get into these things. It has been a very good series at a time we needed a very good series and I really do congratulate you on what has been, after all, a huge achievement. I shall miss the series; and equally will welcome it when it returns.
> Yours sincerely,
> Huw

Success had its penalties. With the high ratings and good audience reaction, Peacock decided to squeeze in another 13 programs just after New Year, 1967. Gatward was dispatched to Amsterdam to film for the first episode, Jenkins to the north of Scotland to lose Izard and Stead in a snowstorm, Frankau to a marine terminal in West Wales, and Proudfoot to Stoke-on–Trent to begin a quiet little story of how the death of a poverty-stricken lost aunt upset the Easter plans of smart Alec Stewart, and, in the word of the *Daily Mail*, "proved he had a heart."

The critics were back with superlatives. Peter Knight in the *Telelgraph* noted "the style and brilliance which sets this series miles ahead of its nearest rival, assuming alertness and intelligence in its audience with sweeping technical assurance—a fine example of teamwork." Our scriptwriters made the rounds of refineries and tanker harbors and shipyards and oil rigs and village petrol pumps and found more real and human plots in the labyrinthine empires of oil. But no sooner had we finished the run in April than Peacock ordered another 26 for the autumn.

We were running out of stock film sequences. But we had scarcely touched the Far East. British Airways offered us four bargain seats to Hong Kong, returning via Bangkok, Delhi, Agra, and Beirut, and our authors joyfully created new plots to fit these locations. I contacted Ernie Christie, the BBC's Hong Kong cameraman, Mark Tully, our stalwart in India, and Bryan Langley, United Nations cameraman based in Lebanon, and prepared to set off with director Moira Armstrong, Tony Read, and our rugged Thornton, Ray Barrett.

We had been voted "TV Series of the Year" by the readers of *Weekend* magazine and had to attend their awards ball the night before we left. Ray had somehow failed to get to bed and was not the prettiest sight as he staggered up the aircraft steps for the 23-hour economy flight. Helped by the hospitality trolley, he managed to sleep most of the way, but he woke up very irritable as we flew through the narrow gap between skyscrapers to land at last in Hong Kong. "Where are we?" he shouted. "And what time is it?"

In London it would have been about 9:00 A.M., but here it was four o'clock on Sunday afternoon. We were greeted by Bryan Salt, another old friend from documentary days, and the redoubtable Ernie Christie, a tough South African. While Ray was packed off to bed in the Mandarin on Victoria Island, Bryan drove Moira, Ernie, Tony, and me around the various locations in mainland New Territories. (We were attempting another Trinidad exercise, but this time I didn't have to hump the camera.)

Having driven up to the border with China, then firmly closed, and all the way down again, across the ferry and up to the Peak, we had a delicious dinner and decided to make an early start the next day. But on my morning wake-up visit to Ray's bedroom I discovered him in deep slumber. Out of sync with the local clock, he had stayed awake the previous afternoon, wandered down to the bar, and discovered conjurer/comedian Tommy Cooper, booked for the late-night cabaret. Ray had stayed around to watch the show, and had then been taken on a tour of Hong Kong's many nightspots until the small hours. Clearly there would be no filming for him that morning.

We rescheduled and killed time chasing a rickshaw with a special passenger—a double for Tsai Chin, the London-based actress booked for the Hong Kong story. Ray recovered more or less by lunchtime, and we completed the two days' work among the junks of Aberdeen, the tightly packed slums of Kowloon, and the floating squatters' settlement by the harbor. We then flew off to Bangkok with Ernie Christie and his Chinese sound man. Our Thailand contact was to be a third secretary (films and television) in the British Embassy, to whom I had

Action-packed Mogul gushes onscreen. *The Troubleshooters*, 1965.

written weeks before and cabled before leaving Hong Kong.

There was no sign of him at Bangkok airport. Luckily, John Drummond of Shell Oil had given me the names and numbers of all his local representatives, and with one call all our problems were solved. Sam Smith, a genial Australian, took us under his wing, found a doctor for Ray (suffering from "prickly heat"), bought us an excellent dinner, and set up all our locations, as well as gaining us entry into a Buddhist temple to stage an additional scene with Ray and a local actor. With his guidance and Tony's rapid rewrites, we exploited every possible exotic locale: the floating market, the great temples, the huge golden sleeping Buddha, the traffic-choked streets, the silent jungle, the enormous river, and everywhere the smiling people.

On the day we were about to leave, our man from the embassy made languid contact. The arrival of our plane had coincided with a cocktail party he simply couldn't miss. He seemed hurt that we'd done so much without his help, but relieved we'd managed it without spending embassy funds and were now out of his thinning hair.

In Delhi we were met by the young and unflappable Mark Tully, then quite new to his job as the BBC's man in India, and the actors

Sayed Jaffrey, his sister Mahadur, and the beautiful Rani Dube (later Richard Attenborough's associate producer on the Oscar-winning *Gandhi*). The locations in Old Delhi and in the gardens of the Taj Mahal in Agra had already been organized. Our only problem was the local crew. The lighting cameraman and his operator, business partners for many years, had recently quarreled and were suing each other for slander. Neither could afford to turn down a BBC job, but as they were officially not on speaking terms, the cameraman's instructions to his operator had to be conveyed by a third party, usually me. Thus:

> "Kindly inform Mr. Vindaloo that the aperture must be set at F16."
> "Okay. F16, Vindy."
> "Courteously tell Mr. Biriani not to be a silly ass. The stop is F22…"

and so on like a terrible comedy sketch from the *Goon Show*.

India was a revelation—hot, dusty, and terribly overcrowded, but full of nervous vitality. Poor Ray, who had endured Hong Kong and disliked Bangkok, positively hated India, particularly as we stayed in a temperance hotel, but as at that time India enforced prohibition it didn't make much difference.

The Taj Mahal proved to be truly one of the world's wonders, and the quiet scenes we shot with Ray and Rani within the aura of its magnificence were dignified by a quiet grandeur. There was just time for a visit to Akbar's deserted city of Fatehpur Sikri, with its perfect mother-of-pearl mosque, and then we had to fly on to our last destination.

In June 1967, before the ravages of civil war destroyed its very heart, Beirut was a pleasant Mediterranean city with broad boulevards, gentle squares, smart shops, jostling markets, and glistening beaches, almost as one imagines Nice before the First World War. But within a day of our arrival the Six Day War between Israel and Egypt threw Lebanon into turmoil, and we were lucky to complete our last main sequence among the ruins at Baalbeck before being forced to leave in a hurry.

All through this trip I again felt the old anguish of "floating through sewers in glass-bottomed boats" first experienced in Cairo years before. Our crammed filming schedule had allowed us no time

Filming for *The Troubleshooters*, Taj Mahal, India, 1966.

to stand and stare, to meet ordinary people in the various countries or to understand a little more of their lives. This is the curse of most television assignments, the need for swift assessment, leading to superficial judgment, which has to be recorded here and now as fact.

Back at the Centre, the fourth *Mogul* series went smoothly into production. Our regulars were joined by Virginia Wetherall as a footloose girlfriend for Thornton, and Camilla Brockman as a new secretary for Stead, when Phillipa Gail returned to the theater. Isobel Black also entered the series as an independently minded publicity officer, and in a short time married James Gatward.

Beside our regular writers' efforts, we were sometimes sent story ideas from men and women in all branches of the oil business, and many were good enough to develop. Tony also discovered a young schoolmaster desperate to write for us, who only needed a strong theme. For some time I'd been nursing a notion of playing Ronald Fraser, from *The Pot-Carriers*, as a hopelessly anachronistic expatriate Brit who'd spent his life in the Middle East without learning anything about the people of the area, and was about to be fired by the head office for his terrible "wog-bashing" attitude. The unknown author thought about it, and finally delivered *The Misfit*, a delightful character study much enhanced by Ronnie's fruity charm, and all at once Roy Clarke's name was made as a television writer.

The night this episode went out, Dennis Vance, unexpectedly home from Barbados, called me to ask if he might develop it as a series. I could hardly refuse; he and Roy pitched it to Lew Grade, and ATV ran a number of half-hour *Misfit*s with Ronnie Fraser that autumn.

By the end of 1967 I'd made 78 hours of *Mogul* and *The Troubleshooters*, a series that had created a new, crisp way of contemporary storytelling for television, but at the end of that year I had had enough. Tony Read took over and kept the pot boiling for an incredible further 94 episodes in the succeeding five years, as he himself developed from a quiet and thoughtful associate into a positive, even ruthless producer.

The Troubleshooters was part of the BBC's most adventurous period in the 1960s, when, with Hugh Carleton Greene at the helm, Wheldon, Peacock, Newman, and Osborn gave producers the right to fail, or to attempt and sometimes achieve miracles. Within our strict dramatic framework we were free to create controversy, provoke thought, challenge political attitudes, scrutinize big business, question solely profit-seeking motives, and argue for human values of tolerance, trust, and friendship. Throughout, our characters were recognizable as men and women of that decade—optimistic, ambitious, compassionate, and credible. It is unlikely that a drama series as bold and far-reaching would even be considered today, certainly not by today's BBC. One of whose uncaring bureaucrats ordered most of the original tapes of this historic show to be wiped (for "reuse!").

It may be a long time before a finer television series is on offer. I am proud to have had a part in it, and very grateful to John Elliot, whose imagination, courage, and persistence made production possible. John, much loved and highly respected, died in 1997 after a long and debilitating illness. As we stood before his coffin at his cremation service, we all remembered a man of extraordinary integrity and passion, now sorely missed.

7

1968–1969:
Color Blossoms—
and a Dramatic Mystery

Patrick McGoohan's The Prisoner
*heralds color TV—but what does it
mean? And another attempt to win an
international audience.*

Television has few legends. Of all the thousands of programs lovingly written and industriously produced over the years little remains. But one drama series is still remembered and even taken seriously more than 30 years after its inception.

It was called *The Prisoner*. Although when first shown in the United States it failed to gain a large audience and puzzled the few who did watch. When repeated it slowly became cult viewing. *Prisoner* appreciation societies flourished not only in the States but also in Japan, Britain, and other parts of Europe. Yet the idea behind the series was not, I submit, very profound.

In the 1960s Patrick McGoohan was a highly esteemed West End actor whom Lew Grade persuaded to become television's *Danger Man*. Retitled *Secret Agent* in the United States, the very profitable series saw its production extended over many years. But during my brief stint as director I found the pressure of working at top speed on such a series irksome after a few weeks.

For Patrick, carrying the whole show, rewriting indifferent scripts, sometimes working seven days a week, it must have been relentless toil. Indeed he became so tired he frequently stayed overnight in his dressing room behind the secure gates of MGM Studios, a virtual "prisoner" of his own success.

I am sure this was his inspiration for creating *The Prisoner*. The story begins with a burned-out secret agent (curiously similar to the character McGoohan had played in *Danger Man*) summarily resigning his post and waking up nameless and without responsibility in a secure model village with all necessities provided—but a place where no one dares to ask the question "Why?" Today Patrick's concept seems banal, but it was different enough then to startle Lew Grade's complacent salesmen into blank refusal. However, he persisted, and in the end Lew agreed to let him make 17 episodes—but at a much reduced fee.

My own involvement was minimal. Between the third and fourth series of *The Troubleshooters*, when we were in active preparation but not in production, Patrick called me one Friday night in some distress. Halfway through the sixth episode of his new series he had decided to fire the director, and he needed me to start reshooting the episode on Monday morning.

This in fact was no great compliment. Years later Patrick explained to my gleeful crew on *Jamaica Inn*, "Why did I ask Peter to direct *The Prisoner*? Because I knew he was quick—and he was *cheap!*" (So much for artistic integrity.)

I protested I was busy at the BBC with my own series. "Who do I have to ask to get you free?" he demanded.

"Sydney Newman, I suppose."

Within the hour he had somehow secured me two weeks' unpaid leave from the BBC, and a dispatch rider appeared the following morning with the script of Episode Six, "The General." Patrick's name was on the script as star, producer, and author as well. The writing was a little ponderous, with the captive hero determined to find whoever was the brain behind the model village. In the end he discovers a computer (a novelty in 1967!) known as "The General," programmed for any eventuality. He destroys it—by the elementary means of asking *"Why?"*—and makes another, inevitably thwarted, escape attempt.

From my experience with *One* I knew how to create an atmosphere of menacing suspicion, but it needed good actors. I was happy with Colin Gordon, Betty McDowall, and Conrad Phillips, but not with the young man Patrick had cast as his fellow prisoner, Number Six, a suspected ferret for the authorities, and persuaded him to try John Castle, an actor of promise, instead.

George Markstein, story editor and espionage expert, helped me unravel the nuances of the script, and I duly started shooting on that Monday with most of the old *Danger Man* crew, and completed within the allotted ten days. I enjoyed the experience but had no sense of making a work of any significance. I truly believe that it was Patrick's own complete conviction, and not the scripts, that gave the films their apparently hypnotic power.

In a similar short break between runs of *The Troubleshooters* I fulfilled my last contractual commitment to Associated British by directing *Mr. Ten Per Cent*, with comedian Charlie Drake again. It was a very poor script; Charlie was in domestic havoc and not his usual comic self. The result was a failure, which appears every so often in mockery on British television.

Later I was again freed from the BBC to direct *Subterfuge*, with a starry cast including Joan Collins (who was amazingly pleasant and cooperative), Gene Barry (television's Bat Masterson from the 1950s), Richard Todd, Michael Rennie, Marius Goring, and Colin Gordon. This was a complex spy thriller that was supposed to show off the "Adda-Vision" system designed to speed up feature film production. Small television cameras were bolted onto the side of two heavily sound-blimped 35mm Mitchell cameras, and in theory scenes could be filmed full-length covering every angle, using live television's multicamera technique, while delivering film quality in three weeks. The problem was I had no pre-rehearsal or planning time, and though the cast played up magnificently, the result didn't justify all the effort (although Universal picked it up and is probably still selling it).

After *Troubleshooters* Andrew gave me the challenging task of making the BBC's first ever drama series in color as one of the main attractions for BBC2, once the channel had commenced color transmissions in autumn 1967. *The Borderers*, from an idea by Bill Craig, was an exciting prospect.

Filming *The Prisoner*, with Patrick McGoohan, Betty McDowall, 1967.

In the mid-sixteenth century the unsettled Borders between Scotland, ruled by Queen Mary, and England, ruled by Queen Elizabeth, were lawless lands dominated by ruthless cattle barons who burned, pillaged, and stole cattle in a state of undeclared war. Author Bill Craig had created a typical family of the time, the Kers, struggling to live in peace and harvest their crops, threatened by the devious actions of their politically ambitious kinsman, Sir Walter Ker of Cessford. When we showed the format to a sales executive of the newly formed BBC Enterprises, the analogy of this story with early America struck him immediately. "It's a Scottish Western," he declared. "Make it move fast and we can sell it."

But Bill's concept, though not short of theft, murder, and bloody combat, had far more depth than this salesman realized, with a moral core and sense of justice equally relevant to present times. With story editor Martin Worth, I commissioned Bruce Stewart, Allan Prior, Jack Ronder, Sean Hignett, and others to find original stories of character and adventure.

Border country is still dotted with watchtowers like Langholm and Smailholm, and medieval castles Hermitage and Caerlaverock, but we found a much more practical fortified tower for our laird of Slitrig farther north, close to Glasgow at Mugdock, near Milngavie, with plenty of woods and open countryside nearby.

For the crafty Sir Walter Ker of Cessford, equally ready to cheat the English or to connive with Scottish rivals for profit, I chose Iain Cuthbertson, an actor of stature and magnitude. Distinguished character actress Edith McArthur was to be the laird's mother, and for Gavin the young laird I needed to find an energetic actor who could ride and handle a sword as well as strong emotion and violent conflict. A promising Scot was playing Iago at Birmingham Repertory Theatre. James Gatward and I drove up to see him perform. But it was the unknown, brown-faced Othello who caught our imagination, although it was difficult to tell what he really looked like under his heavy makeup. After the show we discovered that Iago and Othello shared a dressing room, which created a diplomatic problem. While I chatted to Iago, making vague "we'll let you know" promises, James had invited Othello (now revealed as pale and good-looking) for a drink at the pub, and I soon joined them.

James told him about the series, but he confessed he couldn't ride or "talk Scottish." However, we offered to arrange riding lessons for him in Birmingham during *Othello*'s run, and the accent would come in rehearsal working with real Scot actors. Thus a slightly dubious Michael Gambon, soon to become one of the finest actors on the British stage (and "Sir Michael," to boot), came to play his first television lead, and astounded everyone with his strength and verve.

In early summer 1968 I directed Bill Craig's first story, "Vengeance," where Gavin's father, laird of Slitrig, is lured to his death while on the track of stolen cattle across the English border, a tragedy that suddenly vests young Gavin with responsibility for the lands and livestock of the Ker family, as he urges his kinsmen to live in peace rather than cause further feud and bloodshed.

Cameraman Brian Tufano shot some glorious backlit sequences in sparkling color, and designer Colin Shaw built rugged-looking interiors of rough polystyrene to be used throughout the series. Moira Armstrong, Gatward, Jenkins, and Frankau all followed up with good stories, and we delivered BBC2 an action-adventure series exploiting the wild Scottish countryside in all its natural hues of green, purple, and gold, against skies that changed from crystal blue to sunsets of blood-crimson.

For me, another opportunity beckoned. A year previously, before setting off for Hong Kong, I'd been involved in constructing an embryo program company to apply for one of the ITV franchises when new contracts were to be awarded in 1967. There was a strong impression that new groups would be seriously considered. Northern England was to be divided in two. If Granada was reallocated, Lancashire alone, Yorkshire would certainly be available.

Some of us discussed the idea of a company run entirely by actual program-makers, the people who knew how television worked and created its income. Accordingly, Joan Kemp-Welch, Cyril Coke, and a few other top talents joined me in *The Producers' Group*, with finance provided by Decca Records, Harrap Educational Publishing, and Howard & Wyndham Theatres (which already owned much of Scottish TV and shares in ATV). We applied for Yorkshire, for which, in the end, there were seven contenders.

We were duly interviewed by members of the Independent TV Authority, under their chairman, Lord Charles Hill, who as bluff wartime "Radio Doctor" had urged the British people to "keep their bowels open," but had featured more recently as a cunning politician. He listened politely as we explained that if producers had more say in management, viewers would enjoy a better mix of programs. "And you'd all have more profits in your pockets," his Lordship quipped, dismissing our expertise as almost a handicap. He obviously considered us a lot of bohemians who could never manage a company, not realizing that the average producer, keeping programs within a budget, had as good a grasp of finance as any overstuffed executive.

Our bid failed. A Yorkshire television rental company and a local newspaper seized the lucrative prize, and then had to scramble around to buy the production talent they so obviously lacked.

There were other surprises in 1967. The franchise for Saturday and Sunday in the capital was given to London Weekend, headed by Aidan Crawley, David Frost, Michael Peacock (who had resigned the day before as controller of BBC1), and Cyril Bennett of Rediffusion. Lavish with promises, poor in subsequent performance, the company rapidly lost viewers with programs that aspired to more than they delivered—unfunny comedy, weak drama, and trite talks. Crawley, Peacock, and other founders soon deserted, and the company plunged down-market to become a game show and situation-comedy factory. Meanwhile ABC and Rediffusion had been merged into Thames TV to provide programs of a little more quality for weekdays in London.

Lord Thomson's "license to print money" holding in Scottish TV was reduced from 55 percent to 25 percent, but he still clung to the franchise, while ATV was instructed to improve its Midlands performance. In Wales and West, the feeble, London-clinging TWW was replaced by a powerful local group headed by Welsh peer Lord Harlech, with Wynford Vaughan Thomas, Richard Burton, Stanley Baker, and Royal Opera's Geraint Evans. Although contributions from the stars were less than hoped for, Harlech Television (HTV) soon made important contributions to the network.

Despite my personal franchise disappointment, I had kept in touch with Peter Donald, chairman of Howard & Wyndham. During the making of *The Borderers* he came to our house with a tentative offer.

Howard & Wyndham was selling off its theaters in order to enter production by forming two new companies, one for stage plays, under Peter Bridge and John Neville, the other for films and television, of which I could be managing director. Donald believed as I did that there was a market in the United States and throughout the world for high-quality British television programs. I warned him that it would take time, money, and patience to create a market, and that it would be best financially if we could involve a well-established British broadcaster, with production services.

He agreed, and we shook hands on the deal. My contract with

the BBC was nearly at an end, and Andy Osborn reasonably agreed to my early release.

But I had made one of the worst decisions of my life.

What I failed to understand was that as chairman of Howard & Wyndham, Peter Donald was presiding over a board of directors who didn't all agree with his changes. Some were only waiting for the schemes to founder to force his removal.

Ignorance was truly bliss. At the end of 1968, clad in a new, dark gray flannel suit, I moved into a smart Mayfair office with walls of matching dark gray flannel. First we had to test Peter's theory that popular plays could be remade as films. Peter Bridge had just finished the successful run of a Russian play, *The Promise*, by Alexei Arbusov, about three teenagers in the grueling wartime siege of Leningrad, with Judi Dench, Ian McKellen, and Ian McShane.

Of the three, only Ian McKellen was now available, but we decided to film an adaptation on a minuscule budget. Commonwealth United, an offshoot of the then-respectable financier Bernie Corfield's empire, appeared mushroomlike in London announcing ambitious European production plans. From them we were easily able to secure an advantageous production-distribution deal, and I offered the film to Michael Hayes, director of the first *Mogul*, who promptly announced that he was not willing to film in Russia but instead could do everything he needed with a local crew and doubles in Helsinki, Finland—which was our first mistake. As we soon discovered, Helsinki in January at minus 20 degrees is not the ideal place for filming, and apart from one onion-domed church, a small square, some half-demolished buildings, and the frozen sea, there were very few natural settings that could easily be converted into a convincing wartime Leningrad, and the rushes looked cramped and cheapskate.

However, studio work was completed briskly on two of Shepperton's smallest stages, and we covered with snow one of the huge old London exterior sets built on the lot for the musical *Oliver!*, and filmed the relief of Leningrad with a couple of tanks, a few old trucks, and a mass of cheering extras. But when it was cut together, I realized that our film still lacked breadth and a realistic reconstruction of the hungry horrors of the siege, so I arranged a short visit to Leningrad, a Novosti film crew, and the local resources of

Len-Film Studios to create a more spectacular opening. (And as Michael still demurred, I went alone.)

The spartan Aeroflot Tupolev from London made a sudden dive at least 50 miles from Moscow and flew at tree-top height until its crunching touchdown in level snow. As the engines died no one moved. The aircraft doors banged open and a slit-eyed giant in a soiled green uniform entered, consulting a clipboard. "*Schott!*" he bellowed, staring hard at each passenger as he marched down the aisle. "*Schott!*"

He stopped and stared hard at me. "*Schott?*"

I realized he was asking my name. "You mean—*Scott?*"

"Da. Schott." He beckoned grimly with a stubby finger. I followed wretchedly out of the plane and down the steps, wondering how I would survive the forthcoming roughhouse interrogation. The giant nodded toward an empty 60-seater bus.

I clambered in and was immediately accelerated alone across the snow to the terminal as my fellow passengers stumbled down from the plane, complete with luggage, to walk the same 200 yards in freezing air.

Inside the terminal I was suddenly grabbed by a strange, stubbly little man and kissed with passion and sour cognac on both cheeks. "Mister Schott. I am Yuri, your production manager. All is ready, tovarich." I was sped through customs and driven very fast through empty streets to a second airport where I was led to the foot of another aircraft. "I leave you here," Yuri said. "They will take you to Leningrad. I follow by train."

I walked up into a totally dark cabin. The plane door slammed shut behind me. I sat in blackness for about half an hour, then suddenly all the lights flared, the door swung open, and a crowd of laughing and chattering Russians, carrying live chickens, dogs, assorted parcels, and dangling wet fish burst into the compartment. The engines rumbled to life, and we were airborne.

In Leningrad I met Ivan, the cameraman, his wife, who carried the camera, and the assistant director. They all had yellowing copies of my shot-list, and the next day we set off in an ancient Volga and, after certain delays, began. Yuri didn't turn up until a day later, looking hungover. "Is he sick?" I asked. Ivan laughed. He had a few more words of Italian than English. "He is *ubriaco.*"

A drunk is a drunk in any language. Surprisingly, I learned that Yuri was in fact in the KGB. Considering the amount of spying he did he seemed a poor bargain.

The rest of the resources the Russians provided were excellent. At last I was able to achieve the production values we needed, with hordes of shabby, underfed extras reenacting the misery of their recent history when Leningrad had survived three terrible winters surrounded by the German Army, cut off from essential supplies.

Despite the intense cold, the city in early spring was an inspiring sight, as the sun glistened on fresh snow and the beauty of its architecture—Rastrelli's Winter Palace, the Hermitage, Alexander's huge column, Peter the Great's towering equestrian statue, the Peter and Paul Bastion, and the graceful Admiralty spire—reflected in the frozen Neva River.

I began to sense some of the power and majesty of old Russia, the artistic and philosophical spirit of this place, where Pavlova and Nijinsky had danced, Mendelev and Pavlov advanced humanity's scientific knowledge, and Pushkin, Dostoyevsky and Tolstoy conceived their masterworks. Leningrad (now St. Petersburg once more) is magnificent, just as Moscow is mean and commonplace, and as we worked around the city I felt enriched in spirit.

But all minds were not so noble, however. At the end of the last day, Yuri led me into a quiet corner of the Astoria Hotel and demanded that I hand over my unspent rubles. When I refused, he glowered, "You may have trouble leaving tomorrow." Later Ivan and his wife took me to a Georgian restaurant loud with music and lusty songs. I mentioned Yuri's threat. Ivan laughed. This was Yuri's personal racket. With impressionable foreigners it usually worked.

Of course I had no difficulty leaving Russia, and the extra sequences gave *The Promise* a special realism it had previously lacked, adding a further dimension to Ian McKellen's stylish performance. We delivered it to Commonwealth just as the firm was reeling from the financial horrors of three badly overspent productions. When it collapsed into inevitable bankruptcy, our negative was seized by the unpaid printing laboratory as an "asset," and to this day our touching little film has never been shown.

Unfortunately, Howard & Wyndham's theater company was

With Ian McKellen and author Alexei Arbusov, *The Promise*, 1969.

also in trouble. After three unhappy flops, John Neville emigrated to Canada to launch a new and distinguished career. Meanwhile, after long negotiations, I had organized two coproductions with the BBC. For the first, a series of Francis Durbridge's *Paul Temple* crimesolving adventures, I arranged a handsome German presale. The second was a set of dramatized Somerset Maugham stories to be produced by Verity Lambert. The BBC would make the shows with a budget enhanced by Howard & Wyndham. We would recoup on foreign sales, sharing any profit with the BBC.

Verity's first, *The Letter*, directed by Christopher Morahan, was soon completed. I flew to New York and went through the time-consuming process of arranging showings for network executives and others, and finally secured a deal of sorts with a major soap company, for a simultaneous Saturday night showing in about 100 cities on independent television stations, with maximum press and radio promotion. The price would only just cover Howard & Wyndham's total investment, but it was a start and would ensure us publicity in the United States.

However, the board of Howard & Wyndham thought otherwise. After all the other disasters they were looking for a quick profit—now. One of the directors confidently declared that for such a high-quality show he could get "a much better deal from my friends in the networks." My verbal agreement was canceled, and, not surprisingly, the Somerset Maugham series was never shown in the States. To complete the insult, when the British Academy (BAFTA) announced its awards for 1969, Christopher Moraham was "Best Director" and Verity Lambert "Producer of Best Drama Series"—for, of course, *The Letter*!

I had no option but to resign as managing director of the Howard & Wyndham television subsidiary, after nearly a year of hard toil.

Meanwhile, television technology had leaped ahead. President John Kennedy had provided enough space-exploring resources to land a trio of astronauts on the moon, in itself a feat so astounding that scarcely anyone remarked on the amazing triumph of being able to send and receive clear television pictures of the event in color as it happened a quarter of a million miles away from the Earth—all this less than 50 years after John Logie Baird's first fumbling attempts to transmit a smudgy image from one office to the next!

Personally I had plenty of work on offer. Before the end of 1969 I was asked to remake *Murder in Shorthand* (which I had produced for Rediffusion seven years before) as a full-length television film (*The Word of a Witness*), using the "E-Cam" system (similar to "Adda-Vision" but with smaller Arri cameras instead of heavy Mitchells). With George Maharis, Jane Asher, and Rupert Davies, I made it through my own company at Wembley Studios, and the foreign sales trickled in rewardingly over the next few years.

At the beginning of 1970 Andrew Osborn asked me to return to the BBC to direct two episodes of *Codename*, an undemanding thriller series with Anthony Valentine, Alexandra Bastedo, and Clifford Evans, and I spent the early summer on an enjoyable Children's Film Foundation effort (for Saturday morning matinees), *The Magnificent Six and a Half*, with a host of old-time comedians like Jimmy Edwards and Cardew Robinson.

But as we left for Spain on our annual holiday, I was still saddened, not by failure but from sheer frustration that a good idea for international coproduction at Howard & Wyndham had foundered, partly through

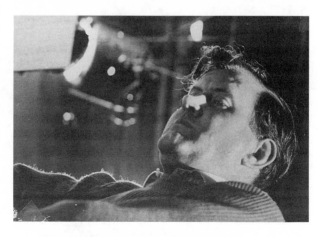

Problems at Howard & Wyndam, 1969.

bad luck, but mainly because of mean-minded mismanagement, and I had thus wasted what might have been two good and productive years.

My anguish was premature. Within a very short time both the BBC and the ITV companies would begin to recognize the value, indeed the necessity, of coproduction and bigger foreign sales. I had simply been too far ahead of the game, or perhaps I had just mixed with the wrong people.

And I was about to be offered one of the best chances of my entire career.

8

1969–1975:
The Onedin Line
Sets Sail

*Sunshine and storms—at sea and on
shore.*

Andrew Osborn generously invited me back to the BBC at the
beginning of September 1970 on a long-term contract. But the corporation had changed from the producers' realm of the mid–1960s.
The Golden Years were already past. Never again would program-
makers enjoy the freedom known under Director–General Hugh
Carleton Greene.

From 1960, in less than a decade, Greene had restored the BBC
to its rightful place as the least afraid and most adventurous television service in the world. He also made enemies, among them
Prime Minister Harold Wilson.

Chairman of BBC Governors, Lord Normanbrook, a shadowy
figure who had scarcely affected our lives, died in 1967, and in a
lightning stroke of vengeance Wilson transferred Lord (Charles)
Hill from chairmanship of the Independent TV Authority to "sort
out the BBC" as its chairman. It was, as David Attenborough
observed, "as if during the Second World War Churchill had
appointed Field Marshal Erwin Rommel to replace General Mont-
gomery to command the Eighth Army!"

At first Greene found some common ground with the wily

doctor, but within a few weeks he resigned to be replaced as DG (director general) by the unknown Charles Curran. A former editor of *Fishing News*, and briefly a radio talks producer, Curran showed little interest in programs, preferring paper-patting as an administrator, seeking to "withdraw as DG from the prominence achieved by Greene." "Withdraw" he certainly did. He made no effort to meet producers or indicate any approval of their efforts, preferring to hide away in Broadcasting House in Central London playing in-house politics with Hill, assuming that in the distant television studios loyal workers were eagerly grinding out daily programs of impeccable taste and objectivity. Where Greene had directed and inspired, absentee landlord Curran merely hid and conspired.

It is difficult to think of any other industry where such complacent disregard of prime product would be possible, let alone a medium of communication. In a leaderless BBC such a creative vacuum ensured a drying up of adventure in programs. Hard-hitting series like *The Troubleshooters* were no longer acceptable. Drama began to look backward to the Victorian era and the certainty of the Second World War. (*Colditz* was a typically soft series showing how British officer prisoners-of-war joked and tunneled while the Russian people fought and bled.)

Peacock having departed to London Weekend Television (LWT), the new controller of BBC1 was Paul Fox, a heavyweight ex-paratrooper who had done well on *Sport* and *Panorama*. Andrew Osborn persuaded him to invest in four series pilots: *The Regiment*, a "by jingo!" salute to Britain's imperial redcoats of the 1890s; *The Venturers*, merchant bankers in their own power game; *Here and Now*, Tony Read's contemporary concept of a freelance news crew (sadly never developed); and a fourth idea that suddenly caught my imagination, embracing the strong popular lure of the ocean with a chance to expose the cruel hardships and ruthless ambition that dominated Victorian life. The title had a certain enigmatic quality: *The Onedin Line*.

A few months before, Liverpool bus driver Cyril Abraham, who had sailed as an apprentice on the sail-training ship *Conway*, had sent Andrew Osborn a rough idea, "The Birth of a British Shipping Line—From Sail to Steam in 13 episodes."

Andrew's dramatic instincts leaped at the possibilities—the visual power of huge sailing ships coupled with a complex family conflict. He rapidly persuaded Cyril to forget the steamship part and backdate the story to the great age of fast clippers and iron-fisted shipmasters, and commissioned the first script. When I returned to TV Centre in autumn 1970, this trial episode was already in active preparation, but the temporary producer, Anthony Coburn, had already expressed a preference for *The Regiment*, and *Onedin* would be mine once the pilot was complete.

First, I had to extricate my old army colleague Royston Morley from difficulties on a series that had to have three "South American" episodes urgently filmed in Malta. The action-packed rags-to-riches-and-back-to-rags story of Brett, gunrunner, hobo, property tycoon and murder suspect, was cheerful hokum, but as one of the scripts I inherited was by John Elliot, it was not completely without some distinction.

With Patrick Allen as Brett, and Hannah Gordon and Peter Bowles in strong support, I had an enjoyable couple of weeks in Malta, and returned to complete studio work on the three parts in December. But my mind was already full of the greater potential of the coming series—of the courage and endurance of seamen, of tea and tarpaulin, storms and stress, trade winds and billowing sails, a swift prow slicing blue water, high canvas black against red dawn, the rhythmic percussion of taut rigging, a setting sun scattering rubies over a luminous cobalt sea—plus all the high romance and adventure promised by *The Onedin Line*.

On seeing Coburn's pilot, Paul Fox had duly commissioned me to produce 15 episodes, dubiously expressing concern about the high cost if I persisted in filming long sequences at sea. But I was in no mood for caution. If *Onedin Line* was to work, there had to be plenty of exterior action and I would have to learn economy on the unpredictable ocean.

John Fabian, my new assistant, told me of the difficulty he had had finding the first seaworthy ship, telephoning every harbormaster from Dover along the south coast, always drawing a blank, until at last, at Dartmouth in Devon, he again wearily asked, "Have you anything resembling a Victorian sailing ship?" After a slight pause a rich country voice answered, "If I lean my head six inches to the left I can just see a three-masted topsail schooner on the other side of the river." Thus the *Charlotte Rhodes* was discovered, a sad, rundown hulk with torn sails and ragged ratlines, scuffed paint and rotting taffrail. Built in 1904 at Svendborg, Denmark, the schooner had battled the gales and storms of the Atlantic for years with cargoes of salt cod from the United States. The ship was 130 feet from bowsprit to stern, about 90 feet on the waterline, 22 feet wide, drawing 8 feet, and unlike many tublike Baltic traders her bows had the lean lines of a small clipper. Even in the few shots in the pilot episode she had a fine photogenic quality.

In 1968 Captain James Mackreth, a British Airways pilot who had graduated from biplanes in the Hebrides Islands to Trident jets, was about to retire. On the regular Copenhagen run he became fascinated by the old sailing ships rotting in the harbor, waiting hopelessly for a last buyer. He began to inspect them seriously and one day saw the *Meta Jan* (as she was then), her elegant lines spoiled by a clumsy wooden wheelhouse. The price was low, and despite never having sailed anything of that size before, Mackreth bought her, hoping to use her in his years of leisure for voyages of discovery.

Armed with an ocean yachtmaster's certificate, and helped by his son and a couple of friends, he began the difficult voyage home across the wild North Sea, finding his skills as an aerial navigator of little use in unpredictable waters. After two days the ancient engine broke down, and the amateur crew battled all night to sail the ship through the narrow and perilously overcrowded English Channel to safe harbor in Dartmouth, where for the next two years the brave captain astounded the locals by slaving away single-handed in all weathers, attempting to turn the near-wreck into a respectable craft. Ropes were restored, a new wooden wheel adorned the poop deck, the ugly deckhouse became firewood, and a brass bell was hung bearing the new name, *Charlotte Rhodes* (after Mackreth's great-grandmother, a fiery lass who ran off to marry her father's horsemaster). Mac continued to dream of the day he might sail off to Madeira or the Caribbean, but tackle was costly and his funds ran out. With some relief he agreed to lease his ship for the single trial *Onedin*, not realizing that he and his craft would one day be world-famous.

For some reason Tony Coburn had based the filming for his pilot at Plymouth, 50 miles west of Dartmouth. The weather was unkind, the ship was hard to manage with a temperamental engine, makeup girls and actors were seasick, and the comforts in the bare, dark hold below were zero (simply a bucket instead of a marine toilet!). Consequently the material he achieved was somewhat limited and disappointing.

In January 1971 John Fabian and I drove through thick snow to Dartmouth. At the first sight of the bedraggled old vessel shrouded in icicles my heart sank. If we were to film major sequences day after day at sea with a unit of 20 for 15 episodes, this ship would have to be rapidly put into decent order. Urgently the sails and rigging needed replacement and the rusty engine rightly belonged in some museum. But Mac's cheerful enthusiasm was infectious. We subdued defeatism and visited sailmakers and chandlers, but the prices they quoted for the most elementary improvements made the blood run cold.

But—Andrew wanted the series, and I was determined to give it to him. At last we evolved a financial scheme to amortize the cost of new sails, rigging, bilge pumps, a thorough overhaul of the ancient engine, plus a simple Calor gas cooker and a reliable marine toilet, all from the scenery budget for the series.

Dartmouth, less crowded than busy Plymouth, was obviously a better filming base, boasting a fine ready-made quayside at Bayard's Cove complete with period customhouse. Dartmouth Council agreed to remove a No Parking sign, a modern concrete seat, and ugly streetlamps and plant genuine Victorian gaslights, which are still there. In the town we found an old church and several good squares, and across the river at Kingswear there was a working nineteenth-century railway with a station and a large quayside area that in time would become every sort of waterfront from Baltimore to Shanghai.

We also discovered a superb run of old-time warehouses, period shops, a lifeboat shed, and a pub a few miles away alongside the Maritime Museum at Exeter. David Goddard, the museum's energetic director, arranged for the adjacent canal to be dredged so that we might bring the *Charlotte Rhodes* and two smaller ships around from Dartmouth. Unfortunately, a motorway was in construction nearby, and after the first year, when we staged Hollywood-sized crowd scenes on the Exeter waterfront (still being edited in years later), it became impossible to move big ships up the canal,

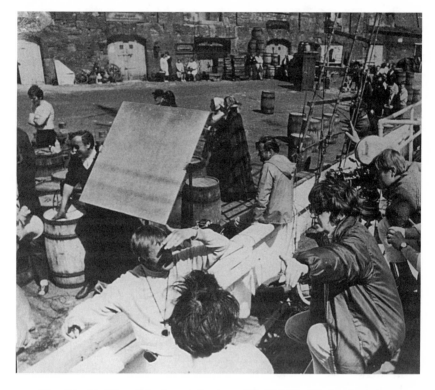

The Onedin Line: **Filming at Exeter with director Moira Armstrong, 1971.**

and our Exeter shooting remains only as a well-photographed memory in David's museum.

Beside crew comfort we also had to be serious about safety. For filming at sea we always had two fast boats alongside, one a camera platform, the other a safety boat. Life jackets, hot and cumbersome though they were, would be worn, or would at least be within arm's length of everybody. We had a first-aid expert on the crew, and a former naval safety officer, and in three years of filming in all sorts of weather, there were no accidents, and only very occasional seasickness.

With work going ahead on the ship, I needed to build a library of general sailing shots. Apart from some excellent helicopter angles of several fully rigged clipper-type ships, including the Swedish

Staatsrad Lemkuhl, shot by Nat Crosby at the start of the 1970 Tall Ships' race, and used in the opening title sequence to the strains of Khachaturian's "Spartacus" (which I had first heard on a visit to the Bolshoi Ballet with, of all people, Charlie Drake), we had nothing—no shots of sailors climbing rigging, hands heaving ropes, sails dropping into place, yards swinging to catch the wind, and steersmen at the wheel—none of the bits and pieces of visual magic that were vitally needed to flesh out the many voyages of *The Onedin Line.*

Then I heard that Philip Donellan of BBC Birmingham was quite independently planning a documentary about the rigors of life under sail in the nineteenth century. We soon agreed to share the cost of a location trip with his cameraman John Williams on the magnificent white square-rigged Danish training ship *Danmark* from the Azores to Europe. With John and Philip I flew out to San Miguel, one of the volcanic and strangely fertile Portuguese islands far out in the Atlantic, a place of green hills, black-and-white houses, bubbling, sulphurous geysers, huge white arum lilies growing wild along the narrow roads, and cultivated pineapples in greenhouses. In among our luggage were the assorted sailor costumes that Philip had promised to get the cadets to wear during filming on the long voyage home.

The ship arrived from Florida, we met the always cheerful Captain Hansen, and from a hired tugboat we spent three days capturing stunning shots of the ship in fair and foul sailing weather.

At last I bade Philip and John "bon voyage" as they sailed away from San Miguel in the *Danmark*, and I flew back to London to face the major problem—scripts. Barry Thomas, a likable Welsh author with a sudden, unpredictable maniac laugh, was to be my story editor, and though Cyril Abraham was to write six of the episodes throughout the series, we had to find writers for the other nine. We gathered Alun Richards, Allan Prior, Ian Kennedy Martin, Bruce Stewart, David Weir, Roy Russell, and Michael Bird in for a session of potted history and a rundown of the main characters. Cyril had set his pilot in 1870, but as I wanted to include a story about the Union blockade of the Confederate states during the American Civil War, we were now starting in 1860. In any case I wanted to remake the pilot as episode one. Though Peter Gilmore, in the lead as James Onedin, Jessica Benton, as his sister, Elizabeth, Howard Lang, as faithful mate Baines, Edward Chapman, as rival shipowner Callan, and others wanted to stay on the show, the lady who played James's wife did not. (Years later she told me how much she regretted her hasty decision!)

This gave me a chance to cast an actress I had admired for some time, Anne Stallybrass, whose down-to-earth North Country warmth and truth became an outstanding feature of the series. The remake also enabled me to improve sailing sequences and toughen up some of the marshmallow performances.

In 1860 Britain was the supreme colonial power, whose sprawling empire spread red patches right across the globe, its mines, foundries, and factories supplying the world with coal and cloth, iron and engines. British yards built ships for merchant adventurers to send goods over vast and hazardous oceans, making and losing fortunes. But wealth was shared by few. Life expectancy for a city child was a mere 17 years, with poverty, starvation, vagrancy, prostitution, and disease a decaying core within the rosy apple of "prosperous" Britain. Over 2,000 seamen died annually in accidents, their wives and dependents receiving no compensation, until at last, within the period of our story, public conscience stirred, a seamens' union was formed, Prime Minister Gladstone's Education Act promised free universal tuition, and successive Parliaments gave the working man new status and protection. All this was to be told in our saga of the ups and downs of a Liverpool shipping family.

In the beginning, James Onedin, a young sea captain tired of the lack of profit as skipper of a Callan Line ship, secures the ownership of the rundown schooner *Charlotte Rhodes* by marrying Anne, plain but prudent daughter of a drunken master mariner. He tricks his shopkeeper brother into financing a voyage, and snatches the Portuguese wine trade from his ex-employer. The story would follow him through sickness, mutiny, storms, and strife, at sea and on land. But Barry and I had a surprising conflict with Andrew Osborn over another plot line we were keen to pursue. To give us some family interest, we wanted Onedin's sister, Elizabeth, to become pregnant by ship's mate Daniel Fogarty, who in ignorance sails off to Australia. She then seduces rich shipowner's son Albert Fraser, a designer of experimental steamships, and persuades him to marry her. In time, of course, he discovers the child is not his.... But Andrew felt we were needlessly introducing "sex" and demanded removal of the idea. Late one night, halfway down the whiskey bottle, we had a serious disagreement for the first time in our long and amicable association, Andrew insisting that the illegitimate baby should be cut out, despite my protests that it was vital to our plot, involving not only Elizabeth and Albert, but also Fogarty, James, and the rest of the Onedin family. Finally Andrew rose unsteadily and theatrically pointed to the door. "Peter," he said majestically. "If you go out of this office determined to retain your little bastard, you need never return to this corporation."

Unable to match his dramatic powers, I stood and said as clearly as I could, "Sorry, Andrew, but I think it's essential." Andrew turned his back on my unimpressive exit. I made my way home, my head clearing rapidly. Had I really fired myself from the BBC over a trivial story detail? But it wasn't trivial, that was the point. My series had to be truthful, about real emotion and genuine human problems, not soft and sentimental.

The next morning I drove back to the center, and walked slowly along the corridor to my office, hoping to pass Andy's own sanctum unobserved. But the door was open, and as I drew level a familiar figure appeared, blocking the light, face grave in shadow.

I stopped. Our eyes met. "Good morning, Andrew," I ventured. "Morning, Peter," he answered casually—and went back in his room. Our row was never mentioned, Elizabeth Onedin duly became pregnant, and the subsequent family squabbles over the baby's paternity and Elizabeth's tangled loves became part of the show's great appeal.

I was pleased to discover that production pressure had eased since *The Troubleshooters*. For each 50-minute episode we were now allowed ten days, rather than seven. In addition we had two whole weeks' filming at the beginning, and two other similar breaks that should give us about ten minutes' action at sea in each episode. Despite all subsequent financial pressure from fearful bureaucrats, I held on to this pattern for the next three years, and am sure it was a major contributor to the show's long-lasting success.

Frankau and Gatward were unfortunately elsewhere, and Moira Armstrong could make only one episode as she was in demand for single plays, but there were plenty of willing directors like David Cunliffe, Roger Jenkins, Ben Rea, Frank Cox, and Gerald Blake. We began filming episodes one, two, three, and four in Exeter in late April. The sun shone every day, a good omen, and as the dockside action was no different from ordinary filming, there were few holdups until we tried complicated maneuvers with the *Charlotte Rhodes* and other ships in the narrow canal.

The real test came when we moved west to Dartmouth to start a daily schedule at sea. The weather turned ugly. Our precautions proved necessary, and *Charlotte Rhodes*'s horrible diesel engine continued misbehaving. Somehow each day's work was more or less completed. However, for Alun Richards's episode five, when Captain Onedin's trusty mate, Baines, is tricked and shanghaied onto a Callan clipper, we planned a dramatic encounter, as Onedin, hearing the Callan vessel has set sail, pursues it in his ship and finally manages to tack right across its bows, forcing the skipper to heave-to.

I had discussed this in detail with Captain Hansen of the *Danmark*, and arranged an early morning rendezvous in Torbay as the ship arrived from the Azores (with Philip and John, and, I was pleased to see lots of footage of sailing material). It was agreed we would use the vessel for only two hours and of course pay for any accidental damage. Against my will I had been assigned a BBC staff director for this episode and been unimpressed with his preparatory work on episode two. A couple of days before we were to shoot the near-miss at sea, he came to me in Dartmouth and said he "disliked the script" and wanted to be replaced. I knew his real reason. He was scared of staging the complex action accurately enough to avoid a collision. There was no time to find a replacement. I took over, and at 5:00 A.M. on that day I set off with cameraman Ken Westbury (and my 12-year-old son, Robin, as passenger) on the camera boat following the *Charlotte Rhodes* (its engine having started in time for once), motoring majestically out of Dartmouth past the strange Victorian castle at the harbor entrance, to feel the welcome roll of the open sea as we headed east along the Channel past Berry Head into the calmer waters of Torbay, where Captain Hansen's fine ship already lay anchored.

We exchanged "good mornings" by radio, and *Charlotte*

Rhodes moved into start position starboard astern of the *Danmark*. Mac's team set their sails as we motored our camera boat ahead of both ships, with both cameramen ready. A third operator was hidden under a tarpaulin on the foredeck of the *Charlotte Rhodes* to film an audacious close-up (I hoped!) of the *Danmark*'s looming prow as the smaller ship swung past. *Charlotte Rhodes* eased forward, Hansen hauled up his anchor, and on a command to the cadets clinging high above in the yards, his huge white sails fell into place in perfect order, billowing out splendidly as the wind caught them. The great ship turned toward us, gathering speed. There seemed little chance of *Charlotte Rhodes*'s catching her up even with all sails and engine flat out. But Captain Hansen knew what he was doing. Calmly he engaged his engines full astern, slowing the huge vessel to less than walking pace as sails strained against diesel power. All cameras rolled as *Charlotte Rhodes* began to gain on the fully rigged clipper, and at last, when her bow had edged a good half length ahead, Mac gently swung his wheel to port, heading across the bigger craft's course.

The camera boat closed in to give a greater impression of speed as the dwarfed red-sailed schooner surged under the high white prow of *Danmark*, missing the tip of her bowsprit by less than a foot as she swung past, our camera boat suddenly having to swerve away fast to avoid a collision. We radioed congratulations to Captain Hansen on his masterly seamanship, for with *Charlotte Rhodes* passing before him only his skill and judgment had prevented an unpleasant accident. "You wish to do it again?" he asked calmly. There was no point. It was unlikely we could ever improve on such a hair-breadth performance.

I waved Hansen and his crew farewell—until next year—and they sailed off into the broad Channel, while the camera team and I sped back to Brixham, where John Fabian had organized a helicopter for aerial shots of *Danmark* and Mac's gallant schooner in full sail.

The next morning, the last day of the first two weeks of filming, I commenced a love scene with Elizabeth and Albert on a hillside overlooking Dartmouth estuary. We completed all the dialogue in bright sunlight, up to the final kiss, when the camera was supposed to tilt up and glimpse, far out at sea, *Charlotte Rhodes* setting off

Filming on hillside, Dartmouth, with Jessica Benton and Philip Bond, 1971. *The Onedin Line.*

on another voyage. But although we'd radioed it to start out from harbor half-an-hour before, there was no sign of it on the horizon. I called up Fabian on the quayside and had no answer but an ominous crackle.

We waited. Then I saw the perspiring figure of my loyal assistant toiling up the hill, to tell us the worst had happened. Perhaps exhausted from the exertions of the day before, *Charlotte Rhodes*'s prima donna engine had at last given up—spectacularly! As Mac struggled again and again to start it, the overheated cylinder had suddenly exploded, showering the engine room with red-hot shrapnel. Luckily Mac had escaped serious injury, but he had been taken to the hospital with minor burns—a sad end to our initial two weeks' filming.

The first five episodes were completed in the tranquil atmosphere of the studio. I was pleased to see how well Peter Gilmore and Anne Stallybrass were interacting, and that the whole cast was performing with an energy and reality that lifted the story high above usual television melodrama. But we were all looking forward to our next burst of sea-filming, and in high summer that July we achieved even better results, despite the cost and loss of time each day of having the engineless *Charlotte Rhodes* towed out to sea by a hefty tug before sails could be set. The sun-tanned crew enjoyed every day, as new cast members John Thaw, Iain Cuthbertson, Peter Jeffrey, and John Phillips joined us for short voyages, performed, and departed. We improved the onboard catering, running a hot lunch out daily from Dartmouth by fast fishing boat. At midday mackerel lines appeared, crew members displayed unknown angling skills, and buckets of fresh fish improved many a hotel menu in town.

Designers Oliver Bayldon and Jeremy Bear, who had created Liverpool and London docksides, were now asked for more ambitious feats—a New Guinea village, an African market, a New England port—and all were accomplished either on the banks of the river Dart or at multipurpose Bayard's Cove. Local inhabitants realized frustrated theatrical ambitions by donning ragged costumes and dirtying their faces as scripts demanded. *Charlotte Rhodes* was painted white overnight to stand in for deck scenes to be cut in with long shots of bigger clippers. David Goddard lent us a Papuan dugout canoe from Execter Museum, which almost capsized as our imported Brixton extras learned to paddle under the lashing tongue of a petty officer from the nearby Naval College, and even David himself once became a fearsome Arab maneuvering the lateen sail of an authentic Arabian dhow.

The second batch of five was recorded at TV Centre, and we returned to Dartmouth in late September for the last film sequences, some demanding deck scenes in a raging storm. It was impossible to wait for a real tempest, even if our fair-weather crews could have worked in foul conditions. We had to find a way of creating our own typhoons, to be switched on and off as required.

Fabian and I devised a system of mooring the ship about 50 yards out from the quay and tying ropes to the tops of the masts. Teams of crew members could pull the ropes from onshore and cause a rocking motion. Then, with the aid of huge wind-machines

With Howard Lang, Anne Stallybrass, Peter Gilmore, Dartmouth, 1971.
The Onedin Line.

and fire brigades from all over Devon, a glistening curtain of hosepipe rain would blot out the harbor background and lash rain on the unfortunate actors in the foreground. The effect worked remarkably well. Many an old salt wrote in to ask how we managed to film in such truly terrible weather!

The last episodes of the 15 were shot and edited at TV Centre. But no one had seen our results, and rumblings of disquiet were heard from above. In those days BBC costings didn't arrive on a producer's desk until weeks after the money had been spent. I knew we had had a great deal of unbudgeted expenditure: the hire of the tug to get the disabled *Charlotte Rhodes* to sea over four weeks' filming, the fees of frogmen to clear camera boat propellers of plastic flotsam, electricians' overtime to recharge batteries, the cost of wardrobe assistants' working all night to dry soaking costumes for the next day's shoot, the constant financial drain of caulkage and

Filming at sea, off Dartmouth, 1971. *The Onedin Line.*

cordage, pulleys and bolts, special props, extra wigs, lost anchors, lifebelts, broken spars, and the thousand and one unusual items that were expended on an *Onedin* episode. But I was still unprepared for the final staggering figure, a serious overspending (for the first time in my career) of over £60,000 ($90,000), astronomical in those pre-inflation days. Of course, we had built up a library of valuable shots for the future, but for the present the series confirmed Paul Fox's worst fears that *Onedin* was simply "too expensive" in spite of Andrew Osborn's continued support.

The bad news spread rapidly through the corporation. For a couple of weeks I became a friendless non-person. I could enter an elevator full of old acquaintances, bid them "Good Morning," and watch their eyes lift to the ceiling as they unanimously ignored me.

People avoided me in that most convivial refuge, the BBC Club. I could take the last seat in the crowded TV Centre restaurant and clear the table within minutes....

Then someone in BBC Enterprises showed a couple of episodes to the German ARD First Network. They bought all 15 for a sum that made my overspend look puny. People started noticing me again. "Where have you been?" they would ask.

Transmission began on Sunday nights on BBC1—and the audience responded with an enthusiasm beyond our wildest hopes. Research reported an incredible Reaction Index of 91, letters of appreciation poured in, and the popular critics rattled away about "an epic theme of Big–Screen proportions," "a refreshing breath of fresh sea air," "rugged realism with a salty tang," "vivid action," "sterling work by a hand-picked cast," and even (thank you, Shaun Usher!) "wonderful value for your licence money."

No one actually thanked us for persevering with difficult sea filming, but I firmly believe that if we had taken the easy way out with more scenes in studio cabins and pathetic model shots *The Onedin Line* would have sunk unnoticed after one run. The Germans even wanted us to write in a Hamburg-based mariner and cast one of their actors, but the BBC, concerned with "editorial control," refused.

Dazzled by high ratings, Paul Fox approved another series of 14 for 1972 with a personal tribute:

> Dear Peter,
>
> A note of gratitude for all your work on "The Onedin Line." It's been a wonderfully successful series—not only very popular but also professionally much admired.
>
> Very many thanks to you and all concerned for giving us such a run of excellent programmes. Like millions of others I am looking forward with pleasure to the new series,
>
> Yours,
> Paul

Barry Thomas cast his net wider for new writers and brought in Elaine Morgan to write a couple of touching episodes in which Anne quarrels with James and goes off to try to earn her living as a lone woman in the harsh environment of Victorian Liverpool, to be found at last by a penitent James, almost dying in a pitiless workhouse. Alun Richards dreamed up two stories set on voyages to South America; Bruce Stewart had the loyal Baines, now a captain, loaned out to another line, discovering he is in command of a "coffin ship," intended to sink by ruthless owners bent on collecting the insurance; and Martin Worth involved Daniel Fogarty in a fraudulent ship auction in Ireland.

Cyril Abraham began the second series with a stirring episode about an ordinary seaman (Godfrey James) struggling to wrest better food and conditions from the profit-conscious James Onedin during a hard and

Filming at sea, *The Onedin Line.*

hungry voyage. We still needed bigger and better shots of sailing ships, and for the second year we used not only *Charlotte Rhodes* (now fitted with a secondhand Rolls Royce diesel salvaged from a factory fire pump), but also the Baltic traders *Als, Jylland*, and *Artemis*, the Sailing Training Association's *Winston Churchill* and *Martin Miller*, two Norwegian square-riggers, *Sorlandet* and *Christian Radich*, as well as a working paddle steamer, *Kingswear Castle*, and a stylish small steam pinnace, *Hero*.

A young filmmaker I knew, Robin Cecil-Wright, asked me to advise him whether to invest his savings in a Spanish trader like *Charlotte Rhodes*. Remembering our problems, I told him, "Definitely No!" He went away looking disappointed, but a few weeks later I heard he'd plunged, on a promise from the BBC to use the ship as Darwin's *Beagle* in a round-the-world documentary series about the famous naturalist and anthropologist. He had renamed the ship *Marques*.

Captain Hansen telephoned. *Onedin* had been a great success in Denmark, and we would be welcome to film his ship again on a training cruise around the Virgin Islands in February. As ever, a slightly dazed Andrew agreed, and cameraman Tim Seseman and I flew out to the Caribbean island of Saint Thomas expecting to rendezvous with the ship. Instead a cable awaited us: "Delayed by storms in Fort Lauderdale. Please await our arrival."

A phone call to Florida reassured us that the ship was already on its way. I pictured my jealous colleagues in rainy old Shepherd's Bush as Tim and I ambled around shooting tropical backgrounds, even feeling slightly guilty about wasting BBC money by downing another rum punch, but in fact the delay was a blessing. The *Danmark* brought the bad weather with it and gave us our first chance at shooting a great sailing ship heeling over in really rough seas.

Plunging and rolling, we hammered our way out in a hired millionaire's fishing boat to meet the ship in ten-foot waves as the sky turned black. With our life jackets tied onto the gunwales of our bucketing craft, Tim and I hung on grimly to the camera and tripod as the *Danmark* appeared from the rain-mist, heeling over and majestically righting itself with each succeeding wave, as we crouched and found no shelter from the high walls of water that rose up and drenched us with every new tidal surge. Desperately wiping lens and camera dry after another deluge, we swung about again and again to chase the ship for further angles.

Soon Tim's magazines were all used up. It was impossible to reload on deck, so we raced back to harbor to reorganize. Salt water is a notoriously corrosive enemy of metal. The camera had to be stripped apart, washed down in fresh water, and carefully dried. but we were satisfied with the morning's work (although when the shots of the ivory ship on an ebony sea against a black sky were viewed in Ealing the following week, some dry-footed wiseacre foolishly asked, "Why did you shoot it all in black and white?").

The next day the storm had passed. The sun shone brilliantly from an amazing blue sky onto a sea of pure turquoise. We followed the dazzling white sails of the *Danmark* out between the curiously humpbacked islands, past glowing lagoons lapping cream shallows of coral sand. Single pelicans hung suspended in cobalt infinity above us, watching for the merest glint of silver in the translucent depths. Then with Stuka-sudden speed they would dive and strike, fishtails wriggling and disappearing into their great pouchy beaks as they soared again cerulean-high. The boat skipper called the names of the islands as we passed: Jost van Dyke, Great

Thatch, the long mound of Tortola to our port, Peter Island, Salt, Ginger, Fallen Jerusalem, Beef, Scrub, Great Dog, and, at last, the strangely domed sandstone rocks of Virgin Gorda, flanked by palm trees, sea grapes, white sand, and a glass-clear ocean.

The *Danmark* anchored, and we were hauled aboard for lunch. Captain Hansen invited us to join his crew for a swim, throwing me a mask, a snorkel, and a pair of huge feet-flippers. Equipped, I dived over the side into a brilliant marine kaleidoscope of jostling, strangely shaped fish of every hue, suddenly incandescent as the sun's rays caught them. Parrot fish, trumpet fish, and squirrel fish swam and swarmed in massed ranks, and huge, sheetlike manta rays in solitary splendor followed in an endless parade of flashing chromatic forms, copper, silver, and aquamarine, sparkling small monsters and glittering dragons dazzling my unaccustomed eyes.

At last it was time to surface and return to work, until nature rewarded us with a glorious sunset on the way back to harbor. The following day Captain Hansen planned to sail away north of Puerto Rico. I still needed a few more aerial shots. There was no helicopter available in Saint Thomas, but I managed to rent a beat-up single-engined Cessna from Ed, a tattooed Second World War veteran.

Tim and I thanked the captain and his crew once again and watched them sail away from Charlotte Amalie harbor, then drove to the airfield and piled into the cramped Cessna. Ed had helpfully removed the doors on either side so that Tim could film unimpeded. After a certain amount of delay, we made a shuddering takeoff and headed west over the sea, expecting soon to sight the white speck of sail on the vast blue expanse to the north of the green mounds of Puerto Rico. But the whole ocean was empty.

After a while we realized that Captain Hansen must have decided to change course and was heading south of the island. Ed swung 90 degrees to port, and soon we were bumping through turbulence over mossy green mountains dotted with white houses. "How long before we get to the south coast?" I asked.

Ed considered. "Maybe an hour, maybe less." It was more, but eventually we saw sea again, and there was the *Danmark*, serenely speeding west. Ed circled the ship, gradually losing height. A flash from below told us we had been recognized. Tim wanted to film but needed to go more slowly. Ed obliged, losing speed until a sudden loud klaxon told him we were close to stalling. We repeated the maneuver around the moving vessel, klaxon screaming, until Tim was satisfied.

At last we headed for home. As we came in to land, the engine coughed ominously. Ed laconically pointed at the fuel gauge, needle on zero. "Right out of gas. Glad we made it." In three days Tim Seseman had provided *The Onedin Line* with a new library of unsurpassed sailing shots in fair and foul weather which were to enrich the series for years until the very end of its long run.

Back at home scripts were progressing. As I had enjoyed directing episode five the previous year, I decided that from now on I would direct the opening and closing episodes. Because Edward Chapman was no longer available as James Onedin's rival, Callan, Barry and I started my episode with a spectacular fire at Callan's warehouse, complete with period fire engine, which would dispose of both the old ship master and his son and heir. Thus the wealth of the Callan Line would be inherited by his young and beautiful niece, Emma. This would create a new conflict involving mate Daniel Fogarty (Michael Billington), who returns from a long voyage home to find James Onedin's sister, Elizabeth, not only carrying his child but married to wealthy Albert Fraser.

Nursing a powerful hatred for James, who he believes contrived the marriage to create a business advantage for himself with Fraser's shipyard, Daniel turns his attention to the lovely but spoiled Emma Callan. When eventually married to the heiress, Daniel would become James's new and ruthless rival.

For Emma we needed to find a girl of arresting beauty. Like a conjuror, my old resourceful agent, John Redway, introduced a raven-haired 20-year-old, a girl of spirit and great potential called Joyce Frankenburg—"But we're changing her name," John added quickly. "To what?" I asked. He paused, "*Jane Seymour.*"

Trained as a dancer, with little previous acting experience, Jane rapidly developed in rehearsal, discovering a strong emotional range. She had a natural camera sense. Studio operators seldom had to ask her to "turn just a little more to the left, please," to improve the angle, particularly in her close-ups.

After the first few episodes had been shown, the inevitable happened. Jane was spotted by producers Cubby Broccoli and Harry

Jane Seymour debuted in *The Onedin Line*. Pictured here in *Jamaica Inn*, shown on ITV in May 1983.

Saltzman and asked to play the lead opposite Roger Moore in the next James Bond movie, *Live and Let Die*. But their start date clashed with our planned recording of the last two episodes of *Onedin*, in which Jane had major scenes with James Onedin and Daniel Fogarty. Strictly speaking we had a contract, and Jane should have had to turn down her big film chance. Harry Saltzman asked me to come and see him, and made a great plea "for Jane's own sake." So, with my other directors' help, I agreed to record all her scenes for 13 and 14 during studio time for episode 12, and released her three weeks ahead.

"I'll never forget this," Harry Saltzman said, with nearly genuine tears in his eyes. "And I'll see that you personally get some benefit." Naturally I never heard from him again.

Jane's rapid rise to stardom didn't please some of the cast, who, with good scripts and a smooth-running success, had also become household names. But this company of previously unknown actors now began to rumble with discontent. Only Howard Lang, Onedin's stalwart Baines, continued to enjoy developing his character from an agreeable support to a powerful figure in all the stories. Saddest of all, Anne Stallybrass, whose gentle influence and occasional blazing anger had made James's wife a real life woman, was personally suffering from marital stress and decided she didn't want to continue. For weeks I tried to persuade her to reconsider, arguing that she was confusing her domestic troubles with her professional career, but her sturdy North County mind was made up.

Cyril, Barry, and I conferred anxiously. Could the show survive the loss of one of its main strengths, the woman behind James Onedin? It had to, but if Anne was going to leave, she must make a dramatic exit. The story for the last episode (14) had her enduring a difficult pregnancy at sea onboard a tea-clipper, with James racing home against Daniel Fogarty in a frantic bid to win enough Onedin shares to regain control of his company. As they reach port, after storms and conflict in the fo'c'sle, Anne is delivered of daughter. "Anne has to die in childbirth," Cyril said with a sigh. Anne was his favorite character. And so it had to be.

That summer, as I filmed the sequence of the unconscious Anne being carried by stretcher from the clipper deck to a horse-drawn ambulance on the quay at Bayard's Cover, I felt a tug at my sleeve.

It was the head waiter from Dartmouth's Royal Castle Hotel. His face ashen. "She's not ... going to *die* ... is she?"

I reassured him, unconvincingly, but I should have been warned. Losing Anne Stallybrass bewildered our faithful audience, who felt suddenly cheated. Unhappily, the following year Anne visited us at Dartmouth and admitted how wrong she'd been—but it was too late. However, shortly afterward she married Peter Gilmore, no doubt solving one of her problems.

The second series was otherwise well received, and Paul Fox ordered another 13 for 1972. In the middle of our spring preparations John Elliott surfaced with a pilot script, *The Team*, about Formula Ford motor racing, which he'd sold to Bill Ward of ATV. Typically, John's characters were unusual and well observed, so of course I grabbed the chance of filming on dry land, begged a few weeks' unpaid leave from Andrew, spent a hectic weekend with my actors mingling with the crowds around the pits and on the track during a Silverstone Trophy meeting, and completed recording at Elstree. James Laurenson played an embittered team manager unable to race himself because of a serious injury, and Stephen Sheppard (who afterward gave up acting to become a successful Hollywood screenwriter) was his arrogant driver. Bill Ward was enthusiastic and wanted to make a series right away, but both John and I were too busy. A year later, when we might have obliged, Bill had left ATV and the project died.

Caroline Harris, who played Laurenson's lover, did so well that I booked her to play opposite James in the third *Onedin* series, and I also found young Kate Nelligan at Bristol Old Vic to play a rival for the newly widowed captain's affection.

I assembled the crew and cast in Dartmouth for filming once more. The scripts, ranging from ice-bound Sweden and a Turkish earthquake to tropical Amazonia, were still vital and original, the conflict between Caroline and Kate's character, Leonora, building steadily throughout the episodes (though Kate's hard-hitting North American acting sometimes left the rest of the cast floundering), and the year passed pleasantly enough. But somehow the ghost of Anne Onedin hung over the production, and I began to feel that perhaps I had said all I wanted to about the vigor and injustice of Victorian life and needed to return to contemporary drama, where I belonged.

I was distracted from these solemn thoughts by the need for a strong action climax for episode 13. We had shown enough of the dangers menacing seamen on long voyages. Stuntmen had plunged from high yards, men's hands had been mangled in tackle blocks, sailors had been sent flying by loose booms, but now we wanted something more spectacular.

"I suppose we could have a man fall overboard and get gobbled up by a shark," Barry suggested facetiously. I grimaced as expected, and then thought, why not? If we had a stuntman swimming in a frogman's suit just below the surface with a credible shark's fin

Wet but happy. *The Onedin Line,* **1973.**

strapped to his back, visually it would establish a sinister threat. The sailor would fall into the water, see the shark's fin and scream for help as it sliced through the waves toward him. As the shark "attacked" its victim, the man would disappear under the water struggling for life, and the fin-wearing stuntman would burst a blood bag just below to gush to the surface. Presto!

Jeremy Bear visited the Natural History Museum and designed a monstrous black rubber shark's fin. Stuntman Roy Scammell and I went to the Highgate open-air pool on a rainy September afternoon to try it. The pool was empty except for one or two hearty city-gent all-weather swimmers, one of whom, ponderously trudgening from end to end, suddenly reacted with a drop-dead double take as he saw the black fin of a killer shark aiming straight toward him!

Confident and assured, we transported the fin to Dartmouth. The cameras rolled, the ship heeled over, a seaman fell into the choppy sea, a black fin appeared, the sailor screamed for help, the shark struck, the victim disappeared, the boiling sea turned red, as planned. I was so pleased with this sequence that I showed it to divers Hans and Lotte Hass, who happened to be in London. They watched in silence. As the lights went up I was foolish enough to expect amazement. Instead Hans simply sat staring at the blank screen, looking bewildered. At last I put the question: "How do you suppose we did that, Hans?" He shook his head. "I have no idea." He looked at me keenly. "But tell me. How on earth did you make the shark swim backward?" In the excitement no one noticed that Roy had put the fin on back to front!

The third series was undoubtedly the best, but Andrew Osborn decided we could take a break while riding high. A couple of years later it was revived by another producer, who was forced to reduce sea filming and who then cut in all my library shots once more.

Before I left it, *The Onedin Line* won the TV & Radio Industries Council Programme Award for 1973 and was nominated for Best Drama Series by the British Academy. As the BBC had at last grasped the idea of marketing abroad, it was sold to more than 85 countries, including the United States (although BBC salesmen never made enough effort to secure a network deal). The Germans showed every episode no fewer than five times. The BBC repeated them from 1972, and again to start its daytime schedules in 1987 — 16 years after production!

British satellite channels are still running the episodes, and in 1992 the BBC re-edited eight three-hour videos out of my first 29 episodes and made another profit of half a million pounds ($750,000)—all a remarkable tribute to the late Cyril Abraham, Barry Thomas, John Fabian, cameramen Ken Westbury and Max Samet, and all the actors, writers, technicians, makeup, set, and costume designers whose enthusiasm and hard work earned this long-lasting triumph for the BBC.

It confirmed my belief that a British television series with a leading man utterly different from the usual mid–Atlantic spy-sleuth could be enjoyed by millions all over the world. But now I needed to return to the present, and reflect the leaner and harsher 1970s.

Which was to prove more difficult than I had thought.

9

1976–1992:
On American Screens
at Last

*A small company in the West of
England provides dramatic hits for
U.S. TV networks.*

Mediterranean blue sparkled in bright sunshine. Before us the
Bay of Cannes opened out to reveal the distant flat earth mysteries
of the Isles of Lerin. Below, traffic and eager pedestrians crowded
the Croisette, to the right the dim outline of a medieval fortress, the
harbor a forest of expensive masts and cordage.

It was April 1976. I listened intently to my companion as we
stood on the roof of the Palais de Festivals, a brave flutter of multicolored flags at our feet. In four busy floors below, the International
Television Market ("MIP") was in full cry.

At last British television programs were being properly publicized and sold all over the world, seven years after my first attempts
with Howard & Wyndham. In about 500 tightly boxed-in exhibition stands the Americans, the French, the Germans, and the rest
loudly competed. The noise within was quite deafening. From the
ground floor, where a newly invigorated BBC Enterprises had the
largest stand, to the top, where the English and Americans refought
Bunker Hill in stereo, rock blared, sopranos hit high notes, heavy-
lidded Ibsenites groaned in Norwegian, gunshots whined, Napoleonic

cannon thundered, ponderous views on ecology clashed, as Japanese equipment makers counted their yen.

There were oil-rich sheiks with little home production but lots of cash, and men from poor countries who'd blown a month's national income on a "prestige" film no one could be bothered to watch, black men in red robes, yellow men in dungarees, every shade and shape of humankind, wheeling, haggling, bickering, inflating the price for the all-too-easily-won prize of this strand, that series, another 52, the adjective "Great!" flung around like a magic password.

No one had time to view the programs. At most, buyers would sample two or three minutes, pick up the literature and ask around. The United States had the most, selling on big names. The British dealt with Australia, Canada, and the friendly parts of the old Commonwealth. The French too had their "traditional" markets: Morocco and Martinique, Senegal and Tahiti. The Germans perspired and moved fast, speaking perfect English, the Scandinavians relaxed, enjoying release from their long grim winter, the Russians showed endless folk dancing and made the odd sale to the Third World, the Japanese smiled at all their hardware in use, and the Chinese spoke to no one, bewildered by the kaleidoscopic audiophonic nightmare.

My last two years had not been pleasant. First, Andrew had asked me to take over *Quiller*, based on novels by Adam Hall, featuring a loner spy. Told mainly in first-person interior dialogue, the stories were difficult to translate into dialogue and action. My story editor John Maynard and I endlessly discussed ways of making a contemporary political thriller with worldwide backgrounds from this uninspiring source. Unfortunately it was not the time for us to think of making any sort of searching and hard-hitting series at the BBC.

In the summer of 1971 a satirical program, *Yesterday's Men*, lampooned members of Harold Wilson's government. Although few viewers actually saw it when transmitted late at night, it convinced the touchy prime minister of a BBC bias against him. Since Parliament had to approve the level of the annual television license paid by viewers, it was made clear that the BBC would have to tread more warily in future.

Lord Hill had been replaced as chairman by Sir Michael Swann, an academic not renowned for any keen interest in television. Charles Curran had retired, unnoticed, and former news reader Ian Trethowan had become director-general. In drama series we lost a doughty fighter in Andrew Osborn, who retired to be replaced by a man of different caliber. Sydney Newman too was no longer head of drama, again exchanged for a poor substitute.

Our new series chief expected to read every script in draft as soon as it arrived and to comment on all subsequent developments in casting, set design, and so on. He was particularly worried by my concept of *Quiller* as a vehicle for relevant and trenchant comment on contemporary world events and demanded drastic changes in our first scripts. At his behest, stories set in war-torn Lebanon or Cyprus in revolt against the British had to become vaguely "Middle East"; South Africa and Rhodesia (soon to become Zimbabwe) were not to be identified in tales of Africans in rebellion; and Red Brigade terrorism in Italy and Palestine Liberation Forces in Israel were strictly untouchable. Thus a series that might even have matched *The Troubleshooters* as a dramatized commentary on important contemporary conflicts was reduced to routine adventure. I was left with filleted scripts that made the average *Danger Man* look bold. For my leading man I was also pressured to choose Michael Jayston, an actor of charm and presence but quite unlike my original idea of our tough and cynical hero.

However, I had a better budget than most series producers, for I had persuaded 20th Century–Fox to make a small investment that just allowed us foreign locations. We traveled to Agadir and Taroudant in Morocco to chase Quiller through Arab bazaars, to Munich for an action climax in the middle of the raucous October beer festival, to St. Lucia for an encounter with Caribbean voodoo, and to Vienna on the trail of a dissident Russian scientist; but glossy and expensive production values failed to conceal the hokum of the scripts.

To make life more difficult, the BBC was beset with industrial problems throughout 1974, our recordings were delayed, and it was not until autumn 1975 that our 13 programs were all ready for transmission. John Frankau, Michael Ferguson, Alan Gibson, and David Proudfoot all directed their episodes well enough, and Moray

Watson, Richard Johnson, Oscar Homolka, Keith Barron, and a sadly wasted Sinead Cusack all gave of their best. The series held on to a respectable 10–12 million viewers throughout the run, and 20th Century–Fox managed to get the first two shown as "TV Movies of the Week" on ABC in the United States and more than recoup its stake, but in the end it all seemed a shocking waste of effort.

By Christmas 1975, despite offering at least six good and workable dramatic ideas, all rejected, I had nothing new to prepare. My BBC contract was due to expire soon. To fill in time I directed a couple of episodes of *The Expert* from scripts by Brian Clemens and Michael J. Bird with Marius Goring as a quirky forensic scientist, supported by Elizabeth Spriggs and Lisa Harrow.

I had at least gained some interest from a major Australian television company for *The Flying Forresters*, an idea of my own about three families in Britain, Germany, and Australia involved in the beginnings of civil aviation from 1919 up to the Second World War, and was waiting for a meeting with them in Cannes in April 1976 when I met Patrick Dromgoole.

Years before, Patrick had been directing *Armchair Theatre* at ABC when I was making *The Avengers*. We enjoyed each other's company and had kept up socially. Having directed Joe Orton's first successful play in the theater, *Entertaining Mr. Sloane*, Patrick had recently been appointed controller of programs for HTV (West) in Bristol.

His chairman, Lord Harlech, who brilliantly combined the skills of business and politics, and had been British ambassador in Washington during the Kennedy administration, was seriously concerned that while American programs often dominated our television peaktime, quality British material found little exposure in the United States. Unimpressed with the feeble efforts of BBC "Enterprises," he was determined to seek more presales for the international drama that HTV could be geared to produce.

He had a willing disciple in Patrick Dromgoole, who was shortly to display remarkable flair in creating profitable opportunities for coproduction, and had already made two successful series at HTV, *The Pretenders* and *Arthur of the Britons*. I was of course fascinated with his vision of the future, which so neatly fitted in with my own unfulfilled hopes.

By the end of the afternoon he had suggested I should join HTV as soon as possible, initially to produce and direct a seven-part children's serial, *Children of the Stones*, by Trevor Ray and Jeremy Burnham, which would give me an idea of the expertise of HTV's present crew, and then I might possibly suggest anyone else who should be brought in to bring them up to the standard of Hollywood's best—and he was not joking!

The highly original script made up my mind. Set in Avebury, a Wiltshire village surrounded by a great ring of huge neolithic stones, it revealed a present-day population held in psychic captivity by the strange emanations of the ancient circle, dominated by the lord of the manor, Hendrick, an astronomer wielding uncanny and awesome powers. A scientist, Adam Brake, and his young son come to live in the village and slowly discover that their minds are being taken over by the unnatural aura. Their attempts to break free conflict with cosmic and extraterrestrial forces, climaxing in the destruction of the evil Hendrick, and mental release for the villagers.

The summer of 1976 was particularly warm and brilliant, and with a cast including Iain Cuthbertson as Hendrick, Gareth Thomas as Brake, Freddie Jones, and Veronica Strong, plus Kate Levy, Peter Demin, and Ian Donnelly as the leading children, I spent three happy weeks filming in leafy Avebury, making the acquaintance of cameramen Bob Edwards, Brian Morgan, and Roger Pearce, sound mixer Mike Davey, and many others who were to become colleagues and friends for some years.

Used as I was to bored and blasé BBC crews, it was refreshing to work with an enthusiastic team once more, just like the early days at Lime Grove or Rediffusion. Difficult shots were attacked with gusto, camera tracks laid, rostrums built, hefty lamps mounted with energy and precision. Later, when we recorded each of the episodes in a day and a half per week at Bristol, the studio crews responded to each new challenge with similar vigor.

I duly reported my satisfaction to Patrick. With a little more experience his crews could tackle anything. He was pleased, particularly when *Children of the Stones* was successful on the ITV network, entering the Top Ten in Wales and the West and spawning a novel. I was tempted to stay with the sight of another equally good seven-part script, *Follow Me*, by Bob Baker and David Martin, a hectic chase around the Docks, Concorde factory, railway yards, and other Bristol landmarks, ending with a rousing race at sea between a fleeing topsail schooner carrying kidnapped hostages and a broken-down pilot cutter. But our Australian friends had made an offer for *The Flying Forresters* and to me for a longer producing deal.

In November Mimi and I flew to Melbourne to meet Hector Crawford, an amiable and respected producer, and his associate, Nigel Dick. We spent an enjoyable two weeks in Melbourne, in Tasmania, and on Lake Eildon, before having to make a difficult career decision. Australia offered a great deal. Their feature films were attracting world attention, and I was being offered a chance to make my own shows free of restraint.

But in the end Patrick's determination to become a force in international television drew me back to Bristol, to make *Follow Me* in the winter of 1976–77. The story was simple. A young girl runs away from home to try to join her elder brother, a yacht delivery skipper who has unwittingly been hired by a paramilitary terrorist group posing as an electronics sales team, planning to kidnap a visiting African leader. The girl's family calls in a private detective, who alerts Sid Dawes, a ne'er-do-well living with his young son aboard a leaking hulk in the Docks, telling him to look out for the runaway. Sid's son traces the girl, hears her story, and they piece the plot together, enlist Sid's help to chase the kidnappers' schooner and finally release the African dignitary.

For the schooner I was able to locate and hire one of the ships we had used in *The Onedin Line*, the *I. P. Thorsoe*, and had it sailed around from Devon to Avonmouth. With Ronald Fraser as Sid, Ewen Solon a crony, and Kate Levy and Ian Donnelly as the children again, we started filming the sea chase in a February blizzard in the Bristol Channel.

Again the comparatively untried crew proved its worth. In a freezing, storm-tossed sea where many outfits would have demanded a return to dry land, the crew members achieved a thrilling final sequence worthy of a major action-adventure movie. The rest of the filming and stunt work was swiftly accomplished. The critics, alerted by our first effort, appeared to enjoy it as much as the public.

Follow Me. **Filming the Concorde, 1977.**

Patrick now formed an association with Tom Wagner, an ebullient producer from Frankfurt, to make *The Doombolt Chase*, by Don Houghton, another action-packed children's serial, with an enhanced budget, in summer 1977. I was to produce again, but direct only half the episodes, with the other three in the creative hands of ex–*Avengers* Robert Fuest. The adventures of a schoolboy who, with two friends, tries to find evidence to clear the name of his father, a naval commander court-martialed for ramming and sinking a fishing boat with his frigate for no apparent reason, led us through many attractive local locations, sailing off Weston-Super-Mare, pursuing on foot through Cheddar Gorge, and traveling by pony across Brecon Beacons, to discover at last the lair of a rogue nuclear scientist in an old Napoleonic Wars sea fort, ending with a nick-of-time rescue by a company of helicopter-borne Royal Marines.

Royal Marines in action, *Doombolt Chase,* **1977.**

The Royal Navy gave us full cooperation with equipment and landing parties, and even offered us the use of a frigate to sink the fishing boat. But as the ship would be on a tight schedule after appearing in the Queen's Jubilee Review off the Isle of Wight, we had to film *between the hours of 5:00 and 7:00 A.M.* as it approached Plymouth Harbor.

The night before, the normally jovial Tom Wagner and I had a somber dinner in Plymouth before an early night, rising at 3:00 to embark on the camera boat with the crew in pitch darkness. The doomed "fishing vessel"—a collapsible wreck—had been anchored off Rame Head. As dawn broke, we arrived at the agreed rendezvous point outside the harbor. Tom surveyed the gloomy channel dubiously. "Where is your ship?"

I showed him my watch. It was only 4:45. But as the minute hand ticked up to 5:00 A.M. the lean gray lines of the frigate emerged surely through the mist. Radio contact was made, a pinnace lowered, and a chirpy sub-lieutenant motored over. We showed him the anchored target boat, a small speck on the horizon, and alerted both cameras, one on our boat, another much closer hidden by a rock, for the impact.

The officer gave instructions over the radio. The huge battle-ship turned slowly and aimed itself at the small boat, gathering speed as we kept pace alongside. "Like trying to hit a fly with a blunt broom-handle," one of the boatmen muttered. "He'll never do it."

Tom nodded, sunk in Teutonic skepticism, clearly regretting all his deutsch marks being squandered on a fool's gamble. The frigate came on, now traveling at a good 15 knots over the last hundred yards toward the bobbing black hull. Then it was 50 yards away, soon 25. We watched spellbound as the great steel bow closed in on the small black boat—and bisected it neatly like a karate blow in a perfect take! From behind I heard a gurgling sound as our stills cameraman, unable to bear the strain, threw up over the side.

"Anything else?" the sub-lieutenant asked calmly.

"No, that's it," I gasped. "Thank you very much."

The shots made a spectacular opening, and with a cast including Peter Vaughan, Donald Burton, and George Colouris, with Shelley Crowhurst, Andrew Ashby, and Richard Willis as the youngsters, we had another minor hit, which even the *Daily Telegraph* described as "a production of continuous pace and zest," and drew us an enthusiastic letter from Sir Brian Young, chairman of the old ITA, now the Independent Broadcasting Authority, for our "imaginative use of West Country locations."

But autumn 1977 also brought us great sadness.

In October my mother, who had been living a comfortable and busy life in Goring-on-Sea in Sussex, suffered a fatal heart attack. But I am sure it was the sort of swift exit she would have chosen.

Connie Cornish, born without any particular advantage except her own extraordinary will to succeed, had survived a troubled marriage to a man who was occasionally entertaining but at times quite impossible. She had lived for over 80 years, to see her sons and grandchildren prospering in a different world.

She always gave more than she had taken, and the memory of her personality remains, vividly courageous and optimistic. I was lucky to have been born her son.

She had certainly approved of my leaving the BBC for the more adventurous atmosphere of HTV, a creative tonic. Now, with a unit of cameramen, designers, and editors as good as the best, we needed an ambitious international project.

It was not long coming. Toward the end of 1977 Patrick negotiated coproduction of a six-hour version of Robert Louis Stevenson's *Kidnapped* with Telemünchen of Germany and Technisonor,
France, to be shown on ZDF, one of the two main German networks,
and TF1, the major French channel. We had to accept as director
Jean–Pierre Decourt, an English-speaking Frenchman, with my
crew, but we would also provide a second unit to cover the complicated battle sequences, a shipwreck, and other action.

Performance would be in English, but the important part of
David Balfour and five lesser roles would be played by German
actors, and heroine Catriona and one other character, French. (We
would dub the Europeans with authentic Scot actors.) After a series
of tests in Munich and Paris, we chose Ekkehardt Belle as David,
Aude Landry as Catriona, Bernhard Wicki as Captain Hoseason,
and Jutta von Speidel as Barbara Grant. This still left the main lead,
Alan Breck Stewart, and most of the important parts for British
actors. I phoned my friend David McCallum in New York and
offered him Alan Breck. He accepted once I had promised that the
script would stay as close to Stevenson's classic as possible. With
a firm start fixed for March 1, I lined up a strong cast: Patrick Allen,
Frank Windsor, Patrick Magee, Bill Simpson, John Carson, Andrew
Keir, Leonard Maguire, Joseph Brady, Tony Wright, Ewen Solon,
and Edith McArthur.

"Highland" locations in Brecon Beacons and the Mendip Hills
were found, and a superb Elizabethan house, Barrow Court, near
Bristol was acquired, with its many ornate rooms, outbuildings, and
courtyards, to be transformed by designer John Biggs into most of
the interiors and streets we needed. Three sailing ships were chartered to be in Dartmouth for two weeks in June. All we lacked was
the final script, which the Germans had been promising, "from one
of our finest writers," for weeks. When it arrived, in German, a bare
eight weeks before we were to start filming, it was worse than anything I could have imagined. Stevenson's story, with its short, easily adaptable, and filmic scenes, had been twisted into a violent
horror-comic of murder, rape, and plunder that would sicken viewers and turn us into a laughingstock.

Luckily someone at ZDF had a literary conscience too. They
also rejected the script, and the project appeared doomed. Desperately

I suggested to Patrick that as I knew both *Kidnapped* and its sequel *Catriona* well enough I could attempt a more faithful adaptation, introducing Catriona early on but otherwise staying close to Stevenson's clear narrative. With no option Patrick agreed.

I rashly promised a draft of all six hours in four weeks, and retired to a hut in our garden prepared as a comfortable study, emerging only for meals and to send each of four hand-written 90-minute scripts as completed by motorcycle to Bristol for typing. Most of Stevenson's dialogue was preserved. The first book, *Kidnapped*, set in Scotland in 1747, after the disastrous Battle of Culloden, begins as orphaned young David Balfour sets out to find his Uncle Ebenezer. In an alehouse on the way he meets a Culloden survivor, which gave us a chance to stage the whole battle, where the Highland clans, following Jacobite Bonnie Prince Charlie, were routed by the English forces of Hanoverian George II. The action follows David as he meets his uncle, who tricks him out of his inheritance and has him shanghaied aboard the villainous Captain Hoseason's ship bound for the tropics. At sea Alan Breck Stewart is rescued from a sinking boat, then Hoseason's ship strikes a rock and is wrecked. David escapes and witnesses the murder of "Red Fox" Colin Campbell, Alan's enemy, then meets Alan Breck Stewart again, and together they flee from redcoat soldiers across the Highland mountains.

In the sequel, *Catriona*, David is forced to remove Catriona from the influence of her conniving father, James More MacDonald. They travel to Holland, James More catches them up, Alan Breck reappears and has to fight for his life in a final swordfight against More and the English sailors bent on his recapture, before David can bid him a heartfelt farewell and return with Catriona to Scotland.

Somehow I managed to pack all this complex narrative into four scripts, which luckily ZDF accepted gratefully, and we were back in business. Director Jean-Pierre Decourt was a veteran of ponderous French historical epics about Richelieu, Mazarin and Co., and his English, as we soon discovered, was not good enough to detect minor "fluffs" or misread lines. However, the cast, notably David McCallum and Patrick Allen, both experienced directors, held the performances together while Jean-Pierre worried about complicated and meaningless tracking shots. Unfortunately, his old-fashioned Continental style, playing complete scenes all in long shot, would have bored our audience rigid. I had to insist that he cover every important line in close-up, so that we could impose a faster tempo in the cutting room. He now complained that the extra coverage would make it difficult for him to complete shooting six hours in the allotted 16 weeks. "It is not possible!" became his daily refrain. Bob Fuest and I had already shot most of the real action scenes with the second unit, including the swordfights and various horses galloping across the hillsides. Now we had to cover the Battle of Culloden as well.

After seeing Bob Fuest's first day's work on the epic conflict, I realized he would never complete it in the scheduled three days. But that was the most we could afford with all the soldiers and Highlanders. Luckily cameraman Bob Edwards was free, and he and I rapidly became a "third unit," snatching vital cut-ins of explosions, cannons belching flame, troops firing, and Highlanders dying, with whoever we could borrow for a few moments of action that would help to dramatize the violence and horror of the battle.

The rough cut of Jean-Pierre's sea-going sequences also betrayed a shortfall of necessary coverage from his week in Dartmouth with ships and actors. Once again Bob and I set off, picked up the *I. P. Thorsoe* and Robin Cecil-Wright's *Marques*, now fully converted into Darwin's *Beagle*, with three masts and square-rig, and reconstructed the poorly staged scenes with long shots and doubles. I was sorry for Jean-Pierre, but his "style" was just too leisurely for the audience I had come to understand. Naturally he disagreed.

Shooting was completed by late summer 1978. With four editors, one for each 90-minute segment, we were soon able to view a rough cut. It was far too long, but handsomely staged and well photographed. David McCallum was outstanding as Alan Breck Stewart, by turns witty, arrogant, charming, and heroic, far more credible as a Scot than Londoner Michael Caine had been in an earlier erroneously tartan-clad feature film. The Germans, Ekkehardt Belle, Bernhard Wicki, and Walter Braus, all stood up well against the experienced British, and French Aude Landry was a fresh and charming Catriona.

However, despite our lush Welsh and Mendip locations, I still felt a lack of genuine Highland flavor. With cameraman Brian Morgan and a small unit, I flew to Glasgow, picked up a couple of doubles for David and Alan, and spent a week above Glencoe, Loch Rannoch, Eilean Donan, and other notable landmarks, achieving some spectacular long shots that powerfully set the scene.

During the subsequent re-editing, we were able to impose a much faster rhythm on Jean-Pierre's original material, and then, by carefully selecting good Scottish actors like Bill Paterson, Brian Pettifer, and Frank Duncan to revoice the Germans and French, and adding a rich musical score especially composed by Vladimir Cosma, finally delivered six hours of highly polished entertainment that was enjoyed by huge audiences in Britain, Germany, France, Italy, Scandinavia, Australia, and Canada; and it soon became the first classic series to be shown on cable and satellite throughout the United States.

Made on a tight budget, *Kidnapped* was probably the first genuine coproduction among Germany, France, and Britain, positively applying the talent of all three countries, rather than adopting the usual British approach of "give us your money and you can have our film," and its critical success encouraged Patrick Dromgoole to seek further international ventures. It was also extraordinarily profitable to HTV. Early in the 1970s the British Treasury had imposed a 66 percent levy on the high profits of ITV companies from showing commercials. But to encourage ambitious productions, they allowed a rebate of this tax against the cost of any production pre-sold to a bona fide foreign broadcaster.

The "above-the-line" cost to HTV (not including crews and studio facilities) was £850,000 ($1.275 million), but the Germans and French had paid £450,000 ($675,000) of this, leaving HTV to find £400,000 ($600,000). But the levy rebate was credited to 66 percent of the whole cost of £850,000, which is £566,666, showing a paper profit of £166,666 before any income from ITV and American and Commonwealth sales, which probably amounted to a further 100 percent of the original cost.

Patrick was emboldened to look for bigger and better prospects. We thought we had a deal to make a 13-part series about the Rothschild family, but after we had invested a fair sum in scripts

With Leonard Maguire and David McCallum, *Kidnapped*.

by John Elliot, Alexander Baron, Bernice Rubens, Julian Bond, and Malcolm Bradbury, the deal collapsed, and none was ever made.

The summer of 1979 was also blighted by an 11-week strike by ITV technicians for more pay, eventually settled with 40 percent increases.

Sudden freedom gave me time to fulfill a small ambition to write a political thriller, *Dragonfire*, which was published by Macdonald-Futura in Britain and Pinnacle Books in New York (and sold 86,000 copies in paperback) and commissioned a sequel, *A Feast of Vultures*, similarly successful in the early 1980s. Both were optioned by a Hollywood major studio but alas, owing to management upheavals, never made.

Soon after the end of the strike we were approached by

Columbia Pictures Television, impressed by *Kidnapped*, to collaborate on a two-hour dramatized special for NBC on the discovery of King Tutankhamun's tomb in Luxor, Egypt, by archaeologist Howard Carter, backed by Lord Carnarvon.

Many of the priceless treasures discovered, including the great golden mask of the boy king, had recently been exhibited in Britain and in the United States and had created enormous public interest in the way they had almost accidentally been unearthed. Lord Carnarvon's untimely death shortly after, and the unhappy fate of several of the other people involved, had nurtured a legend of a strange curse upon anyone disturbing the dead ruler's last resting place. The film was thus to be *The Curse of King Tutankhamun's Tomb*.

First, designer John Biggs had to recreate every item of the boy king's treasure: three huge gold sarcophagi (coffins) fitting inside one another, a gilded chariot, and a gold throne with carved lion's heads on each arm, its back bearing a charming picture of the handsome young king being anointed with perfume by his bride. Then there was a bed with heads of cows, lions, and hippopotami at each corner, treasures of lapis lazuli and cornelian, a vulture and a cobra, a crook and flail, a beautiful canopic chest with four tiny golden goddesses on guard around its base, scepters, alabaster jars, wigs, fans, small boats with lifelike figures on board, a black jackal-faced Anubis, rings, jeweled belts, amulets, collars, scarabs, and brooches of turquoise, jasper, and obsidian: a great hoard of glittering beauty that had to be made, perfectly—and quickly.

Somehow John found sculptors, model makers, and jewelers able to reproduce the amazing treasures in detail well enough to be examined by a camera's prying eye, while I planned the production with our new partners. Many of the people at Columbia were old friends. Senior Executive Herman Rush had been my agent during my brief sojourn in the States in 1964. Tim Vignoles from *Mogul* had left MCA and was now Columbia's vice president in London, and Seymour Friedman, friendly codirector on the George Raft film in 1954, was now, 25 years on, a confident head of production at Burbank.

Unfortunately, this concentration of goodwill was offset by the erratic behavior of Executive Producer Hunt Stromberg, Jr., who owned the rights to the script. Son of one of Louis B. Mayer's producers (responsible for some of Greta Garbo's best films), Hunt, Jr., had all the worst flaws of a rich man's son. Mother-pampered and overindulged, homosexual, ultra-wealthy but unloved, alcoholic and drug-addicted, he was capable of sudden manic rages over tiny problems, becoming in seconds a screaming small boy of 56. Yet in a calmer, sober mood he could be transformed into a charming man of acute artistic knowledge and perceptive wit. For a short period Hunt had been an executive at CBS, hiring and firing producers like a medieval princeling. He had set his heart upon making *King Tut* but professed no idea of the limitations of a television budget. Any sensible suggestions for cast were treated with regal scorn. He believed that good actors could be picked up at the last minute, their costumes somehow run up overnight by willing slaves.

Unfortunately he had promised both NBC and Raymond Burr that the *Ironside* star would play a leading part. But it was evident that, fine character actor though he was, Raymond could be neither the aristocratic English Lord Carnarvon, nor the fussy and epicene Howard Carter. In the end Hunt agreed to expand the part of an unscrupulous art dealer dogging Carter's progress, and Raymond made the most of what little it offered.

Hunt was equally confused over Carnarvon's daughter, Evelyn, for whom he suggested several unsuitable California bimbos. In the end he was persuaded to accept the delightful Angharad Rees, but undeterred he created a completely fictitious female reporter involved in an unlikely romance with Carter, and imported Academy Award-winner Eva-Marie Saint for a part unworthy of her considerable talent. Hunt's final act was to cast cocksure Ian McShane (who had given me a splendid performance as a working-class soldier in *Redcap* years before) as the cautious intellectual Howard Carter.

But despite Hunt, I was able to engage powerful actor Harry Andrews as a more likely Carnarvon, dignified Dame Wendy Hiller as a spiritualist medium who predicts his death, Faith Brook as Lady Carnarvon, and Tom Baker and Rupert Frazer in support. The present Lord Carnarvon, who had been an army subaltern in India summoned to Cairo at the time of his father's death, was now a

With Raymond Burr, Luxor, Egypt, *The Curse of King Tutankhamun's Tomb*, **1979.**

sprightly 82. I wrote to him; he was delighted to help and invited us to lunch as Highclere Castle, the imposing family home near Newbury, Berkshire, where his own son, Lord Porchester, was now the Queen's horse-racing trainer.

Hunt and his companion, Joe, arrived by Rolls on best behavior. We were shown around the stately home and admired his lordship's Van Dycks, Romneys, and Gainsboroughs. I asked permission to film scenes in the magnificent library and entrance hall, and

Carnarvon agreed at once. Then Hunt spoiled it all by making a tactless offer to buy a Joshua Reynolds he fancied—"in *cash*, my lord"—and we were practically thrown out.

Diplomatic relations were subsequently restored. But our filming at Highclere was only to be allowed "if that damn Yankee nancy-boy stays away!" (We were happy to comply!) While Hunt was persuaded to loiter even longer around the sale rooms of Sotheby's and Christie's, designer John Biggs, cameraman Bob Edwards, and I flew to Cairo (a very different place from the smart city I'd left 32 years before) to penetrate the bureaucracy and corruption for filming permission, and to engage an Egyptian film company to provide assistant directors, construction workers, drivers, vehicles, and special props.

Then we flew on to Luxor to negotiate with the local ruler for camels and locations. The Valley of the Kings and Tutankhamun's Tomb were too busy as tourist centers to be possible for filming, but we were allowed to create an alternative and authentic digging site, matching Carter's photographs, in the "Valley of the Monkeys," a similar canyon nearby. More labor was recruited, and everything from a mobile kitchen with a carpeted marquee-restaurant to handy desert toilets were imported from Europe.

We returned to Britain hoping that at least Hunt would finally have chosen a director from several interesting suggestions we had left him. He delayed until too many were lost, and in the end had to offer the film to Philip Leacock (certainly not my first choice), a 62-year-old British director from 1950s Pinewood who had gone to Hollywood to direct episodes of *The Waltons* and *Buck Rogers*. As he was of an earlier generation, without having had live television's gift of experience in camera-fluency, Leacock's work seemed to me dull and utterly predictable, and I longed for more originality and adventurousness in staging and performance. Alas it was never to be seen in *King Tut*.

I also wanted several improvements to the script, and here at least I had Leacock's support. Together we could have carried them out, but Hunt thought otherwise, and as the original writer was not available, he insisted on sending to Hollywood for a "rewrite man." When this unfortunate arrived, we were deep in problems of small-part casting, crew visas, and import licenses for all the equipment, including the period cars and an old but still airworthy biplane. Thus the rewrite man's suggestions fell on deaf ears, and although he followed us to Luxor, none of his work was used, as Leacock and I found it simpler to rewrite the necessary scenes ourselves.

The unit was duly installed in a new hotel on the banks of the Nile, ready for a daily crossing by steamer to the tomb sites on the west side, where John Biggs had nearly completed all the sets. But Egyptian customs had impounded all our cameras, lights, generator, and sound equipment on arrival because of some new or invented ruling, and it took a week of hard bargaining by our local associates to secure a complete release.

But at last we could start, with some fairly simple scenes of Ian McShane as Carter in a native market and driving his motorcycle past picturesque ruins at Karnak and Memnon. By the third day all seemed to be going well on a scene at Carter's house on a rocky promontory, so with Mimi and Harry Andrews I drove on to the Valley of the Monkeys where John Biggs was adding the final touches to our "dig" from which all Tutankhamun's treasures would gradually be produced. Everything seemed on schedule, but as we drove back toward Carter's house we could see a cluster of people around the foot of the jagged hillside, with Carter's period Model A Ford suspended on its nose, having obviously been driven over the edge.

Closer, we saw Ian McShane, ashen with pain, being carefully lifted onto a makeshift stretcher and gently placed in the back of a Land Rover to be driven slowly to the ferry and back to the hotel. On the way the crew doctor told us how the accident had occurred.

Leacock had finished the main scene between Eva-Marie Saint and Ian at a lunch table outside the house, ending as Rupert Frazer drove up with bad news from the dig. As scripted, Ian as Carter decided to return immediately, climbing into the driver's seat, with Eva-Marie and Rupert in the back. At that point Leacock cut the scene and wanted another take quickly as the light was fading.

Ian should have jumped out of the car and let the owner-driver take it back to the start. Instead, perhaps with a sense of urgency, he had started the engine and attempted to make a U-turn in the narrow track. But he didn't know that the controls of that model Ford are reversed and the accelerator was where he expected the brake to be. Out of control, the car sped toward the edge of the steep escarpment. Rupert and Eva-Marie leaped clear, but Ian hung on until, too late, he attempted to jump out just before the impact, and smashed his leg in the wreckage as the Ford hit the main track below.

At the hotel Ian was thoroughly examined by our doctor. The leg was severely fractured and needed expert attention. We rapidly organized a hospital jet from Switzerland, and he was flown back to the London Clinic first thing the next morning for the best treatment available. He would clearly be unable to complete the film. I phoned Patrick in Bristol. He went into action immediately, and within a couple of hours he had arranged to fly out a respectable substitute, Robin Ellis, who had had a great success in the BBC's adaptation of Winston Graham's *Poldark*, and might well have been considered more sensitive casting for the moody archaeologist.

Hunt Stromberg of course disagreed. "I don't care if he's Laurence Olivier!" he screamed. *"He's not playing the lead in my film!"* Production was stopped, Columbia was informed, and the unit and cast, including just-arrived Robin Ellis, flew from Luxor back to London. Patrick and I had a couple of days of meetings with Seymour Friedman, and we showed him some of Ellis's work; our decision was approved over Hunt's head, and we returned to Egypt to start again.

One evening, after a heavy day's work in the hot sun, we were all having reviving cold drinks on the terrace of the Winter Palace Hotel. Raymond Burr, who had long since realized his part was scarcely necessary to the main story, had disliked Ian, and now, with Hunt, treated newcomer Robin Ellis with lofty disdain. Not in the best of moods, having been called to the location early and not used until late afternoon, he strolled over to Robin and handed him his own rewritten sketch of the scene they were to shoot the next day. Robin quickly scanned it. Originally it had shown Howard Carter questioning Burr's character, a shifty antiques dealer, about a valuable stolen papyrus. In Raymond's new version, the dealer led the scene, admitting ownership of the document and trying to make a deal to sell it, while Carter remained noncommittal. Robin handed it back. "I can't do this."

Raymond tuned puce. "What do you mean, you little flea? Are

you insulting a super-star?" Robin calmly informed him that the new piece had nothing to do with the script he had agreed to play. At this Raymond gave a theatrical gasp, clutched his chest, and slowly collapsed to the floor, slapping his hand hard on the marble. Hunt leaped up and rushed over to Robin. "My God! You've killed my star!" But Raymond groaned loudly and gradually raised himself to a sitting position, muttering, "I will not appear with that actor."

The scene was dropped from the location schedule, and a sort of peace was re-established, enabling us to shoot the contested sequence later (as originally written) in a library in England. Curiously enough, from that moment production went reasonably well. We completed in Egypt within the revised schedule, including a dramatic escape in a light aircraft by a native digger (Tom Baker) making off with some of King Tutankhamun's artifacts. We had had to import an old Tiger Moth in pieces, reassemble it, and bulldoze a desert runway near the tombs, staging a spectacular explosion (by permission of the local governor, the army, the police, and even the Luxor fire brigade) as the plane appeared to crash on the other side of a hill shortly after takeoff. I had worked with film specialist pilot Captain John Crewdson before, but only with helicopters. Sadly this was our last collaboration, for within a few months he was killed in an aerial collision on another film.

Meanwhile, back in England John Biggs had converted a country-house school in Grittleton near Bath into the luxurious 1920s interior of the Winter Palace Hotel, Luxor, and had also built the whole of the great tunnel leading to the tomb in a huge aircraft hangar rented from the RAF nearby at Coleherne. After temperatures exceeding 100 degrees in Egypt, we finished the film swaddled in thermal underwear, with deep snow in drifts outside.

Despite the melodramatic liberties taken with historical facts, the true story of Howard Carter's tenacity and the eventual discovery of Tutankhamun's treasures was enough to attract and intrigue a huge audience. To the despair of some critics—"With a script like this who needs curses" (Elkan Allan); "A barrage of balderdash" (*Mirror*); "A load of old hokum" (*Sun*); "Tut! What a curse!" (*Washington Post*); "Sly parody of an old Hammer horror film" (*Hollywood Reporter*)—it commanded an outstanding audience on ITV

John Crewdson's deliberate near miss, *Tutankhamun*.

and was number five in the American Top Ten for the whole month of May 1980 when shown in peaktime coast-to-coast on NBC, a first-time achievement for any British-made television film. It was a pleasure for us to read in *Variety* that it had "knocked 'Dallas' out of first place and reduced this mega-hit to its lowest ratings of the season," along with well-deserved praise for Bob Edwards's location photography and John Biggs's outstanding designs.

More importantly it had taught us how to deal with a multi-million-dollar coproduction. Never again would we put up with the tantrums of a prima donna like Hunt Stromberg. Columbia was all set with another offer when negotiations had to be abruptly stopped. Some busybody in the Independent Broadcasting Authority (originally ITA) began questioning the value of the levy rebate that made these large-scale ventures possible. For the next two years our chairman, Lord Harlech, argued at the highest government level and eventually succeeded in getting the rebate restored. But in the interim we could at least make intelligent children's drama, and the Bristol studios had just been reequipped with new color television cameras and mixers that offered immense possibilities for visual effects.

Writer Bob Baker and I rapidly devised *Into the Labyrinth*, in which two boys and a girl exploring a cave in the Mendip Hills hear weird noises coming from a deep grotto and rescue a curious immortal, Rothgo (played by Ron Moody), entrapped in heavy stones by the spell of a glamorous sorceress, Belor (Pamela Salem), who had stolen the source of his powers, the Nidus, and split it into five parts. Unless he can regain all the pieces and make it whole again, he will slowly fade away into oblivion.

Every week the children were to be dispatched by the ever-weakening sorcerer into some other time and place to challenge Belor for another piece of the elusive talisman. We mobilized writers like Anthony Read, Ray Jenkins, Andrew Payne, Robert Holmes, John Lucarotti, Christopher Priest, and Martin Worth to create fantastic adventures among the Druids, in Sherwood Forest, the English Civil War of the 1640s, the French Revolution, and the Labyrinth of Knossos in Crete, with Rothgo and Belor appearing in ever more period disguises, causing walls to vanish, carpets to fly, and people to be reduced to pin-size—every pictorial trick our writers could devise, effectively conjured by designer John Read, the brilliant lighting effects of John Burgess, plus Sydney Sager's imaginative music, and the skill of our inventive crew.

Thus, *Into the Labyrinth*, intended for only a short run, became a cult program, rivaling the BBC's established *Doctor Who*. Ron Moody was persuaded to stay for a second series, into the Nibelung saga, Guy Fawkes and the Gunpowder Plot, the Battle of the Alamo, ancient India, Sherlock Holmes's Victorian London, the 1565 Siege of Malta, and Tutankhamun's ancient Egypt (another use for our special props). Ron Moody had to create a new character for "Rothgo" to assume every week: a Druid priest, a mountebank seized by Robin Hood, an Arabian grand vizier, a Cavalier on the run, a French aristocrat escaping the guillotine, a high priest at Knossos, a Wagnerian blacksmith, Guy Fawkes, an Indian mystic, a Tower of London Beefeater, a rival to Sherlock Holmes, a heroic Knight of St. John, and an Egyptian royal chamberlain—all showing his mastery of characterization and comedy timing. Unfortunately, the pressure was too great, and he refused the third series, where I introduced Chris Harris as Lazlo, another magician in distress, in tales of Treasure Island, Jekyll and Hyde, Inca gold, Marco

Polo, and the secret of King Arthur's sword, Excalibur. Two of the stories had been sent in by young viewers, one, the Phantom of the Opera, by 20-year-old Gary Hopkins, now a well-established writer; and the other, about the Great Fire of London, by 15-year-old Jane McClosky (produced on her sixteenth birthday), who soared upward to a career as a television producer of note, becoming program controller for Westcountry TV in 1995 at the age of 29.

During these years when our international ambitions were at stalemate, there had been another reallocation of ITV program contracts in 1980. With David Elstein I was involved in an unsuccessful bid for Southern, which was trumped by my old associate James Gatward (until 1991, when another reshuffle handed Southern to a new company, Meridian, now part of United Media).

But in late 1982, Lord Harlech at last untangled the levy misunderstanding, and Patrick was able to arrange a new coproduction of *Jamaica Inn*, from Daphne du Maurier's haunting thriller. This rousing adventure among Cornish shipwreckers in the early nineteenth century was scripted by Derek Marlow as a three-hour version for ITV and as four hours for Metro-Media and U.S. Primetime Syndication. The director was Lawrence Gordon Clark, whose work I wholeheartedly admired. Jane Seymour, now a bankable name in the United States, was to play heroine Mary Yellan, who, when her sea captain father is murdered by shipwreckers after a storm, goes to live with her aunt in a mysterious inn on Bodmin Moor, and slowly discovers that her uncle, Joss Merlyn, is one of the leaders of the deadly wrecking gang.

Patrick McGoohan agreed to return from Hollywood to create the villainous Joss, Billie Whitelaw was to be the terrorized aunt, and another old friend, Peter Vaughan, the squire. Trevor Eve as Jem, Joss's gypsy brother, and John McEnery as the vicar, headed a very strong cast. Designer Ken Jones built the inn on a windy hillside on Dartmoor, not far from the grim prison for long-sentence prisoners. Since the story was to begin with the wrecking of a huge, ocean-going sailing ship,and another was to be destroyed halfway through, Lawrence began muttering about "models" until I persuaded him that the most realistic way of staging the wrecks would be to equip a condemned hulk with breakaway masts and sails and to drive her onto the rocks in bad weather (as we had done in *Kidnapped*).

As we were using *Marques* again, I asked the owner, Robin Cecil-Wright, to help. Searching the southwest coast, he discovered the *Beechgrove*, an 85-foot former naval supply vessel lying half buried in mud near Penryn, abandoned for many years since the Department of Trade had pronounced her unseaworthy. The ship was refloated and towed around to Padstow in North Cornwall, our base for coastal filming, and the carpenters went to work, making her a rough-and-ready soft-hulled double for the elegant *Marques*. A false prow and bowsprit, hardboard poopdeck, and stern cabin were all nailed on. The *Marques*'s distinctive white gunwale with gunports was reproduced. Three old telegraph poles were lowered through holes in the deck and roughly secured as masts. Sails made of easily torn cotton were hoisted, with hemp rigging and light wood yards, all designed to crack and splinter on impact. The rotten hull was broached and patched with thin planks that would give way as she struck rock, causing the impressive-looking ship to heel right over.

When all was ready, we prepared to film at 7:00 A.M. one wet October morning. Robin and a crew of three volunteers, armor under their shirts, crash helmets concealed by straggly wigs, were towed out to sea on the doomed *Beechgrove* against an onshore wind that would speed them back toward the rocky shore on the incoming tide.

If ever a shot was "one-take," this one was. We watched the old craft being slowly hauled into place and saw the sails set. Slightly nervous, Lawrence called, "Action," over the radio.

For a few moments nothing seemed to happen. The tug, cast off, sped out of shot. The cameras started rolling. Then slowly making way the *Beechgrove* began to move toward us, acquiring a curious dignity in the last short voyage she would ever make. The waves rolled in over jagged limestone teeth as the ship came on, closer and closer yet.

Then, with a crashing and tearing sound, the hull struck rock and burst open, the sails ripped, masts crashed onto the deck, and with elephantine grace the great vessel lurched over to settle at last at an ugly angle of 45 degrees. Lawrence and his cast of stunt men now had to work really fast staging the attack on the stricken ship by the Cornish wreckers, "killing off" any member of the ship's crew attempting to escape through churning surf to shore, before they made off with the cargo.

As the tide receded again, he had to film the aftermath, the seamen's bodies lying in the sand, as the squire rides up to inspect the damage and utters a condemnation of the outlaws who had lured the ship onto the rocks with false signal lights and murdered innocent seamen in their greed for goods.

By lunchtime it was already low tide. With beach scenes completed, Lawrence and the main film crew departed for scenes on the nearby cliffs, while our riggers secured the beached wreck with four strong anchors, and I stayed with the second camera team for more shots of bloodied sailors floating in the surf. The plan was to leave the wreck anchored in place overnight, and patch it up in the morning for a second wrecking on another rocky beach after we had refloated it on the morning tide.

The wind was rising. Our camera was suddenly swamped by a wave from the returning tide. Cameraman Mike Hastie hurried back to the hotel to dry his equipment while I ran to the temporary production office in a boardinghouse overlooking the sea to change trousers. Glancing out the window, I saw the stormy tide thundering in again, making the wreck of the *Beechgrove* shudder ominously, and I dashed down to join a group of watching locals. High seas were already surging dangerously around the stricken hulk. "Them anchors of yours ain't gonna hold her," one of the boatmen declared.

I ran back to the hotel. Clad in a bath towel, Mike had his camera in pieces on the bed, and was slowly and carefully wiping each part. "Get your clothes on—and bring the camera!"

I radioed Lawrence on the cliffside and told him our ship was about to wreck itself a second time. Within a few minutes we had three cameramen set up along the cliffs filming the huge ship as it was picked up like a toy by wind and raging sea and flung back against the rocks. But daylight was failing fast. From among the small crowd of spectators our gaffer electrician emerged to make an amazing offer. "Shall I get the generator and a couple of H.I. arcs round here, Guv'nor?"

"What about your meal break?"

To which he replied (a sentence never before spoken in the

The wreck at Padstow by day, *Jamaica Inn*.

long history of British film production), *"Bugger our meal break, you've got to get your shots!"* And as darkness fell two bright lamps sputtered onto the breaking wreck as it smashed to matchwood, giving us an unforgettable second-act climax far better than any special effects team could ever have devised.

We continued filming all through cold and dismal November and December, capturing an authentically bleak view of the desolate moors. Jane Seymour was frequently soaked and freezing for much of the day, including one afternoon when a group of Royal marines, fresh from the rigors of the Falklands War, passed close by, retreating to barracks because they found the weather too rough! But we soldiered on.

I also took my unit to sea in the *Marques*, and for the first time, as she heeled rather too violently, I felt strangely unsafe aboard the large sailing ship and immediately ordered her back to port.

Shown on ITV in May 1983, *Jamaica Inn* was a resounding success, repaying all our effort. Jane Seymour, Patrick McGoohan, and Billie Whitelaw were acclaimed, and the show was number five in the National Top Ten that week, gaining a far greater audience than, for instance, *Brideshead Revisited* ever achieved. In the United States the *Hollywood Reporter* praised "impressive action sequences, a suspenseful story, cogent performances and vigorously effective execution."

People magazine averred that Patrick McGoohan's Joss Merlyn "held our attention better than any villain since Sweeney Todd, and deserves the highest honor in television today." It wasn't Patrick but the whole film that won a major drama award that year at the New York Television Festival.

By spring 1983 we were already busy with another coproduction with Columbia, a three-hour version of *The Master of Ballantrae*, by Robert Louis Stevenson, set in the same historical period as *Kidnapped*. It was scripted by William Bast, with Larry White as executive producer and Hugh Benson as producer for Columbia, all seasoned professionals, quite different from the neurotic Hunt Stromberg. We were able to assemble a magnificent cast, headed by Sir John Gielgud, Michael York, Richard Thomas, Timothy Dalton, Ian Richardson, Brian Blessed, Nickolas Grace, and the attractive Finola Hughes, who had just scored in *Staying Alive*, dancing energetically with John Travolta.

As the only American in a British cast, Richard Thomas (the friendly "Johnboy" from long-running *The Waltons*) was concerned about acquiring a credible Scottish accent. Luckily, Iain Cuthbertson was recovering from an illness and agreed to take the whole cast in hand (including the once-formidable Sir John), and in the end through perseverance Richard was one of the few actors to achieve an authentic Highland burr.

Douglas Hickox, who had a unique visual style, was director, but as we had to cover the whole Battle of Culloden again (but with a bigger budget than for *Kidnapped*), a sea battle between a pirate vessel and a Royal Navy warship, and many adventures in canoes, rapids, and trackless forests, we set up a second unit once more for the complicated action sequences.

We had used St. Catherine's Court, a Victorian Gothic mansion in the hills north of Bath, for the squire's house in *Jamaica Inn*. Jane Seymour and her (then) husband, David Flynn, had admired the property, made an offer, and were now proud owners. It was a perfect choice for the Ballantrae family home; a deal was negotiated, and Douglas made full use of its elegant rooms and library, the conservatory and the rolling grounds.

For the two ships, we found that in addition to the *Marques*, Robin Cecil-Wright and his new partner, Mark Litchfield, had converted another Spanish trader, the *Ciudad de Inca*, with a similar period square-rig. They were planning a voyage to the Caribbean with both vessels, but by increasing the charter fee we persuaded them to film with us in Dartmouth first.

The sun shone and all was calm for our three-day sea chase and fierce engagement with heavy cannon. Stuntmen reeled bleeding from the rigging, the air was loud with the cries of the wounded and thick with smoke and the reek of cordite as the two great sailing ships charged each other again like white bulls in slow motion, let fly with their cannonballs, retired, went about and lined up to prepare for the next take—until at last Douglas was satisfied.

Near Symonds Yat, where the river Wye flows fast and deep, John Biggs built a primitive North American stockaded village on the river bank, which even Larry White, a native of New York State, pronounced authentic to the last split log. Valiant Bristolians had their heads shaved and their bodies painted to become convincing Adirondack Indians tracking our heroes, Michael York and Timothy Dalton, through the thick woods of the Forest of Dean, to bury their stolen treasure under a gushing waterfall. And when it rained too heavily, we sheltered in John Gielgud's trailer to enjoy his fund of outrageous stories.

The actors loved it, swordfights, cannon fire, and all, and when it was shown on ITV the following year Richard Last of the *Telegraph* described the sweep of the story and varied locations as "scrumptious—in the same dramatic mould as HTV's earlier success, *Jamaica Inn*."

Once again we gained high ratings, and were, not surprisingly, number one in Scotland. In the United States, shown for a full three hours from 8:00 P.M. on CBS nationwide in January 1984 on the "Hallmark Hall of Fame," the film gathered some impressive reviews:

Filming *Marques* at sea off Dartmouth for *Ballantrae*.

"Well acted, swiftly paced and eminently watchable"—*New York Times*.

"A sure winner"—*Variety*.

"An Epic Adventure—*Hollywood Reporter*.

"Riproaring hugely entertaining swashbuckler. I fell completely under its boisterous spell"—*Los Angeles Herald*.

"That completely rare commodity—intelligent escapism"—*People* magazine. (Praise indeed from the toughest television critics in the world.)

But tragedy struck soon afterward. The elegant *Marques*, which I had failed to dissuade Robin Cecil-Wright from buying all those years before (but no less a fine ship, which I had been glad to use many times since), was on a voyage in the Caribbean when it was struck by a sudden squall, swamped by a freak wave, and overturned and sunk in minutes. Of 28 people aboard, 19 were lost, many of them our friends, including the captain, his wife, and small

Filming the *Marques*, with Ray Gallard, *Ballantrae*.

baby. Secure as my crews had always been, with a safety boat close at hand, we could all too easily imagine the horror of these last moments as the unpredictable sea suddenly rose up violently to claim a few more victims. Even recently the other boat we had used on *Ballantrae*, the *Inca*, now owned entirely by Mark Litchfield, and renamed *Santa Maria* after many exploits all over the world, finally sank in 1996 quite near Padstow where we had staged our own carefully organized wreck for *Jamaica Inn*. A sorry end indeed.

Our next production, again for CBS, with executive producers John Newlands and Ted Rayner, was entirely different in style and theme from Stevenson's rich adventure. *Arch of Triumph*, set in a Paris full of refugees fleeing from the German Nazis just before the outbreak of the Second World War, had been written in deep depression by Erich Maria Remarque (renowned author of *All Quiet on the Western Front*).

The doomed love affair of Ravic, a refugee German surgeon forced to earn money by secretly performing difficult operations

Dartmouth again, Bayards Cove, *Ballantrae.*

Filming at sea aboard the *Marques*, for *Ballantrae*.

for less gifted doctors, and Joan, a shiftless nightclub singer, was told with a power and truth not revealed in a pathetically romanticized film version made in about 1948 by aging Lewis Milestone, with Charles Boyer, Ingrid Bergman, and Charles Laughton. But a new television script by Charles Israel magically conveyed the novel's dark atmosphere, while at the same time creating a certain optimism, in contrast to the threat of war.

Anthony Hopkins agreed to play Ravic, Lesley-Anne Down was Joan, with Donald Peasence an undercover German Gestapo officer, Frank Finlay a White Russian nightclub doorman, Richard Pasco a friendly Parisian doctor, and Joyce Blair a golden-hearted brothel keeper.

Waris Hussein directed. We chose locations in those parts of Paris not yet ruined by modernization, contriving to stop the frenzied traffic normally roaring around the Arc de Triomphe (with amazing police assistance) for important scenes not once but twice, early on a Sunday morning and late on a Tuesday night. We also filmed all one night on a narrow bridge in the shadow of Notre Dame, catching the unique flavor of small hotels, with their cramped and grinding elevators and dark stuffy rooms, of restaurants like Escargot near Les Halles and Julienne in the Rue Saint-Denis, and of nightclubs where sad people tried to drink away unhappy memories.

Designer Jane Martin built lifelike interiors in the hangars of RAF Coleherne, Julie Harris captured the spirit of the period with her attractive costumes, and Bob Edwards's photography brilliantly conveyed the wistfully seedy atmosphere. Anthony Hopkins was powerful and moving as Ravic, inspiring Lesley-Anne Down to one of her finest screen performances as Joan, with riveting support from Pleasence, Finlay, Pasco, and Blair.

When it was shown on peaktime CBS in the autumn, *Variety* found the film "a striking example of intelligence at work by all hands," and the *New York Times* called it "that unusual primetime phenomenon—an adult story told with the minimum of audience-research distraction." Despite these comments, the American public found the story and subject "too sad" and switched to other channels. However, in Britain the ITV audience loved it, giving us number six in the weekly Top Ten.

Night filming in Paris with Anthony Hopkins *(right). Arch of Triumph.*

Three international successes created a dangerous euphoria. Our next assignment for Columbia, *Jenny's War*, was an unfortunate mistake. This was the true story of a North County working-class English woman, Florence Barrington, married to and separated from her German photographer husband before 1939, whose RAF pilot son was shot down in the early years of the conflict. She decided to use her German passport to make the difficult journey through France and Switzerland to discover his fate, was subsequently arrested and tortured by the Gestapo, and was finally released. She found her son at last in a prisoner-of-war camp, then cut her hair to take the place of an escaping prisoner inside the camp until the war's end. It was an enthralling tale of courage and persistence.

After the story was fictionalized in a novel by *Daily Mirror* writer Jack Stoneley, the idea of turning it into a four-hour television miniseries had hung fire until someone in the networks decided it could be made palatable by making the woman American and

Filming in a real Paris street. *Arch of Triumph.*

casting film star Dyan Cannon. Of course it was unlikely that any-one as attractive as Miss Cannon would be working as an under-paid schoolmarm in Bristol, England, but no matter. Columbia said, "Jump," and we jumped.

As unashamed melodrama, Stephen Gethers's script worked. He was also appointed director. We arranged to fly the last RAF Lancaster bomber (it should have been a Wellington, but by 1984 none existed). Wartime German railway engines and carriages were found in working order in the privately run Nene Valley Railway near Peterborough, and designers Bruce Grimes and Hazel Peiser converted a disused army camp near Ollerton, Nottinghamshire, into a grim POW camp, complete with barbed-wire fences, parade grounds, and watchtowers fitted with menacing machine guns.

We filmed every day during the wet and cold months of win-ter. Because of a national coal miners' strike, our huge camp, which should have been empty for our use, was filled with policemen sent north to keep order at night, sleeping during the day. As Ollerton was one of the few coal mines still working, there were frequent

The prison camp, Ollerton, *Jenny's War.*

disturbances and pitched battles with flying pickets nearby. Being so close to suffering and deprivation added a sense of unreality to our work in the camp, and a genuine feeling of release as we escaped through the gates each night to the comfort of a local hotel.

Despite the not exactly inspired script, our cast, headed by Robert Hardy, Elke Sommer, Nigel Hawthorne, Richard Todd, Christopher Cazenove, Michael Elphick, Oscar Quitak, and even a young Hugh Grant as Dyan Cannon's RAF son, made the most of the opportunities offered.

The highlight of the fourth hour was a camp concert staged by the prisoners to ease the aching boredom, coinciding with a Gestapo search for Jenny through the huts, forcing her to mingle with the hefty transvestite "showgirls" singing on stage to avoid being recaptured. But as Gethers had spent the war in the Pacific, he had little idea how to stage a truly appalling British Army concert. For once my army service paid off, and with Adrian King I devised probably the most vulgar and outrageous drag show ever seen. Gethers had simply to point his camera.

At last shooting ended, and Gethers presented his fine cut. Many of the action sequences needed further work, and after consultation with coproducers Lou Rudolph and Bob Chenault, I recalled some of the actors and reshot for eight days, recutting other material to heighten dramatic impact.

I need not have bothered. *Jenny's War* was not particularly successful in the United States, and in Britain the critics had a ball, rubbishing everything from Dyan Cannon's unconvincing Eton Crop wig when posing as a "man" to the glaring inaccuracies and incredible situations in the script. Having lavished superlatives on our earlier efforts, they reversed their energy into outraged abuse. But our audience supplied a different judgment. Whether attracted by so much adverse publicity or from sheer curiosity they watched in huge numbers. For four weeks *Jenny's War* stayed near the top of the Top Ten. But Florence Barrington's real, human story remained untold.

Our 1985 coproduction was, alas, no happier—an experimental joint venture with Telecip of France, Primedia of Canada, Klaus Hardt of Germany, and no fewer than 12 other European partners. The original plot of *Frontier*, or, as it appeared in English, *The Adventures of a Lady*, was conceived by a Frenchman, but it went through many minds and hands before a final multicolored script, much rewritten, emerged as a ragbag of international tosh.

In the eighteenth century, we were asked to believe, the noble Lady Anne Howard, wrongly tried and condemned for the alleged murder of her husband, is apparently hanged but really secretly released, having agreed under duress to travel to Nova Scotia on the trail of dissolute French Baron Griffard and his half-Indian companion, Faucillon, who are suspected of being spies on a mission to turn the Iroquois Indians from loyalty to the British, then occupying much of Canada, to an alliance with France. Forced by the captain's mistake to share a cabin with Griffard on the outward voyage, Lady Anne sees him robbed of his funds in a rigged card game by her accomplice, evil mercenary Captain Richter. Arriving penniless in the fortified town of Louisbourg, the baron is flung into jail, but Faucillon helps him escape, and they eventually join Lady

Filming at Gloucester Docks, *The Adventures of a Lady,* **1985.**

Anne's party making the journey inland. After being captured by unfriendly Indians, they finally reach the Iroquois, but instead of carrying out their task, they are arrested by British redcoats, to be returned to Britain for execution. On the voyage home, Lady Anne, now obviously in love with Griffard, contrives his escape by lifeboat during a storm, but is led to believe he has been drowned.

In London they meet once more, but Captain Richter thwarts their return to France. Lady Anne, dressed as a boy, is seized by a navy press gang while Griffard fights his way back to France, is denounced as a traitor, but decamps to Louisbourg again, to be miraculously reunited with Lady Anne (released by a gallant Royal Navy captain), and the couple set off for a new future in Canada.

Obviously only speed, panache, and a reckless disregard for improbability could make this six-hour farrago presentable, but at the time it seemed worth a try, particularly as we had nothing else on offer. I was able to cast Mel Martin as Lady Anne, with old friends Ronald Fraser, Douglas Wilmer, Peter Copley, and Clive Merrison in support, but then had to hope for the best from foreign actors like Daniel Ceccaldi (France) as Griffard, Matt Birman

Filming in Bath, *Adventures of a Lady*.

(Canada) as Faucillon, Mathieu Carriere (Germany) as Richter, and Paolo Baroni (Italy) as a Catholic Father.

To handle the far-fetched tale with, we were promised, all the energy of a pace-conscious British or American director, we had to accept Victor Vicas, who proved to be exactly the opposite, an old-fashioned French hack, as obstinate as he was slow-thinking. What we didn't know at the time was that he was also very ill. He somehow managed to avoid the stringent medical examination that our British insurers normally insist upon for directors, but produced some sort of health certificate just before the first day of shooting.

This was to be in Louisbourg, in the north of Nova Scotia, which Canadian Parks has restored exactly as it was in the 1740s, complete with Citadel, Governor's Palace, chapel, and many streets of houses and taverns, as a tourist attraction populated with local inhabitants in period costume as villagers, fishermen, and soldiers, ready to explain their working day to all. We had generously been given filming permission for 18 days, but Vicas, after two years of preparation on full pay, grumbled that he could never shoot a whole hour of action in that short time. (At home we allowed ten days!)

On the first day of shooting, Vicas asserted his independence by wasting a couple of hours on a pointless long tracking shot of extras unloading bales from a ship, while his leading actors waited in the rain. After a few days, slipping well behind schedule, I telexed Patrick Dromgoole in Bristol asking for him to be replaced, but apparently the main finance depended on having a French director. However, it was finally agreed with Pat Ferns of Primedia that young and talented Canadian director Alan Kroeker would take over after Louisbourg in the Canadian forest locations and Vicas would resume in France in December.

Somehow Vicas stumbled through the simple scenes in the Citadel city. The main battle sequence was taken over by a special effects team in my hands. Kroeker then made the next two one-hour episodes on time, obtaining remarkable performances from real Canadian Indians, one of whom, Graham Greene, went on to play a big part in Kevin Costner's *Dances with Wolves*. In France once again Vicas commenced with a French unit in a tumbledown château on the river Marne, while I gritted my teeth in frustration at his infuriating delays.

I returned to Bristol on the Friday of that week. On Sunday afternoon I had a call from an unhappy Patrick. Vicas had apparently had a heart attack the night before. Investigation had shown that it was by no means his first. I was to fly to Paris at once and take over the following day. I arrived on location that Monday morning to a sullen crew full of "pauvre Victor" moaning. The scheduled scene was quiet stuff, so to wake them up I decided to shoot a chase through the woods, with Indian Faucillon hotly pursued by a posse of horsemen. The slow-paced French wondered what had suddenly hit them. I made sure they didn't stop running until lunchtime, when, with 25 setups in the can, they paused for a Gauloise-wreathed break muttering sourly, "*Les Anglaises sont fous!*"

But the ice was broken. They forgot the sick director and began to work for quality at a proper pace. At the end of the week, well up to schedule, I handed over to writer-director Pierre Lary, who added some style, finished the French episodes, and came to England for the last four weeks at Bristol, Longleat, Gloucester Docks, and Bath. A few days later we heard the sad news that Victor Vicas, having concealed the fact that he had been suffering from a serious heart condition for some time, had died during an operation. Tragically, none of us had had any idea that he was so totally unfit for the strain of a multifaceted production. Had we known, of course, he would never have been allowed to start.

When at last edited to six hours, the film suffered from its muddled script and many different styles of direction. Even when the foreigners had been skillfully dubbed by good British actors, notably George Baker (Baron Griffard, whom he could have played so much better on-screen!) and June Barrie (as Faucillon's alehouse-keeper sister), some of the performances remained substandard. The film was, however, shown successfully in Canada, France, and the other countries. We slipped it into ITV in half-hour segments for 12 Sunday afternoons. It did us no harm, but no good either.

On the positive side, I had enjoyed working with energetic and enthusiastic Canadian crews, but I could see that in any future coproductions with the French we would have to be more involved from the outset in concept, script, and choice of director.

In 1986 Columbia came to our rescue with a couple of comedies, *The Canterville Ghost* and *Three Wishes for Jamie*. For the first, based on Oscar Wilde's short story, we suggested John Gielgud as the tetchy 300-year-old ghost condemned to haunt his castle and frighten away any would-be occupants as a punishment for causing his own wife's death. I sent him the American script, and a few days later drove with costume designer Robin Fraser-Paye to his small but perfect country house, originally a Palladian-style music room, in Buckinghamshire.

Sir John welcomed us, but the atmosphere was slightly frosty. He admired Robin's designs for his main costumes, but lunch, excellent as always, was eaten with less of the usual Gielgud gossip. After coffee he picked up the *Canterville* script. "Have you read this?"

I admitted I had. "But have you studied the original Oscar Wilde?" he asked. "Because I seem to remember some rather good ideas that aren't in this version."

Luckily I had brought a couple of photocopies of the short story. Together we combed through it, discovering at least three good scenes that had somehow slipped from the adaptation, which I promised would be included.

When Paul Bogart arrived, a rotund and cheerful director I liked on sight, I broke the news. He too had reservations about the script, and together we drafted new material, sent it to the writer for approval, and took the result to Sir John for a much more festive lunch. Gielgud knew and liked Bogart, who had directed a live New York television version of his one-man show of Shakespearean monologues, *The Ages of Man*, many years before.

For the American family which inherits Canterville Castle, updated from Wilde's turn of the century to the 1950s, we cast three interesting comedy actors: Andrea Marcovicci as the stepmother, Ted Wass, late of *Soap*, as her husband, and the delightful 14-year-old Alyssa Milano from *Who's the Boss?* as the daughter who strikes up a warm friendship with the lonely old ghost. In real life the unspoiled Alyssa charmed the distinguished Sir John so much that he would never allow a take to be printed before checking that she, the inexperienced girl, was satisfied.

Main filming was at Eastnor Castle, near Malvern, Worcestershire, a reproduction trumpet-towered "Norman" castle built by Sir Robert Smirke from 1812 onward, with an interesting fan-vaulted ceiling in the huge drawing room by Pugin and Bernasconi bearing a great bronze chandelier, and a Renaissance-style library by G. E. Cox. Though freezing cold in March, it was an inspiring place, and every night in his favorite restaurant in Worcester Sir John would hold court until 10:00 P.M. precisely, relating his indiscreet and ribald stories and even singing a verse or two of *The Good Ship Venus*.

We took a good deal of trouble with special effects. Every appearance and disappearance of the old ghost was made in a different and humorous way, and the scene where a manic ghost-hunter (Bill Wallis), using every bit of electronic equipment we would string together, conjures up not just the ancient Canterville but his murdered wife as well, finally climaxed in a mighty explosion that shook the old ramparts to their foundations.

The result was shown the following Easter Sunday. For once even the *Daily Express* reveled instead of reviling us:

> The beauty of this highly-inventive family film was that
> it could be enjoyed on two levels. There was enough

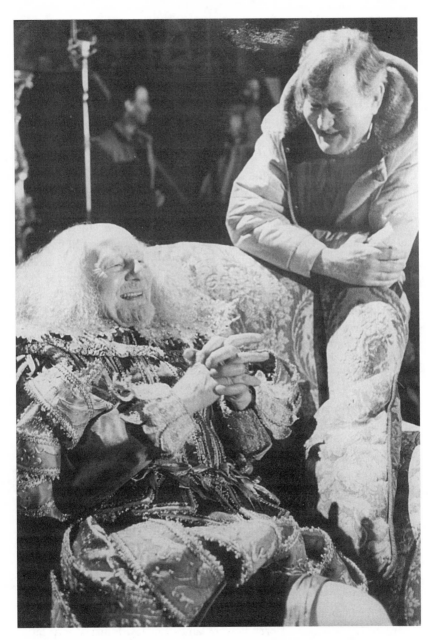

With Sir John Gielgud, Eastnor Castle, *Canterville Ghost.*

> technical wizardry to captivate the most computer-conscious child, but also a sly script full of in-jokes for the adults.
>
> "*Actors!*" boomed the 17th-century Sir John, when told of television's mysteries. "Why, even the King's Players are renowned as the very scum of London!"
>
> I swear that I heard the ghost of a laugh in the voice of one of our greatest living thespians as he spoke Oscar's words....

Fair enough as praise, but those words weren't in fact penned by Oscar Wilde but were a last-minute addition of my own!

The American public enjoyed the joke too, coast to coast.

Soon we embarked on *Three Wishes for Jamie*, to star Jack Warden, from *Crazy Like a Fox*, as Owen Tavish, a wily old matchmaker on the west coast of Ireland at the turn of the century. Based on a 1950s Broadway musical (which flopped!) and a novel by Charles O'Neal, Laurence Roman's whimsical script had great charm but precious little originality.

Tavish finds a rich bride for young Jamie M'Grew to save his family from penury. But Jamie has dreamed he is to be given three wishes by Una, queen of the fairies. He promptly wishes for travel, the girl of his dreams, and a son who will speak the ancient Gaelic tongue. Angry at Jamie's refusal, the girl's six brothers pursue Tavish and Jamie for miles, and over a rickety bridge, which collapses, throwing the old man and the boy into a raging torrent.

Presuming the two fugitives dead, Jamie's brother takes his place as a suitor. The M'Grew farm is saved from the bailiffs, and Tavish and the boy Jamie sneak off to the United States, where of course our young hero meets the girl of his dreams, unfortunately already betrothed to another, and after many more complications the second and third of his wishes are finally granted.

The paper-thin plot needed a visual stylist to bring it to life, and I was able to offer it to a talented director I had admired for some years, Robert William Young.

Full of rich characters and colorful incidents, the film was a gift for Dublin's fine range of actors. Marie Conmee, Barry Lynch, Liam O'Callaghan, Derry Power, James Bartley, Fiona MacAnna, and Gillian Hacket all contributed rich comic cameos under Robert's direction during two weeks of unexpectedly sunny weather on the green coast of Connemara near Clifden. The Guinness flowed, lobster and turbot came fresh from the Atlantic to the table, and our crew returned in good health and spirits to the woods and lakes of Woodchester in Gloucestershire to complete the sequences in "early America."

Shown on Saint Patrick's night across the United States in 1987, the film gained a huge and appreciative audience, with special praise from *Variety* and other papers as "lovely and authentic," "with the charm and buoyancy of a good Irish tale," and so on. It continues to be reeled out every Saint Patrick's night on some channel or other.

The year ended on a high note for HTV and all the hard-working members of my film crews when we were awarded the coveted "Queen's Award for Export Achievement for 1986," which was cited as "a tribute to the talented production teams who make outstanding programmes for Worldwide sales."

Our company was expanding fast—too fast, as it later transpired. Having built a £14 million ($21 million) studio complex at Culverhouse Cross, Cardiff, partly to serve the new Welsh-language fourth channel S4C (Sianel Pedwar Cymru), the cramped Bristol studios that had no less satisfied all our needs over the years were rebuilt at a cost exceeding £4 million ($6 million). The refurbished premises were opened on December 2, 1986, by Her Royal Highness Princess Anne, who paused on her tour in the cutting rooms to watch scenes from *Three Wishes for Jamie*. On that happy day not one of us dreamed that the good times might be coming to an end....

Suddenly, at a stroke, Margaret Thatcher's government abolished the levy rebate, which had supplied two-thirds of our large budgets for programs sold overseas. We thus had to turn to Europe for different financial partnerships on smaller-scale films. The first two I produced in early 1987 were *Hand in Glove*, directed by Peter Duffell, with Nicola Paget, Helen Cherry, and Helen's husband, Trevor Howard, in his very last screen appearance; and *The Hospice*, directed by Dominique Othenin-Girard (a good French *metteur en scène* for a change!), with Jack Shepherd and Marthe Keller, both in association with Hamster Productions of Paris.

With Jack Warden, Clifden, Connemara, Ireland, *Three Wishes for Jamie*, 1986.

These were followed by my final film for Columbia, for peaktime NBC, *Wall of Tyranny* (or *Freedom Fighter* in the United States), directed by Desmond Davis, with Tony Danza, from *Who's the Boss?*, David McCallum, Geraldine James, and Syd Caesar. This was filmed partly in the shadow of the hideously real Berlin Wall, but mostly against a huge replica we built across a large stretch of the city of Bradford, Yorkshire, because of its Teutonic-looking architecture.

Though it gained a good audience on ITV and in the United States, this had to be the end of my friendly association with Hollywood. Seymour Friedman left, and Columbia was sold, first to Coca-Cola, then to SONY.

However, coproductions with Hamster meant much less interference, though on smaller budgets. In the summer of 1988 I was able to commission John Elliot and his daughter, Julia, to write *A Chance to Dance*, an original romantic story of the pains and passions in a struggling Bristol ballet company, Their script (sadly, the last John wrote before his untimely death) called for the creation of a short new ballet. I contacted Christopher Gable, who had just

Opening of rebuilt HTV Bristol Studios. With Her Royal Highness, Princess Anne, watching scenes from *Three Wishes for Jamie*.

taken over Northern Ballet Theatre, and with his choreographer, Michael Pink, he devised "Memoire Imaginaire," based on the tempestuous affair between Impressionist painter Edouard Manet and his sometime model Berthe Morisot, which was danced for us on film by Mireille Bourgeois and Anthony Harith, doubling for principal actors Judi Trott, Patrick Ryecart, Emma Sutton, and Dominic Hawksley, who had to learn to become credible dancers for close-ups.

Having planned an intricate camera-script for each ballet sequence, intercutting real dancers and actors, I decided to direct this one myself, and spent an enjoyable four weeks in and around Bristol with my talented young cast.

Immediately after it was finished, I produced Peter Duffell's *Some Other Spring*, a thriller filmed in Istanbul, Turkey, with Jenny Seagrove and Dinsdale Landen, again completed in four weeks. I next produced *To Each His Own*, a powerful drama about twin boys, one of whom was given to the wrong mother at birth, and the complications that ensued when the mistake was discovered some years later; it was scripted by Bristol writer Rosemary Mason and directed by Moira Armstrong in newly developed Cardiff Bay, featuring Julia Watson and Hilton McRae.

Though made on the tightest of budgets, each of these two-hour productions showed up well in the Top Ten. But HTV's powerful position as a major supplier of top-quality drama had been eroded, and the company's finances were further unbalanced by several ill-judged purchases by the Board of Modern Art. Galleries, television facilities, poetry publishers, and other unrelated enterprises all suffered badly in the slump from 1990 onward. With no hope of ever repeating earlier ambitious projects, I felt the time had come for me to leave HTV, after 16 happy years.

With Bristol Old Vic Theatre I had been involved with a scheme to help new local writers, and as a final flourish I produced on minuscule budgets two half-hour plays: *Starstruck*, by Peter Kesterton, about a manic entertainment officer (played by Bryan Murray) in a rundown seaside resort, desperate to create a full-scale planetarium at the end of a rotting pier; and *Just Like Eddie*, by Catherine Johnson, with Academy Award-winner Brenda Fricker as a suburban housewife obsessed with a fantasy that she spent a night of passion with rock singer Eddie Cochran the night before he was killed in a car crash near Bristol. Both were neat and effective, shown on ITV, and led to better assignments for both authors, particularly Catherine, who enjoyed success in theater and television, and authored the hit ABBA musical "*Mama Mia!*"

Meanwhile, a new national network had been successfully launched, the product of much thought, argument, and aspiration: a second commercial television outlet, the long-awaited *Channel Four*.

10

1970–Present:
The Birth of
Channel Four

*A showcase for originality—but how
long can it continue?*

Today the cheerful visual signature of Channel Four bounds
onto our screens, assured and proud. But the conception and birth
of this infant service, the last quarter of British television, was
fraught with as much disagreement and doubt as the original plan
for commercial television.

The Independent Television Authority had always agreed that
a second competitive advertising channel was technically available,
but the ITV companies, determined to maintain their profitable
monopoly, invariably rejected the idea, until, as profits mounted
and pressure on slots in popular programs increased, the advertisers themselves began to demand an alternative outlet. The ITV companies grudgingly agreed, provided they could run the second
channel as well.

But many producers (and I was one) could see a chance for a
channel that was in every way original and different from ITV,
allowing space for independent and regional producers, and catering to neglected minorities. But both Labour and Tory governments,
in power through the 1960s and 1970s, dithered and held back from
boldly establishing the channel we wanted.

The indifference accorded to the considered views of program-makers was clearly demonstrated at a meeting in 1973 at the House of Commons attended, as council-members of the Association of TV Directors and Producers, by David Elstein, then a distinguished documentary maker, Mark Shivas, the award-winning drama producer, Christopher Nupen, an outstandingly successful producer of classical music on television, and myself. The ruling Tory "Media Committee," listened to what we had to propose in somnolent silence and did nothing further.

Yet slowly the momentum grew. People from all walks of life began to support the crying need for a television channel that could give access to any citizen with something of value to say. Rather than continue to pretend that this powerful visual medium of communication could be effective only in the hands of trained writers and directors, we, the practitioners, wanted to demonstrate how easily television could be used as a language for all.

At last, at the beginning of 1980, the Independent Broadcast Authority (IBA) called a meeting of those of us involved in the public debate. Every sort of program was discussed, and the authority was able to discover at least 400 teams willing to become small production companies ready to submit ideas. Then, in April, before Parliament could discuss and approve a possible Channel Four company, a new lobby, Plaid Cymru, the Welsh Nationalist Party, demanded a separate Welsh-speaking channel alongside the new one, to redeem a promise made in a Conservative Party election manifesto. Whole communities refused to pay their license fees, transmitters were attacked, and party leader Gwynfor Evans threatened to fast unto death if the pledge was not honored.

The government hastily reconsidered, and when it sanctioned a Channel Four company it also agreed to set up Sianel Pedwar Cymru (S4C). Though the costliest-per-viewer television station in the world, the use and understanding of the old language increased, with a varied mix of drama, documentaries, advice and entertainment for the handicapped, agriculture, events like the National Eisteddfod (Festival of Music and Poetry), education, religion, children's programs, and a comprehensive service of news and current affairs—all in Welsh.

The main Channel Four was established with Jeremy Isaacs,

former program director at Thames, appointed chief executive with Paul Bonner, former BBC head of science and features, as controller of programs. They promised that the new channel would create a vitally new television experience by encouraging programs from independent producers from all over Britain, which would open up choice for viewers, and even at times further a broad educational purpose—a channel that would be unlike any other in existence.

But who would pay for this brave new venture? Initially we had proposed that the Independent Broadcasting Authority should fix a reasonable budget annually and levy a proportional charge on each of the ITV companies, which should be empowered to recoup the extra cost by selling Channel Four's commercial time in their own areas. Which was, in the end, after a great deal of hard bargaining, the way the channel was funded. Starting broadcasting in November 1982, after a rocky first year, the tabloids had field days of cheap abuse—CHANNEL SNORE! CHANNEL BORE! and even CHANNEL-FOUR-LETTER-WORD! Under Jeremy Isaacs's wise guidance the new service didn't swerve from its avowed purpose of providing "something different for everyone," gradually building a loyal audience for its programs, almost all commissioned from newly established independent producers. Programs included an hour-long evening "news in depth," documentaries on our threatened environment, racial prejudice, the arguments for and against nuclear weapons, the problems of the young unemployed gays, and old people ending their days in poverty, as well as the Open University and Schools TV programs, and of course lighter entertainment—new comedians like Paul Merton, Dawn French, Jennifer Saunders, Rik Mayall, Robbie Coltrane, Stephen Fry, Jimmy Mulville, Harry Enfield, and Paul ("Crocodile Dundee") Hogan. Original series appeared, like *Drop the Dead Donkey*, lampooning a typically hectic television newsroom, and full performances of opera and ballet and a vivid version of Dickens's *Nicholas Nickleby*.

Along with *Brookside*, Phil Redmond's popular, everlasting, three-times-a-week serial made completely in a newly built crescent of houses in Liverpool, which dealt with searingly real contemporary human problems and also found a number of excellent hitherto-unseen actors, a number of dramatic series, usually socially concerned, were specially commissioned. These worthwhile productions included Robert Knights's *Porterhouse Blue*, Horace Ove's *The Orchid House*, Peter Hall's *The Chamomile Lawn*, Graham Theakston's *The Politician's Wife*, and Patrick Lau's *The Fragile Heart*.

Because Channel Four had no studios of its own, most of its major drama programs had to be made on film, largely on location. This led to the rapid development, under the guidance of David Rose, of a new type of British feature film that commanded considerable respect. Examples include Merchant Ivory's *Heat and Dust* and *Howards End*; Mike Newell's *Dance with a Stranger*; Alan Bennett's *A Private Function*; Neil Jordan's *The Crying Game* and *Mona Lisa*; Mike Leigh's *Life Is Sweet*; David Hare's *Wetherby*; Peter Chelsom's *Hear My Song*; Mike Radford's *Another Time, Another Place*; Stephen Frears's *My Beautiful Laundrette*; and John Huston's last film, *The Dead*. In 1990 David Rose was succeeded by David Aukin, whose ambition and imagination led to even greater world success, with Alan Bennett and Nicholas Hytner's *The Madness of King George*, Mike Leigh's *Secrets and Lies*, and Mike Newell's *Four Weddings and a Funeral*.

Nothing about Channel Four had been simple or safe, but after many disasters and several genuine triumphs it was soon accepted as a vital part of British television.

Despite the ITV companies' reluctance to sell a rival's time against their own, the advertisers had soon responded to Four's growing popularity and the access it offered to a higher-income and better-educated public. Channel Four's management personnel began to realize that perhaps they would profit more if they were allowed to sell their commercial time themselves. However, nothing was done until 1987 when Jeremy Isaacs handed over to new Chief Executive Michael Grade (Lew's nephew, former controller of London Weekend, then director of television, BBC), who ran a relentless campaign to secure a right to commercial sales.

Eventually the IBA changed its rules, and from the beginning of 1993 Channel Four was permitted to sell its own commercial breaks, but the cautious IBA had insisted that if Four failed to reach a certain annual figure, the ITV companies would have to subscribe to support Four's budget. If of course Four exceeded the "security net," it would have to pay half the surplus in proportionate amounts to the companies. To everyone's surprise, despite a serious recession, Four topped the net figure with an impressive profit from its first year of solo trading, and unwillingly had to pay half to ITV.

Michael Grade argued that instead of financing better programs on Four (which he promised would happen if Four were allowed to keep its cash), the extra money would simply pour into the pockets of ITV shareholders. He now began to campaign against the IBA's "net" system, finally succeeding in having it canceled in 1997. In the future, Four would have all its own earnings to spend on programs it believed in. Much of the commercial success had been due to Michael's shrewd scheduling (even running repeats of ITV's popular *Inspector Morse*, with John Thaw, in peaktime, along with American and Italian football, and sophisticated and well-written series like *Friends* and *Seinfeld*. The improved viewing figures caused an outcry from ITV managers, claiming it was never part of Four's remit to be "popular."

This was not the only reason ITV companies faced a declining audience. In 1980 the IBA, when renewing broadcasting licenses, exchanged Southern (owned by the Rank Organization, Associated-Newspapers, and comic-paper publisher D. C. Thompson of Dundee) for James Gatward's locally funded TV South, dropping dull Westward for promising TV Southwest, and substituting modern Central for tired ATV in the Midlands. ITV had also announced a new franchise for Breakfast Television, following the BBC's intention to start television broadcasts at 6:00 A.M. daily.

Boasting a dazzling lineup of well-known presenters—Anna Ford, David Frost, Robert Kee, Michael Parkinson, and Angela Rippon—the new company, TV-AM, wanted to start transmission alongside Channel Four in November 1982. But the IBA held them back until February 1, 1983, which gave the BBC a chance to mount its own "Breakfast Time" two weeks earlier and capture the available audience with a show of deliberate popular appeal.

Peter Jay, who had been the British ambassador in Washington when his father-in-law, James Callaghan, was briefly prime minister, was the brain behind TV-AM and held serious views on the morning program's "mission to explain" the issues behind each day's news. Worthy aspiration though that might be, his company had to pay its own way by selling commercial airtime, and cautious advertisers rapidly concluded that, given the BBC's successful start and commanding lead, Jay's solemn offering was not for them.

TV-AM was soon in deep financial trouble. All the famous faces departed, except for David Frost. Another Australian newspaper magnate, Kerry Packer, bought a major share-holding and appointed Bruce Gyngell, former deputy to Lew Grade at ATV and then controller of Australia's multilanguage "ethnic" channel, to replace Peter Jay.

Reverting to a matey "G'day" approach, Gyngell introduced an engaging hand-puppet, "Roland Rat," as a presenter, and rapidly out-tabloided the BBC with down-market popular guests. Within a few weeks TV-AM was ahead in the ratings and on the way to showing a profit at last. Indeed, nothing is truer than the old adage that "no one ever lost money by underestimating public taste."

By the end of the 1980s the gap in the schedules between breakfast and tea time had been filled, with all four channels running from 6:00 A.M. to well past midnight into the small hours. Despite strong competition from BBC2, Channel Four still improved its viewing figures under Michael Grade's skillful scheduling and enhanced budgets.

When Michael Grade departed to become chief executive of First Leisure Corporation in 1997, young Michael Jackson, formerly his rival controller at BBC2, took over. He faced the interesting problem of how to hold on to the viewers his predecessor had left him. In 1997 advertisers were finally offered a further outlet, virtually the second ITV they had always wanted, Channel Five.

Unfortunately, to receive the new channel, viewers' sets had mostly to be retuned, and so far many potential customers have not bothered. With a diet of cheap magazine programs, fifth-rate television films, dull interviews, and inane game shows, Five has had a struggle to attract even the miserly 5 percent of the available audience that had been hoped for. Yet on those occasions when it has managed to capture a major film of note, or an international football match, Five has found the larger audience it needs, waiting out there for something good.

So, with a new, dynamic approach, Five's performance may well improve. We can only wish it well.

TV broadcasters now have to face competition from satellite, digital and cable sources. In the 80s, Rupert Murdoch, a successful Australian newspaper owner persuaded the Thatcher Government to issue licenses for alternative TV broadcasts from satellites flying over Britain. Swiftly absorbing a rival, Murdoch established Sky stations' monopoly, offering mainly easy viewing "lifestyle" and "human interest" programs, but with a strong tabloid news output, all well-publicized by his newspapers.

The idea caught on slowly, but once he had the prospect of a million homes fitted with satellite dishes Murdoch began to charge a monthly subscription slightly more than the cost of the compulsory BBC license. With the funds raised he was able to make high bids for football cup finals and other special sporting events and new popular feature films, charging a further viewing fee for each, but leaving his BBC and ITV competitors floundering.

With the advent of a digital technique of sending several programs simultaneously on single terrestrial wave-bands Murdoch also commenced digital transmission of Sky channels, with each subscriber's TV set fitted with a special "top box" converter initially provided free, The BBC and a consortium of larger ITV companies also simultaneously started digital transmission on a multitude of outlets followed by new cable companies led by Cable & Wireless.

This development was widely advertised as a great cultural revolution, providing the British public with an almost unlimited choice of television worth viewing. Unfortunately the effect has simply been total confusion over so many different program titles suddenly on offer. The comparatively few viewers venturing into new channels have simply reduced the body of mainstream audiences, with a consequent reduction of ITV revenue and a certain resentment against the legally enforced BBC license fee, currently nearly £100 ($150) per annum but increasing every year.

11

The Present:
The Bandits Aren't Just
Coming—They're Here!

Satellite, cable and digital diversity—
for better or much much worse?

Over the last few years, a darkness of spirit has overtaken British television. Once lively and innovative, programs are now dull and predictable. In drama there are too many police and crime series and too many fictional lawyers and doctors—as if to suggest that our vivid and multifaceted society contains nothing but law-breaking and pain.

In a medium once vigorous and flourishing, a combination of circumstances has corrupted and confused British television's maturity. The spread of video-players split off some of the audience who prefer to rent feature films. Satellite, digital and cable also offer more choice, without necessarily exciting the imagination or improving quality.

Sky, first of the satellites, presents a range of up-to-the-minute news, sports, pop music, and uncut Hollywood films, and has enlarged its subscription audience by paying huge sums for rights to important sporting events. New digital and cable outlets of all kinds reduce main-channel numbers by appealing to viewers interested in history, cartoons, cooking, travel, wildlife, and re-runs of classic television programs.

With its audience on two channels shrinking to 30 percent or less, and fearful of a consequent possible cut in its license income, the BBC has made stringent economies, even closing down its invaluable departments of scenic design, costume, and makeup. Though each round of job cuts is trumpeted with brave words about "a leaner, more efficient organization," in reality it means fewer resources for experiment, originality, and adventurous production.

The ITV is beset with problems too. Apart from the increasing competition for viewers, some sense has to be made of the chaos caused by the IBA's incredible mistake of holding an "auction" for franchises in 1991, resulting in two rich companies, Scottish and Central, with no opposing bidders for their television territories, each having to pay only £2,000 ($3,000) annually for their license to broadcast, while hotly contested companies like HTV (practically bankrupt through mismanagement) are forced to find over £20 million ($30 million) a year for Wales and the West of England.

Nowadays, program commissioners make decisions far too late and far too cautiously, motivated by fear of the consequences of costly errors of judgment. An ambitious drama will be approved only on perceived sure-fire appeal. Serious documentaries on important subjects (and smaller budgets) are banished to unfriendly hours.

Newly rich companies dominate the ITV network. London weekday holder Carlton has taken over Central in the Midlands and Westcountry TV in Devon and Cornwall, to command 35 percent of the total U.K. television advertising revenue. Granada from the North has swallowed London Weekend, Yorkshire, and Tyne-Tees. Meridian, successor to TV South, now part of United Media, owner of the popular *Daily Express*, has seized Anglia in the East and HTV (now financially recovering but depleted in quality staff) in Bristol and Wales. Glasgow's Scottish TV has amalgamated with Grampian to cover the whole of Scotland. Only three companies, none of which contribute much to the main network, remain independent of the Big Four: Border, still profitable Ulster TV, and minuscule Channel Islands TV.

With such powerful players controlling Britain's most popular television service, there seems little chance of improving programs for the average viewer.

The immediate future, seen from the chilling present, looks bleak indeed.

12

2000–Onward: The Future

Better television is always possible—
it all depends on producers!

And yet—television still stirs the imagination.

We have advanced from an infant medium using clumsy, heavyweight ironmongery to universal pictorial communication with pocket-sized camcorders. The means to make television are now available to practically everybody in the civilized world. The techniques of lighting, recording, and editing are no longer secrets known only to an expert few. Almost any teacher, writer, scientist, or inventor can present the fruits of his imagination visually to his selected audience.

Let us hope this freedom produces a flood of new ideas alongside the inanities of tabloid television. Programs should never be aimed at a vaguely perceived "illiterate mass." The viewer is all of us, and we want neither the extremes of Marx nor of market-force Mammon.

The hope for another spring in British television must come not from administrators and accountants, but from thoughtful producers and directors encouraged to create an awareness of family values and of peace and international cooperation, and thus enhance the priceless riches of the human spirit. Given the right conditions, we can devise more fantastic, funny, and life-enhancing programs that will enthrall and entertain our enormous audience, and give them something of value to think about.

Television has been very good to me.

It has taken me to places I never dreamed of, and given me some appreciation of sculpture, painting, music, and dance, and a greater understanding of the people on this planet.

I have been permitted to play a small part in the slow but sure creation of real enlightenment that, despite all the falsehood, greed, and corruption surrounding us, has made people throughout the world more aware and more caring than they were 50 years ago.

On balance, I believe this extraordinarily persuasive medium, television, which has dominated, obsessed, and illuminated my entire adult life, will continue to be of genuine and lasting value to all humanity.

Appendix:
Professional Career of
Peter Graham Scott

Television Dramas Directed

1953

Our Marie. Life story of music-hall star Marie Lloyd; with Pat Kirkwood.

William's Other Anne. Incident in Shakespeare's early life; with Irene Worth, John Gregson.

Charles B. Cochran Presents. Life of theatrical impresario before Second World War; with Frank Lawton.

All Our Yesterdays. Coronation special, life of a British family through five coronations; with Stubby Kaye, Vivien Blaine, Sam Levene, Jack Watling.

Desert Adventure. A family lost in the desert; with Mary Jones.

Johnnie's Night Out. Children's play about a young Irish boy's adventures in a strange city; with 13-year-old Sean Barrett, who also wrote the play.

1955

A Call on the Widow. Two detectives call on widow of man found dead in suspicious circumstances, and, trapped by floods, are forced to stay overnight; with Jean Kent, Michael Craig.

The Guv'nor. Respected professor uses encyclopedia sales team as cover for businesslike burglary; with Michael Hordern, Coral Browne, Jimmy Hanley.

All Correct Sir. Wild girl in prison at last responds to intelligent, humane treatment; with Adrienne Corri, Bernard Lee.

End of the Mission. Ex-soldier goes back to France after war to discover which Resistance Frenchman betrayed him to the enemy; with Derek Bond, Zena Marshall.

The General's Mess. A choleric colonel is accidentally locked into the wrong flat and gets tangled in a rave-up; with Leslie Hanson, Jimmy Thompson.

1956

One. By American author David Karp. Dissident teacher in totalitarian "foreseeable future" succumbs (almost) to ingenious brainwashing; with Donald Pleasence, Kenneth Griffith.

Castle in the Air. Desperate Scottish aristocrat rents out his castle, and disaster ensues; with Jack Buchanan, Coral Browne.

Rain on the Just. A once rich and powerful family group face the enforced sale of their estate; with Michael Denison, Marie Ney, Patricia Driscoll.

Ever Since Paradise. J. B. Priestley's satirical sketches on love and marriage; with Donald Pleasence, Helen Cherry.

The Last Enemy. Peter Graham Scott's own script based on Richard Hillary's moving wartime testament of how a Battle of Britain fighter-pilot shot down in flames, terribly burned and disfigured, finally finds kinship with his fellow sufferers; with Peter Murray, Patricia Driscoll. *News Chronicle* Best Play Award.

HMS Drake Will Proceed... Mutinous ordinary seaman fails to have his complaints of bullying investigated, but turns hero as ship's company have to assist survivors of a Greek earthquake; with Clive Morton, Martin Starkie.

Snowball and the Birdwatcher. With Peter Sellers, showing his extraordinary versatility in two contrasting short plays.

1957

The Day of the Monkey. Second television play adapted from novel by David Karp. Powerful conflicts in a West African state about to get its independence from British colonial rule; with Edric Connor, Maurice Denham, Kenneth Griffith.

Evening in Hochsberg. Attractive young girl, lover of imprisoned revolutionary poet in nineteenth-century Central Europe, approaches susceptible town major to plead for his release; with Jeanette Sterke, Robin Bailey, Peter Wyngarde.

The Breath of Fools. Peter Graham Scott's own prize-winning play. An arrogant film director attempts to impose his own cynical interpretation on a truly felt story of a miracle, and faces strong opposition from an inexperienced and innocent young actress; with Marius Goring, Susan Wills.

Summertime. Ugo Betti's light-hearted romp with a picnic party one sunny day in Tuscany; with Michael Meacher, Jeanette Sterke.

A Voice in Vision. The struggle for recognition by John Logie Baird, whose pioneering theory of mechanical television was soon overtaken by the more effective electronic system now in general use; with Michael Gwynne, Leslie Phillips, and a first appearance (screaming!) from Glenda Jackson.

1958

2000 Minus 60. A rocket transporting nuclear fuel goes astray in space, as a team of experts desperately tries to avert global disaster; with John Robinson, June Thorburn, Eric Lander.

Women in Love. Anniversary production celebrating Rediffusion's first three years of London weekday ITV. Six playlets set in European cities—Paris, Rome, Madrid, Munich, Vienna, and Stockholm; with Sean Connery, George Sanders, Daniel Massey, and a starlet from each city. First-ever British drama recorded on two-inch videotape.

The Quare Fella. Brendan Behan's powerful prison drama on the eve of an execution; with Dermot Kelly, Wilfrid Brambell. *News Chronicle* Best Play Award.

1959

The Face of Treason. Adapted by Peter Graham Scott from novel by Storm Jameson. Clandestine Communist secretly influences university; with Adrienne Corri, William Russell, Andrew Cruickshank.

The Violent Years. Anglia TV's opening production. A man on trial for suspected murder remembers his happier days in Vienna, and his mother's love story; with Laurence Harvey, Hildegard Knef.

The Mark of the Warrior. Adapted by Paul Scott from his own novel. Tragic events in an officer-training unit in wartime India; with Paul Massie, Ewen Solon, Robert Harris.

The Boy from the Gorbals. Peter Graham Scott's adaptation from Robin Jenkins's novel. Adventures of a Glasgow slum boy sent on holiday with a middle-class teacher and his family; with Hamish Wilson, James Copeland.

1960

A Moment in the Sun. Middle-aged man has a fling with a footloose teenager on the Spanish Costa Brava; with Griffith Jones, Daphne Anderson, Christin Gregg.

The Darkness Outside. Adapted by Peter Graham Scott from George Johnston's novel. Group of archaeologists in remote site in Iraq on verge of major discovery are disturbed by unhinged man with a tale of holocaust and disaster in Europe; with Marius Goring, Virginia Maskell, Wilfrid Lawson, Jack Hedley.

The Pot-Carriers. Original and authentic prison comedy-drama by milk deliveryman Mike Watts; with Ronald Fraser, David McCallum. (Remade later as feature film.)

1961

Dr. Everyman's Hour. Realistic hospital drama about an arrogant surgeon determined to use a generous bequest for his own research; with Albert Lieven, Adrienne Corri, Glenda Jackson.

A Different Drum. Unpopular schoolmaster discovers a boy's gift for organ playing and clashes with headmaster as he tries to prevent the boy from wasting valuable practice time playing football on the school team; with Eric Portman, Douglas Wilmer.

I, Having Dreamt, Awake. An unloved gas-fitter is unsettled by the return of his wife's obviously successful former lover from the United States; with Timothy Bateson, Jasmine Dee, Dudley Foster.

1962

Murder in Shorthand. Murder mystery. Girlfriend of suspect puts herself in danger to find truth; with Oliver Reed, Justine Lord.

The Second Chef. Mike Watts's second television play. A young man with a mysterious background walks into a roadside café, is taken on as assistant chef, and begins an affair with the owner's wife; with Oliver Reed, Jane Hylton, Ronnie Barker.

The Pinkness of It All. Mike Watts's third television play, about a group of unsuccessful gamblers trying to win enough cash to send a niece to Australia to join her lover; with Ronnie Barker, Robert Lang.

1963

It's All Lovely. Comedy, with music by David Proudfoot. A young man obsessed with a television starlet goes to extraordinary lengths to meet her; with Leonard Rossiter, Tony Tanner, Sally Smith.

1964

The Four Seasons of Rosie Carr. Four plays by Ted Willis. The adventures of a young London Cockney barmaid, through two world wars, marriage to a drunkard, three children, and a final trip to Australia; with Jane Hylton, James Bolam, Kenneth Warren.

Memory of October. Leon Griffith's black comedy about two Hungarian refugees in London incompetently plotting the assassination of a visiting minister from Hungary; with Warren Mitchell, Kenneth Griffith, Alfred Lynch. 1964 Writers' Guild Award for Best Original TV Play.

Redcap. Two episodes of military police adventure series; with John Thaw, Leonard Rossiter, Ian McShane.

1965

The Campaign. Adapted by Gillian Freeman from her own novel. A village priest is tormented by spiritual doubts about the value of a hard-sell fund-raising campaign to save his church; with David Buck, Philip Latham, Fay Compton, Isobel Black.

1969

The Word of a Witness. (Also producer.) Television film version of *Murder in Shorthand* (1962); with Jane Asher, George Maharis, Rupert Davies.

1970

Codename. Two episodes of spy-adventure series; with Anthony Valentine, Alexandra Bastedo.

Brett. Three episodes of action-adventure series in Malta and London; with Patrick Allen, Hannah Gordon, Peter Bowles.

1973

The Team. (Also producer.) Pilot episode for new series on motor racing by John Elliot; with James Laurenson, Carline Harris, Stephen Sheppard.

1975

Dial "M" for Murder. One episode of mystery series; with Brenda Bruce, Valerie White.

1976

The Expert. Two episodes of whodunit series about a forensic scientist; with Marius Goring, Lisa Harrow.

Television Dramas Produced

1960

The Citadel. (Also directed one episode.) Nine episodes of A. J. Cronin's prewar medical novel; with Eric Lander, Zena Walker, Noel Harrison.

1961–62

Tales of Mystery. (Also directed one.) Twenty episodes of horror-mystery plays based on short stories by Algernon Blackwood; with John Laurie as Blackwood, narrating.

1965–67

Mogul/The Troubleshooters. (Also wrote four.) Seventy-eight episodes of worldwide action-adventure series devised and written by John Elliot about the international oil business; with Ray Barrett, Robert Hardy, Geoffrey Keen, Philip Latham, Colin Blakeley, Brian Blessed, Philippa Gail, Isobel Black. Best Drama Series Award, British Academy of Film and Television Arts (1966).

This Man Craig. (Also directed one.) First four (of 26) episodes about an innovative master in a Scottish comprehensive school; with John Cairney, Iris Russell, Leonard Maguire.

1968

The Borderers. (Also directed one and wrote another.) First 13 (of 26) episodes of BBC2's first color series, an action-adventure based on the lawless sixteenth-century cattle-raiding and plunder on the Borders of Scotland and England; with Michael Gambon, Iain Cuthbertson, Edith Macarthur.

1970–73

The Onedin Line. (Also directed five and wrote another.) First 42 episodes (of 91) of worldwide adventure series by Cyril Abraham, of a sailing ship family struggling to make a living in turbulent Victorian Liverpool in the 1860s; with Peter Gilmore, Anne Stallybrass, Jessica Benton, Michael Billington, Philip Bond, John Thaw, and first appearance of Jane Seymour. Best Series Award, Television and Radio Industries Club (1975).

1974–75

Quiller. (Also directed two.) Thirteen episodes of contemporary international spy-thriller; with Michael Jayston, Sinead Cusack, Moray Watson.

1976

Children of the Stones. (Also directed whole series.) Seven-part children's adventure among supernatural happenings within the neolithic stone circle at Avebury, Wiltshire; with Iain

Cuthbertson, Gareth Morgan, Veronica Strong, Freddie Jones, Katherine Levy.

1977

Follow Me. (Also directed whole series.) Seven-part adventure. A boy and girl search for her missing brother in Bristol Docks, and uncover a plot to kidnap a visiting African dignitary; with Ronald Fraser, Ewen Solon, Katherine Levy.

The Doombolt Chase. (Also directed three.) Six-part adventure of three youngsters looking for evidence to clear naval officer father of a charge of bad seamanship, stumbling across a plot to threaten Britain with nuclear destruction; with Donald Burton, George Colouris, Frederick Jaeger, Peter Vaughan, Ewen Solon, Shelley Crowhurst.

1978

Kidnapped. (Also wrote adaptation and directed action sequences.) Six-hour version (shown in the United States by Turner Network as 13 half-hours) of Robert Louis Stevenson's adventure stories, *Kidnapped* and *Catriona,* set in Scotland and the Low Countries, from 1746 onward; with David McCallum, Patrick Allen, Bill Simpson, John Carson, Leonard Maguire, Andrew Keir, Jutta Speidel, Patrick Magee.

1979

The Curse of King Tutankhamun's Tomb. A two-hour coproduction with Columbia Pictures and NBC about the discovery by Howard Carter and Lord Carnarvon of the treasures buried at Luxor within the tomb of the fifteenth-dynasty Egyptian boy king; with Raymond Burr, Eva-Marie Saint, Robin Ellis, Harry Andrews, Wendy Hiller, Tom Baker, Angharad Rees.

1980–82

Into the Labyrinth. (Also devised format with Bob Baker and directed 19.) Twenty-one episodes of a supernatural special effects series where three children are lured from a cave by Rothgo, an ailing magician, into many periods of time and history in search of the Nidus, key to his waning powers of sorcery, stolen by the glamorous witch, Belor; with Ron Moody, Pamela Salem, Chris Harris.

1982

Jamaica Inn. Four-hour action drama set in post–Napoleonic War Cornwall where a young girl, visiting her aunt after the death of her sea captain father, discovers the terrible truth about the gangs of shipwreckers who plunder ships they cause to founder on the rocks; with Jane Seymour, Patrick McGoohan, Billie Whitelaw, Trevor Eve, Peter Vaughan, John McEnery. Shown through the United States by Metromedia. Bronze Medal, New York TV Festival.

1983

The Master of Ballantrae. (Also directed action sequences.) Three-hour coproduction with Columbia and CBS of Robert Louis Stevenson's adventure with survivors of the Battle of Culloden on the high seas and in early America; with John Gielgud, Michael York, Richard Thomas, Timothy Dalton, Ian Richardson, Finola Hughes.

1984

Arch of Triumph. Two-hour coproduction with CBS and Newland-Raynor of Erich Maria Remarque's somber story of love between two refugees in Paris just before the outbreak of the Second World War; with Anthony Hopkins, Lesley-Anne Down, Donald Pleasence, Frank Finlay, Richard Pascoe.

Jenny's War. Four-hour miniseries with Columbia based on Jack Stoneleigh's true story of estranged Anglo-American wife of a German officer during the war, who, when her son is shot down over Germany, finds her way to the prisoner-of-war camp where he lies injured, gets into the compound, and stays with him until the armistice; with Dyan Cannon, Robert Hardy, Nigel Hawthorne, Elke Sommer, Christopher Cazenove, Richard Todd, Hugh Grant.

1985

The Adventures of a Lady. Six-hour miniseries coproduced with Canada, France, Germany, and others. The exploits of a well-born eighteenth-century lady who escapes the gallows to embark on a voyage to Louisbourge in Nova Scotia on the trail of a French spy, joins him and his Indian companion traveling into the interior, is arrested by redcoats, returns to London, and at last establishes her innocence of her original "crime"; with Mel Martin, Douglas Wilmer, Matt Birman, Ronald Fraser, Daniel Ceccaldi.

1986

The Canterville Ghost. From the original Oscar Wilde story, a coproduction with Columbia, a tale of the outraged reaction of an angry ghost when an American family inherits his castle, tempered by his genuine friendship with the young daughter of the family, who finally gains him his release from endless spectral captivity; with John Gielgud, Alyssa Milano, Ted Wass, Andrea Marcovicci, Harold Innocent, Lila Kaye, Bill Wallis.

Three Wishes for Jamie. Saint Patrick's night special coproduced with Columbia. A young Irishman escapes from an arranged marriage in Ireland, seeks his fortune, a bride, and a fine son in early America; with Jack Warden, Anna-Livia Ryan.

1987

Hand in Glove. Supernatural story of a young woman's obsessive fear of death; with Nicola Paget, Trevor Howard, Clive Francis, Helen Cherry.

The Hospice. A traveler whose car breaks down on a dark night in an unknown part of the country finds himself welcomed into a strange establishment of ancient people on the verge of death, and soon knows his own immediate destination; with Jack Shepherd, Marthe Keller.

Wall of Tyranny. (*Freedom Fighter* in the United States.) Coproduced with Columbia and NBC. During the Cold War a young American soldier in Berlin meets and falls in love with a girl from East Germany. His desperate efforts to help her escape to the West end in disaster. Years later he meets her young daughter and hears of her death; with Tony Danza, Syd Caesar, Geraldine James, David McCallum.

1988

A Chance to Dance. (Also directed.) A young girl dancer joins a struggling ballet company in Bristol and falls for the leading male. The choreographer jealously gives her a hard time, but then is forced to use her in a leading role when they open in Barcelona. Because the male lead is injured, the choreographer takes over, and she is too nervous to do herself justice. But on the second night her professionalism asserts itself—and she triumphs; with Judi Trott, Patrick Ryecart, Dominic Hawksley, Emma Sutton.

1989

Some Other Spring. A young divorcée reclaims her daughter from her ex-husband, and they fly off to Istanbul to join her lover, who doesn't show up. She then meets a handsome South American, and only later realizes he is a terrorist. Suddenly she understands the danger facing her and her child; with Jenny Seagrove, Dinsdale Landen, Jean-Claude Dauphin.

1990

To Each His Own. The wife of a philandering university lecturer in Cardiff suddenly discovers that one of her 12-year-old nonidentical twin sons is not hers—the babies had somehow been mixed up in the hospital at birth—and she finds her other identical twin being brought up by a tough café owner in a rough part of town. Her efforts to recover him unfortunately end in bitterness; with Julia Watson, Hilton McRae.

1991

Starstruck. (Also directed.) Pilot for comedy series about a desperate entertainment manager in a rundown seaside town hoping to drum up business with a planetarium at the end of a crumbling pier; with Bryan Murray, Judi Trott, Katie Carmichael.

1992

Just Like Eddie. (Also directed.) Pilot for comedy series about a suburban housewife convinced that on the night rock singer Eddie Cochran was killed in a car crash just outside Bristol she conceived his child; with Brenda Fricker, Robert Lang, Debra Gillett.

Television Films Directed

1959

Danger Man (*Secret Agent* in the United States.) Seven episodes. Patrick McGoohan as a NATO secret agent.

1960

Mr. Riviera. Pilot episode for series set in Monte Carlo.

1962

Sir Francis Drake. Four episodes, with Terence Morgan as the Elizabethan adventurer, and Michael Crawford, Howard Lang, Jean Kent.

Zero One: Four episodes, with Nigel Patrick as an airport investigator.

1964

The Avengers. Three episodes of off-beat spy series, with Patrick Macnee and Diana Rigg.

1965

Court Martial. One episode of American Military Police series, with Bradford Dillman, Peter Gray, Darren McGavin.

1967

The Prisoner. One episode of unusual series. Patrick McGoohan as retired secret agent, trapped in a curious village, where no one dares to ask, "Why?"

Other Television Productions

1953–54

All Your Own. Three episodes of Huw Wheldon's junior amateur talent show.

1957–58

First ITV Programs for Schools. Executive Producer for first year, involved in devising *The Farming Year, Shape in Your Hands, Producing Macbeth, Judge for Yourselves.*

1958

Come to the Opera. Live program of excerpts from popular operas, with Sir John Barbirolli and the Halle Orchestra and chorus, Richard Lewis, Victoria Elliott, Veronica Dunne, Marina de Gabarain.

Documentary Film Directed

1947

Sudan Dispute. Inquiry into the economic prospects and political conflicts as Sudan approached independence.

Main Feature Films Directed

1960

Let's Get Married. Comedy, with musical numbers by Lionel Bart. Anthony Newley and Bernie Winters as two cheerful laundrymen who encounter a girl, pregnant and dumped by her lover, and attempt to solve her problems.

1961

Captain Clegg (*Night Creatures* in the United States.) Starring Peter Cushing and Oliver Reed. A quiet country priest, once a ruthless pirate captain, protects his villagers from starvation by organizing smuggling through the haunted Romney Marshes; with Patrick Allen, Yvonne Romain.

1962

The Pot-Carriers. Film version of highly successful television play (1960) about life in prison; with Ronald Fraser, Paul Massie, Carole Lesley.

Bitter Harvest. Ted Willis's script about young girl's rise to become mistress of a rich industrialist—and her fall; with Janet Munro, John Stride, Alan Badel.

1963

The Cracksman. Comedian Charlie Drake as a master locksmith lured into crime, with disastrous results all around; with George Sanders, Dennis Price, Ronnie Barker, Nyree Dawn Porter, Finlay Currie.

Father Came Too. Comedy about newly wedded couple suffering from interfering father-in-law over rebuilding of their dream cottage; with Stanley Baxter, Sally Smith, James Robertson Justice, Leslie Phillips, Ronnie Barker.

1966

Mister Ten Per Cent. Adventures of comedian Charlie Drake as an unsuccessful playwright being used as part of a tax fraud; with George Baker, Derek Nimmo, Wanda Ventham.

1968

Subterfuge. Spy thriller, with Joan Collins, Gene Barry, Richard Todd, Michael Rennie, Marius Goring.

Awards

Beside awards from the British Academy of Film & Television Arts and Festivals at Banff, Chicago, and New York, Peter Graham Scott was elected a Fellow of the Royal Television Society in 1979, and honored with the society's prestigious Sir Ambrose Fleming Award for "Outstanding Service to Television" in 1984.

Index